Just Kidding

Just Kidding

Using Humor Effectively

Louis R. Franzini

ROWMAN & LITTLEFIELD PUBLISHERS, INC.
Lanham • Boulder • New York • Toronto • Plymouth, UK

Published by Rowman & Littlefield Publishers, Inc.
A wholly owned subsidiary of The Rowman & Littlefield Publishing Group, Inc.
4501 Forbes Boulevard, Suite 200, Lanham, Maryland 20706
www.rowman.com

10 Thornbury Road, Plymouth PL6 7PP, United Kingdom

British Library Cataloguing in Publication Information Available

Library of Congress Cataloging-in-Publication Data

Franzini, Louis R., 1941–
Just kidding : using humor effectively / Louis R. Franzini.
p. cm.
Includes bibliographical references and index.
ISBN 978-1-4422-1336-4 (cloth : alk. paper) — ISBN 978-1-4422-1338-8 (electronic)
1. Interpersonal relations. 2. Wit and humor—Social aspects. I. Title.
HM1106.F73 2012
302.3—dc23
2012007717

☺™ The paper used in this publication meets the minimum requirements of American National Standard for Information Sciences Permanence of Paper for Printed Library Materials, ANSI/NISO Z39.48-1992.

Printed in the United States of America

Contents

Acknowledgments

I greatly appreciated the ongoing assistance of my loving wife, Jessica, who has been an indispensable aid in keeping my computer functioning, detecting writing errors, and reminding me of the boundaries of socially appropriate humor. She is not only the greatest life partner but a laughing partner for life as well. Finally, she has taken on much more than her usual 60 percent of the child-rearing duties with our son, Sam, while I was consumed with the research and writing for this book.

Sam is a very special young man in so many ways. He seems to have acquired great humor skills without ever reading *Just Kidding*. However, I cannot recommend that approach to anyone else. Sam's friends, relatives, teachers, teammates, and parents all agree that he is funny, intelligent, empathic, and on his way to a successful life. His keen sense of humor helps.

Thank you, Jessica and Sam, for laughing so much and for always being there for me.

Introduction

If you're like most people . . . you're probably not planning to perform comedy on a professional basis. More likely, you just want to learn how to be funnier in your personal life: to be more amusing in social contexts, in certain work situations and with the opposite sex. . . . You may simply want to enhance whatever gift for humor you may have already discovered within yourself, to ingratiate yourself with others, [and] to "win friends and influence people."
—Steve Allen, the late comedian-author-songwriter-musician[1]

For professional comedians, the primary goal is to make people laugh. For everyone else, humor can be the envelope in which another message is sent and therefore will be received with pleasure. *Just Kidding: Using Humor Effectively* is designed precisely to help you make your own efforts at humor more effective in achieving the primary goals of your interactions. Your overall goal may be to establish or solidify friendships, to preserve a marriage, to obtain employment, to close a sale, to conduct therapy, to defuse conflict between yourself and someone else, or simply to enjoy life more by sharing something funny.

We are not born with a good, bad, or absent sense of humor. Being funny and appreciating humor is learned. It is learned by practicing telling jokes, riddles, and funny stories and having your listeners laugh and enjoy them. That is the humorist's reward. Kids develop their sense of humor when their parents, teachers, and friends encourage them by laughing in response to their early efforts at humor making and then try to return the favor by making the kids laugh.

From the outset let's acknowledge without dispute that being funny with friends and family or on stage is not limited to one gender. Admittedly, in the history of show business comedy, males have dominated the field overwhelmingly with just a few outstanding exceptions, such as Lucille Ball, Phyllis Diller, Carol Burnett, Gilda Radner, Joan Rivers, and Ellen DeGeneres. However, the emerging generation of stars among professional comedians includes many talented women (in alphabetical order, strangely enough): Samantha Bee, Whitney Cummings, Tina Fey, Kathy Griffin, Chelsea Handler, Lisa Lampanelli, Kathleen Madigan, Amy Poehler, Sarah Silverman, Wanda Sykes, Kristen Wiig, and many others on their way to becoming well-known stars on TV and the comedy club circuits.

Cummings says, "Really, it seems like it's more of an advantage [to be a woman] these days than a disadvantage."[2] There are still many fewer women in the comic business than men. Handler agrees: "I actually think it's easier being a woman in comedy . . . [because] you get noticed more quickly . . . if you're funny."[3] Note to the trailing corporate world: The glass barrier has already been removed from the world of comedy, probably by male remodelers.

Just Kidding includes many examples from the professionals' acts and their candid opinions about humor. However, this book is primarily designed for regular folks, nonprofessionals who want to increase the humor in their lives and use it more effectively in daily interactions. The numerous illustrations from the pros intentionally include both positive and negative models of humor use.

Is this book for you? Try the following nonscientific, self-administered mini-quiz: *Just Kidding* should be helpful to most people but particularly to those who frequently are the last one in the group to get a joke. Would that be you? Or have you been watching a movie or TV show and seriously wondered to yourself whether it was intended to be satire? Are you interested in being more attractive to others? Have you been frequently told by friends or family that you are too serious or need to lighten up? Are you a good appreciator of humor but a poor initiator of humor, who has not yet developed many humor-making skills? Do you believe the myth that funny storytellers and witty people were just lucky to be born that way? If any or all of these qualities seem to fit, you, my new best friend, may be "humor impaired." Unfortunately, this diagnosis will not qualify you for a special handicapped parking placard, but there is a painless and effective treatment available immediately for you. You are holding it. Smile more and worry no longer.

Bookstores and online booksellers already offer countless joke books, biographies of comedians, essays by humorists, funny personal anecdotes, and humorous stories about the author's experiences while parenting, performing on stage, traveling, having sex, and even making love. However, no available book describes the instances when humor has failed or the dangers of using humor in our politically correct (PC-sensitive) society. This book goes on to teach readers how to avoid those pitfalls and then, most important, how to be funny in positive, constructive, and socially appropriate ways.

Even though the concept of a self-help book is itself a bit of an amusing oxymoron, as a society we still readily acknowledge the potentially valuable input from experts. We seek the advice of professionals in the fields of medicine, psychotherapy, finances, theology, athletics, the arts, plumbing, landscaping, architecture, landscape architecture, and most areas of our lives in which we believe experts know more than we do and can help us. Before scheduling expensive appointments, though, we tend to try to do it ourselves first by reading the latest book on the topic.

This book is different. The techniques presented in *Just Kidding* are not situation specific, but rather discussions of general principles provided in an emotionally supportive context. These techniques are generally applicable to many personal and professional relationships.

Just Kidding is a book for adults who enjoy humor and who would like to be funnier themselves. This book is intended for people who want to add humor skills to their personal lives, not particularly for those who have ambitions to perform comedy on stage. Subsequent chapters will take the reader through valuable and practical information about humor processes and how to deliver funny comments effectively.

Just Kidding includes definitions of funniness and examples of both helpful and harmful humor. It describes the relevant comedic and psychological rules for making humor effective. It points out the danger signs to offensive humor and how to make the decision to "say it or stuff it." Finally, the book contains a variety of fun exercises to build skills for effective humor making.

Sharing humor can be a powerful social bond. But it has to be done thoughtfully and sensitively. In some ways, effective humor is like an effective drug. It can be powerful, change-producing, and even potentially addictive. Unlike drugs, however, thoughtfully delivered humor has no negative side effects, needs no doctor's prescription or criminal connection, and is totally free! Humor can be positive, uplifting, and a genuine social lubricant when properly applied. Unfortunately, humor can also be misused, cruel, and destructive, sometimes even when the attempts are well intentioned.

This book discusses in detail the differences between positive and negative uses of humor and how to avoid the latter. It also gives clear guidelines on how to be funny. It discusses political correctness and how it both helps and hinders effective humor. Your humor making will soon be received with laughter, which—trust me—is much better than responses of eerie silence, active derision, or overripe fruit thrown at you (not in that order).

The phrase "Just kidding" has become quite common in daily conversation and carries with it several possible connotations. Most frequently it is used by people who are trying to undo their "humorous" misstatements, which (as was immediately obvious) were unfunny and possibly even hurtful to the listener. "Just kidding" is a quick follow-up comment, known technically as an *eraser phrase*, which becomes necessary in an attempt to preserve the status of the social relationship now thrown into some jeopardy.

A second, somewhat more hostile use of "Just kidding" is when the speaker deliberately misleads the listener with some apparently true but actually false information, in a practical joke format. Then the speaker immediately yells "Just kidding!" to highlight the humiliation of the believer-listener. If any humor can be discerned in these instances, it is enjoyed only by the perpetrator.

Third, Kristen Wiig's new character on *Saturday Night Live*, Judy Grimes, uses "Just kidding" as both a filler and an eraser phrase to cover her nervousness about appearing on TV. Her rapid-fire speech is peppered with "Just kidding" after nearly every sentence to undo her previous anxiety-motivated untrue sentence, all for great comic effect.

Finally, "Just kidding" is often heard as an excuse for bad behavior. In criminal cases it may even be put forward as a legal defense. In neither case does the term follow a genuine attempt at humor. For example, in May 2010 in Concord, New Hampshire, four adults and one minor were arrested for bullying an "intellectually challenged" fourteen-year-old boy and tattooing racist and offensive images on his buttocks. Despite arguing that it all was "just a joke," they each received jail time for a hate crime assault.[4]

Politicians also frequently invoke this phrase to account for some silly or stupid comment they thoughtlessly made during a campaign speech or press conference, even when they obviously had not been joking. For example, a schoolchild named Isis approached California Secretary of Education Richard Riordan outside a public meeting and asked him, "Do you know what my name means?" Riordan replied, "It means stupid, dirty girl."[5] Needless to say, any schoolchild would know that this reply was neither nice nor funny. The secretary of education later explained to the media that his joke had been "misconstrued."

Another frequently used eraser phrase is "No offense," but it sounds so curt and nonempathic that it becomes much less palatable than "Just kidding." By following the suggestions in this book, you will rarely have to try to undo possible damage from your misuse of humor by using eraser phrases.

Psychologically, eraser phrases allow the speaker to *decommit*—that is, to save face after having made an inappropriate or hurtful joking remark. In some cultures, this is an important restorative action to take if you might have offended someone with your humor. In that way, the speaker seems to reassure the target and the audience that the comment was a joke not to be taken seriously and to offer reassurance that their friendship remains intact.

Genuine comedic love means never having to say "Just kidding." Of course, you are very welcome to use the words *Just Kidding* if you are recommending or buying a great gift book for a friend.

You may want to know a bit about me to be assured of my credibility and credentials about humor and human behavior. In brief, I am a clinical psychologist with postdoctoral training in behavior modification and an emeritus professor of psychology. I have devoted the past two decades to researching, writing, and speaking about humor to interested groups and professional humor conferences. I have performed stand-up comedy in a variety of venues, not counting my innumerable appearances in many university classrooms filled with unsuspecting psychology students, where I lectured on and demonstrated abnormal behavior.

One of my previous books, *Kids Who Laugh*,[6] is directed toward parents and teachers who would like to develop their children's sense of humor. Finally, I am proudly the past president of Laughmasters in San Diego, which at the time was the only Toastmasters International Club in the world specializing in humor.

Let's get started with learning more about humor and how to use it in ways that are both personally and interpersonally enriching. And if more fun and laughter in your life brings about world peace as a side effect (as the leaders of the World Laughter Tour proclaim), that certainly is an outstanding outcome. Effective humor is guaranteed to be low cal, legal, cholesterol free, and just plain free.

Just Kidding is intended to be more helpful than hilarious. I can easily guarantee that goal. Surely there will be some chuckles and even laughs from some of the illustrative examples cited. However, this is not a joke book, but rather a book to enhance your life experiences. Our primary goal is to develop more effective humor skills for the nonprofessional comedian who will not be performing on stage but will just be using humor as a way to live life more enjoyably. This book will explain how to do that in ways that will be both fun to read and fun to try out.

Humorist Garrison Keillor reminds us, "Jokes are democratic. Telling one right has nothing to do with having money or being educated. It's a knack, like hammering a nail straight. Anyone can learn it, and it's useful in all sorts of situations. You can go your whole life and not need math or physics for a minute, but the ability to tell a joke is always handy."[7]

Surprisingly, most humor making in our daily lives does not take the form of formal joke telling.[8] *Just Kidding* helps you use *all* forms of humor easily and effectively in your social contacts without the risk of hurting yourself or others. I am not kidding about that.

How can you be sure to remember this book's title when shopping for gifts or recommending it to friends? Just think of this (hopefully untrue) story:

> After thirty years of marriage, a wife asked her husband to describe her.
>
> He looked at her for a while and then said, "You're A, B, C, D, E, F, G, H, I, J, K."
>
> She asked, "What does that mean?"
>
> He said, "Adorable, Beautiful, Cute, Delightful, Elegant, Foxy, Gorgeous, Hot."
>
> She smiled happily and said, "Oh, thank you, that's so lovely. What about I, J, K?"
>
> He said, "I'm Just Kidding!"

The swelling in his eye is going down and the doctor is fairly optimistic about saving his testicles.

NOTES

1. S. Allen and J. Wollman, *How to Be Funny: Discovering the Comic You* (New York: McGraw-Hill, 1987), 2–3.

2. S. Barney, "Women Out Front in Fall TV Shows," *Florida Times-Union*, August 30, 2011.

3. J. Behar, interview with Chelsea Handler, *Joy Behar Show*, HLN Cable Network, August 31, 2011.

4. "CHS Bullying Story Spreads around the World," May 26, 2010, www.concordmonitor.com.

5. "Stupid, Inappropriate Commissioner," July 9, 2004, www.thesmokinggun.com.

6. L. R. Franzini, *Kids Who Laugh: How to Develop Your Child's Sense of Humor* (Garden City Park, NY: Square One Publishers, 2002).

7. G. Keillor, *Pretty Good Joke Book*, 5th ed. (Minneapolis, MN: HighBridge Company, 2009), 9.

8. R. A. Martin, *The Psychology of Humor: An Integrative Approach* (Burlington, MA: Elsevier, 2007).

ONE

The Power of Humor and Laughter

Compliment a woman and, sure, she will smile. But make a woman laugh, and she may get naked.

—Nia Vardalos[1]

Actor and author Nia Vardalos's advice identifies one of the top secrets of effective humor use. It can lead to intimacy in more ways than one—and it's certainly cheaper than ordering a bottle of imported wine. More important, it can be genuine and honest, two terrific traits of attraction in and of themselves.

A keen sense of humor is a quality nearly all of us claim in ourselves and one we seek and highly value in others. We love a sense of humor in our dates and mates, our children, and basically everyone with whom we have social contact. Newspaper personal ads placed by those seeking dates now even feature their own acronym for a good sense of humor (GSOH). When our humor making is successful, we are drawn closer to people and share a bonding emotional experience with them. We enjoy life more, and our troubles seem to lessen instantly. Most important, we like that person even more.

Movie and TV star Jennifer Aniston was named "The Sexiest Woman of All Time" by *Men's Health* magazine in late 2011.[2] Tip to eligible males: Ms. Aniston has revealed that for her the most attractive trait in a man is his sense of humor. He must be able to make her laugh.[3] On an encouraging note, it will be easier for you to develop this quality than to accumulate a huge stock portfolio, obtain the handsomeness of a model from some skilled plastic surgeon, or acquire a Beverly Hills mansion, a Ferrari convertible, yachts on each coast, or six-pack abs.

If Jennifer happens to be no longer available when you read this, be assured that humor's overwhelming power of attraction is also true for thousands of other beautiful, sexy women and men out there just waiting for someone. Please do not write me for a list of their names or numbers—at least not without enclosing a large cashier's check.

There are many proven ways to enhance our sense of humor and our children's. Humor making really can be taught and developed to a very high level in both children and adults, thus increasing their chances for social and even economic success. Comic actor Tom Hanks recognizes the importance of laughter and humor in his own children: "I want my kids to laugh every day. If they don't do it on their own, I'll arrange it for them."[4] Good advice for all parents!

Steve Allen further advises, "If your purpose is to become funnier personally, my first and strongest recommendation is to immerse yourself in the entire business of being funny. . . . You will develop a more sensitive awareness of the various forms funniness can take and an understanding of some of the simple techniques for eliciting laughter from others."[5]

In case my words are not sufficiently persuasive, may I add an adage from the Bible itself? In the Book of Proverbs, we are advised, "A merry heart doeth good like a medicine." Laughter and humor can buffer stress and reduce experiences of pain. We can also take note of some humor research findings from mortal scientists. The use of humor has been shown to be associated with a positive self-concept, higher self-esteem and intelligence, and even the enhancement of enjoyment of positive life events. These relationships have not yet been determined conclusively to be causal, but that certainly remains a most encouraging possibility. The associations are definitely there.

Longtime married couples typically cite their senses of humor as the major contributing factor to their established relationship. More important than mere longevity, laughter can make those relationships healthy and loving in these three ways: (1) laughing at each other in an adorable way, acknowledging that all humans are imperfect; (2) laughing at themselves, showing the humility of self-deprecating humor; and (3) laughing together, sharing humor with smiles and genuine joy. The resulting bond can last a lifetime—truly a lifetime guarantee!

One final motivation to develop your effectiveness at humor making is to negate any of those pesky accusations by friends, relatives, and health care professionals of your mental illness. Psychiatrists and clinical psychologists have long considered the absence of a sense of humor to be a clinical diagnostic sign of emotional instability and perhaps a full-fledged illness. Correspondingly, the return of effective humor making is regarded as a positive prognostic indicator for treated patients. But displaying socially inappropriate humor will only encourage any enemies who are "out to get you." To keep the shrinks away, build up and display your sense of humor effectively and appropriately.

Christie Davies, emeritus professor of England's University of Reading, points out that "most people spend a larger portion of their lifetime in telling, reading, or listening to jokes than they do voting, praying, stealing, or rioting."[6] He is suggesting that what people choose to do with their time is by definition what they feel is important to their life. Therefore, we should study that activity and its functions. Davies's scholarly interests have focused particularly on the meanings and comparative analyses of ethnic humor in subcultures throughout the world. While the activist Political Correctness (PC) Police seem devoted to eliminating ethnic humor by regarding it with unrestrained opprobrium, Davies sees it as quite harmless and highly informative toward a broader understanding of societal cultures.

AMATEURS AND PROFESSIONALS

Throughout this book, I will distinguish amateur from professional humorists. The term *amateur*, as used here, simply means that the person does not make a living at humor making, while *professional* indicates that the person works as a paid comedian or comic actor. These terms do not even reflect a difference in humor skills necessarily. We have absolutely no intent to disparage amateurs—that is, nonprofessional humorists. Many amateurs, in fact, are (or can become) very funny people. They may already understand how to create and perform humor just as well as many of the professionals. They just have other primary jobs. This book provides a number of illustrations of good humor from professional comedians along with some major humor bombs from them and other public figures, such as politicians and athletes.

The principles of humor and its smooth delivery are the same for everyone. What is socially acceptable for certain forms of humor, though, can be very different for the nonprofessionals as opposed to the pros. See chapter 3 for an extended discussion of the real effects on humor making that arise from the influence of PC values.

For nonprofessionals, the guidelines for appropriate humor must be much stricter. Friends, relatives, and strangers are not necessarily expecting brazen or obscene humor in everyday social situations. They will be very prone to discomfort and annoyance at amateurish attempts at humor, especially if they are off-color or worse. The boundaries for good taste in everyday social interactions are definitely more stringently drawn and enforced for nonprofessional humorists.

Just Kidding: Using Humor Effectively is primarily intended to help amateurs who want to incorporate more humor into their daily lives more successfully. Certain situations very rarely call for humor—for example, eulogies at a funeral, homilies by the clergy in places of worship, responses to media queries about a tragedy or crime, business proposals, formal presentations to the public or business contacts, contributions at company meetings, interviews with the police, or sworn court testimony.

Certainly, canned jokes are not in order. Occasionally something humorous may happen in one of these settings by accident, and consequently it
becomes even funnier because of the great disparity with the expected
serious decorum for that event. We will later discuss some instances of
unintentional humor, but by definition you cannot plan to be spontaneous in your humor making or anything else.

As with most skill-based behaviors, sharpening your humor-making
skills involves study and practice. Some people mistakenly believe that
you have to be born funny. Of course, humor skills can be rather hard to
learn, especially to reach world-class levels. In the same way, you are not
born as a world-class tennis player, golfer, artist, mechanic, plumber, or
anything else, but require many hours of studying the profession and
good coaching to direct your practice. Similarly, to be able to use humor
more effectively, the same diligent approaches in preparation must be
applied to achieve your desired level of expertise. Top-tier comedian and
late-night-TV host Conan O'Brien admits, "I've spent tens, hundreds,
thousands of hours thinking about what's funny, trying to be funny, and
it's still a struggle. It's *always* a struggle."[7]

Rosie O'Donnell, comedian and former talk show host, offers some
insight into her professional roles: "My talent is linked to laughter. My
core desire is to connect with people in the raw realness of their lives. I
always remember this, that my work is about connection, and timing;
about story, revelation, and comfort."[8] Her perspective is useful to amateurs as well, because she emphasizes how humor can bring people together and touch them emotionally. You don't have to be a paid comedian to do that.

So you need not aspire to a career in comedy that could bring you
worldwide fame and millions of dollars. Who wants that anyway, with
all those intrusive paparazzi and increased income tax burdens? But if
you simply want to get better at using your humor, Allen's and O'Brien's
advice is particularly valid and valuable. Understand as much as you can
about the structure and techniques of humor and then practice and practice some more. Your best feedback comes from your audience, whether
it numbers just one person or more. Did they laugh? Then it was funny.
Did they laugh loud and long? Then it was very funny and not just a
courtesy laugh. You will feel great, and rightly so!

HUMOR INITIATION ISSUES

Whether humor will be acceptable and appreciated becomes a very complex equation involving the status (e.g., age, sex, sexual orientation, social
prestige, religion, ethnicity, education, abilities/disabilities, political affiliation, emotional state, and assorted other variables) of the speaker, the
topic being discussed, the immediate social setting, the status of the lis-

tener(s), the degree of conformity with the ever-changing boundaries of political correctness, and the form of the humor (e.g., satirical, sardonic, sarcastic, silly, sexual, ironic, aggressive, ethnic, intellectual, physical, in-group, plays on words, and so on). Will the intended joke or humorous comment be taken as funny or not? And to what degree? Ultimately, those outcomes can never be predicted with 100 percent accuracy.

Interestingly, in this dimension the amateurs have the advantage over the pros. Nonprofessionals are usually dealing with their friends and family, while professional comedians have to win over total strangers who have paid money to hear their performances. On top of that, their audiences may be half drunk, not at their sharpest cognitively, or pursuing other social agendas at the time. This book will provide you with some excellent guidelines in making your own humor efforts more likely to be judged as appropriate and therefore effective.

GELATOPHOBIA

Gelatophobia is *not* a fear of gourmet Italian ice cream. Fortunately, there is no such fear plaguing people seeking delicious desserts. *Gelatophobia* is a term coined by German psychologist Michael Titze, which refers to the psychological disorder of a serious fear of being laughed at and not taken seriously.[9] This phobia is not yet specifically listed in the official diagnostic manual of mental disorders, but it is a real source of social discomfort and can be a genuinely inhibiting factor in humor interactions. Some of the most prominent characteristics of gelatophobes are the inability to distinguish ridicule from playful teasing, difficulty in discerning the social cues for smiling and laughter, extraordinary levels of shame and fear, and often childhood experiences of humiliation and bullying.

The person with gelatophobia is typically also very shy and unassertive, and avoids other people. That person may appreciate humor as much as anybody but will be very unlikely to repeat a joke or a humorous observation to other people. Such individuals tend to be hypersensitive to criticism, and if they should try to say something funny, their overwhelming fear is that any resulting laughter will be *at* them, not *with* them. Hence, they usually do not even try humor making.

Psychologist Willibald Ruch of the University of Zurich surveyed over twenty-three thousand people in seventy-five countries to determine the incidences of gelatophobia. He has developed a forty-six-item questionnaire to measure people's fear of laughter. He has reported that in Europe the disorder was far and away most common in Great Britain (insert your own joke here). The U.S. incidence was 11 percent of the population.

This new field of study has been expanded to two new humor-related concepts: *gelatophilia* (the joy at being laughed at) and *katagelasticism* (the joy of laughing at others).[10] We might predict that professional comedians would score high on each of these attributes and low on gelatopho-bia, although this research has not yet been done. Science *can* be fun!

To the extent that the pain of being laughed at begins early in life, there is a book that may be helpful for kids ages six and up. *Don't Laugh at Me* addresses the issue of being different in some visible way and perhaps becoming the brunt of teasing and bullying.[11] Intervening early with these children may allow them to avoid gelatophobia and other emotional scars arising from early negative experiences.

Is there an available effective treatment that does not include medica-tion or hospitalization? Yes! Regardless of the possible childhood origins of this problem or how it may have been learned at the family dinner table or during a speech class, I would highly recommend consulting a competent licensed behavior therapist. The techniques of cognitive be-havior therapy should be able to eliminate this kind of phobia in fairly short order. When the fear is gone, the person will be free to make and keep friends with ease and, in the process, will also become an effective humor initiator.

LATTE-BREAKING NEWS: IS THERE A COFFEE EFFECT?

If you would like this humor skills course to move more quickly, James Freeman suggests drinking more coffee. Freeman is a self-described "cof-fee lunatic" and happens to be the founder and owner of Blue Bottle Coffee, a small chain of specialty coffee houses with a unique brewing process. Freeman unabashedly claims, "Coffee will make you funnier."[12] (It is not clear whether this effect results only from his company's coffee.)

I mention his suggestion here just to give comprehensive coverage to our topic. Most likely, any brand of strong coffee will serve as a stimulant that can give someone the energy to assertively speak up and attempt humor. I also cannot guarantee that such humor attempts would neces-sarily be very funny. Since he also mentioned that coffee would make you more intelligent and sexually attractive, Mr. Freeman may merely be trying to sell us more of his brand of coffee. In fact, sir, it is our effective humor skills, rather than our brand of coffee choices, that make us more sexually attractive.

HUMOR AND YOUR IMMUNE SYSTEM

Scientists have in recent years found that there is a genuine interconnect-edness between your mood and your immune system. A whole new specialty area of interdisciplinary study has been formed with the jaw-breaking name of *psychoneuroimmunology*. Without reviewing all the lat-est research results here, we only need to know that there really is a relationship between a person's positive mood and a greater protection from diseases. That protection is probably more effective against fatigue and the common cold than against cancer or AIDS. Similarly, negative moods (depression, anxiety, anger, bitterness, and so on) are associated with susceptibility to physical illnesses.

Belief in these associations between a person's emotions and well-being is growing stronger and more widespread throughout our society. Promoting the positive use of humor and laughter is known as the "humor and health movement," or simply "humor therapy."[13] To be fair, we must acknowledge that certain claims are frequently being made that extend well beyond what scientists have conclusively proven thus far.[14] Nevertheless, there has been a notable increase in clowning and comedy rooms in hospital settings and even the hiring of professional humor consultants by businesses and health care facilities such as hospitals, convalescent and nursing homes, and hospices.

Some medical settings offer a special room for patients and their family where a variety of humor materials is available for their use as desired. Sometimes an aide brings a comedy cart to the patient's room, which typically includes choices of funny movies, tapes, joke books, and other amusing materials. There is little risk in introducing humor in any of these settings after permission from the patient has been granted. If clowns and humor materials can help alleviate pain and increase the cheerfulness of patients residing in institutions that are often much less comfortable for them than being at home, let's do it. It is an extraordinarily powerful and effective way to use humor.

CAN USING HUMOR MAKE YOU MORE PERSUASIVE?

Most people believe that using humor appropriately will make it more likely that you will be able to persuade other people to buy your product or to vote for you or to adopt the point of view you are championing. This is certainly a reasonable expectation. In fact, approximately 25 percent of TV commercials now incorporate some humor.[15] Apparently, the very bright and highly paid executives of major advertising agencies believe that using humor in ads helps sales.

However, research results on this proposition are quite mixed. Some studies indicate that humor does help in persuasion, while other studies show no effect in either direction, and at least one study showed that humorous ads were actually less effective than serious ones. It may be that the humor in the ads is remembered well—but at the expense of the nonhumorous material, such as information about the product or its price. For example, to assess the impact of humor in advertising, researchers must examine several different aspects: the communication goals, the message factors, the best audience, and the specific product factors.[16] Clearly, the question itself turns out to be quite a bit more complicated than you might at first anticipate.

LAWYERS WHO USE HUMOR TO PERSUADE

We are all aware of the plethora of lawyer jokes, typically with the lawyer as the butt of the humor. However, there is at least one credible study in which lawyers themselves were able to apply humor in court for the direct benefit of their clients. Pamela Hobbs, an attorney and university lecturer with a doctorate in applied linguistics, conducted the study examining the use of humor by lawyers in two divergent settings: mediation hearings and oral arguments before the U.S. Supreme Court.[17] Hobbs summarized the potential advantages of humor in the courtroom:

1. As litigators, lawyers are professional performers who can fit humor into a variety of conversational styles.
2. Humor injects an element of surprise into the proceedings, making the presentation more memorable.
3. Using humor effectively displays creativity and daring.
4. Humor showcases the attorney's rhetorical skills.
5. Humor can be part of a calculated strategy to discredit allegedly frivolous claims.
6. Humor can destroy opposing counsel's credibility and neutralize arguments.
7. Using humor as a defensive strategy implies that the court should not consider the opponent's position seriously.
8. Humor can penetrate hypocrisy and express disapproval and ridicule of the inherent incongruity of plaintiffs' claims.
9. Humor allows one to call attention to problems with what are the accepted behavioral norms.
10. Humor becomes an ideal and public method for producing social criticism.

Hobbs's arguments above are indeed persuasive and should encourage more lawyers to become skilled in the use of humor. They must select specific cases carefully so that its use will most likely be effective—that is, persuasive (preferably on behalf of their clients). It is a clever way to demonstrate that the plaintiff does not have a serious case without simply announcing it directly. If humor can be successful in cases before the U.S. Supreme Court, there is no reason to avoid such a potentially successful strategy in any lower court, where humor has long ago been officially declared "missing in action."

One important caveat regarding Hobbs's message has been generated for this non-attorney author. In building her case for greater use of humor by lawyers in the courtroom, Hobbs cites the frequent use of humor by famed criminal defense attorney and TV personality Mark Geragos during his client Scott Peterson's capital murder trial for the deaths of his wife and their unborn child. Geragos often produced laughter from jurors, spectators, and even the judge. What Hobbs does not mention is that Peterson was convicted in that trial and now resides on San Quentin's death row in California.

The bottom line of what to take away from the research on humorous persuasion is that using some humor in your own messages and interpersonal contacts is definitely worth a try. Success cannot be guaranteed. Nevertheless, the anecdotal evidence is very strong in support of Nia Vardalos's suggestion regarding the likely benefits of applying appropriate amounts of appropriate humor to your dating life.

Interestingly, professional comedians differ on how useful their humor is in readily producing sex partners for them. For example, Chelsea Handler, an attractive and well-proportioned comedian and TV host, fearlessly weighs in on this discussion: "If you're fat and funny in this country, you can get a hot chick. If you're fat and not funny, go fuck yourself."[18] Her observation is probably accurate and is thankfully quite supportive of the value of our goal of increasing your effective humor. By the way, this phenomenon might also work if you substitute the word *rich* for *fat*.

In fact, British stand-up Billy Connolly confirms this point: "You only get laid when you're successful—and then you get laid for being successful, not for being in comedy. Comedy's the *least* sexy thing in show business! Playing bass badly gets you more women than doing comedy *well* does."[19] Connolly's axiom may not apply to amateur humorists. Or it may apply only to Mr. Connolly. Check it out for yourself.

PRACTICAL EVERYDAY SITUATIONS TO INTRODUCE HUMOR

Most of us, of course, do not possess the cachet of the professional comedian. We have to navigate our relationships with whatever personal attributes we already have or can develop further with some practice. Humor is not restricted to joke telling or scripted performances. In our daily interactions, it is relatively easy to add some humor within the conversational context of the main reason for the interaction. At the very least, it makes the business at hand more enjoyable for both parties.

Do *not* add humor specifically for some hidden purpose or to gain some kind of advantage. Obviously, those strategies would be manipulative, possibly exploitive, misuses of humor and so are not recommended. Realistically, though, sometimes you might benefit from your use of humor by receiving an unexpected bonus in some form.

Personal examples of surprises delivered to me without any request after a brief conversation peppered with some humorous wordplay and smiles: airline upgrades to business class, extra snacks and a baby bottle of bourbon (while remaining in the airline's coach seat), free item at the supermarket after it did not scan correctly, a complimentary pound of salmon in the fish market when the original piece had been cut too small, complimentary meals at restaurants when the manager requested feedback on a less than satisfactory meal, an earlier appointment with a physician than the time originally offered, the waiver or reduction of bogus fees in mortgage applications, and various other such positive outcomes. The point is not to try to get something for free (which sometimes will happen fortuitously) but just to make your social and business contacts more enjoyable through the liberal use of humor.

Sometimes you may assertively make a complaint for which you wish some specific form of satisfaction, such as a refund, an exchange, or simply an apology. When that message is delivered in a humorous envelope, you are much more likely to be pleased with the results and with yourself for not allowing yourself to be taken advantage of.

It is important to treat a situation with the seriousness it deserves, while smiling and invoking a light-spirited tone with a bit of wordplay or an unexpected reply to a common courtesy comment. For example, if someone upon parting wishes you "a great rest of the day," you could simply say "Thank you" or even nothing, which is certainly acceptable but not memorable. But what if you returned the compliment along with this statement: "I'll try, but that puts a lot of pressure on me. What if I just shoot for an above-average day?"

When the supermarket cashier asks, "Did you find everything you are looking for today?," what would happen if you replied, "No, I was also looking for love and attention"? It could lead to an interesting discussion or maybe just a laugh. I've field-tested this one, and it works.

Many clerks and casual friends will end a casual conversation with "Have a good one." Courageous males might consider George Carlin's recommended response: "Oh, I already have a good one. I just need a bigger one!" (This reply is not recommended for all situations in which this verbal stimulus might be presented. Judicious discretion is always a good idea.)

Humor can help in many everyday settings, including settings that can be delicate or sensitive in some way. It can ease anxieties, defuse conflicts between adversaries (or spouses), and reduce the stress on both sides. Here is a partial list of potential social interactions that could be eased by introducing a degree of humor in a casual and gentle way:

1. Discussion of money issues between spouses or partners.
2. Discussion of sexual matters between spouses or partners.
3. Discussion with an elderly parent about limitations on driving and financial affairs.

4. Discussion with an elderly parent about alternative or assisted living arrangements.
5. Discussion with siblings about caregiving responsibilities for elderly parent(s).
6. Making a complaint about unsatisfactory service or a purchased product.
7. Submitting a letter to the editor for publication in a newspaper.
8. Routine interactions with clerks, delivery personnel, receptionists, and waitpersons.
9. Messages sent or received by e-mail and other social media.
10. Accepting a compliment.
11. Giving a compliment.
12. Introducing yourself to a potential romantic partner.
13. Joining an informal group conversation at a party.
14. Extricating yourself from a personal conversation in person or on the phone.
15. Extricating yourself from an informal group conversation.
16. Requesting help from a stranger.
17. Requesting to borrow something (e.g., phone or small change) from a stranger.
18. Asking your spouse or partner to stop doing something that is annoying to you.
19. Asking your partner to stop doing something that was intended to be helpful to you.
20. Meeting with a physician and medical office personnel (e.g., receptionists, nurses, assistants).
21. Refusing an unreasonable request from another person.
22. Refusing what actually is a reasonable request from another person.
23. Establishing or modifying the division of labor in your household.
24. Responding to the misbehavior(s) of your children.
25. Asking or inviting or pleading with a relatively new friend to sleep with you.

(These listed items are *not* necessarily presented in order of importance!)

THE SCIENCE OF HUMOR

Scientists are only beginning to study humor seriously, despite the increasing frequency of glowing anecdotal reports of its usefulness and helpfulness in personal relationships, hospital settings, schools, industry, and bedrooms across the country. University researchers (ideally those with tenure) have begun studying humor within a large and interesting variety of academic disciplines: psychology, sociology, medicine, nursing, literature, linguistics, speech communication, drama, history, business, and even religious studies. Unfortunately, private and governmental granting agencies are very unlikely to fund humor studies, as long as the complexities and cures of the major physical diseases remain elusive.

Serious scientists fortunately do sometimes study humor. Most of them are active members of the International Society for Humor Studies, a multidisciplinary academic organization that also publishes a prestigious journal for reports of humor research (aptly named *Humor: International Journal of Humor Research*).

Humor scholar Christie Davies suggests that analyzing jokes, especially ethnic jokes that attribute stupidity to groups of people from different cultures in the world, can be most helpful in understanding human society. Specifically, the jokes can reveal a society's areas of "moral ambiguity and ambivalence" and the relationship between the jokesters and the targets of their jokes. Davies explains:

> The jokes thus indicate who is at the center of the culture and who is at the edge and that the culture of the butts of the jokes is subordinate to and derivative from that of the joke-tellers. Ethnic jokes about stupidity are also jokes told at the expense of groups seen as static and unenterprising by those who see themselves as . . . dynamic and competitive. In an open society the jokes indicate the existence of a known and established cultural and economic pecking order of ethnic groups regardless of official rhetoric about equality or pluralism. The butts of the jokes may be liked or disliked, but they are not esteemed.[20]

(Academic theoreticians unsurprisingly tend to be quite prolix in their elucidations of phenomena. May God forgive them, for they do indeed know what they are doing.) In other words, ethnic jokes clearly communicate who is on top and who is on the bottom in a society's structure of subcultures.

THE POLITICAL POWER OF HUMOR AND LAUGHTER

Professor Davies, a keen observer and theoretician about humor processes and effects, gives humor much *less* power than do most social scientists. Specifically, he argues that humor does not *create* stereotypes of groups or nations but is often based upon widespread perceptions. No one really believes that all Greek males are homosexuals, that all Poles are stupid, that all Italians are cowards, and the other unflattering descriptions that frequently appear in ethnic jokes. In his view, humor is *not* a source, or even a vehicle, for expressing hatred of others because it is far too weak for that. True haters have access to more lethal weapons than joking words. Davies's position against censoring jokes is generally accepted in all open societies. When attempts to censor humor occurred previously in history in closed totalitarian societies, they only spawned more humor, such as satire critical of the government's repression. Davies insists that the humor from Eastern Europe was much better when those countries were closely Communist controlled. [21]

China and other countries not particularly renowned for their freedoms of speech and expression are experiencing great difficulties in dealing with uncontrolled communications by their citizens, who are now using the Internet and the new social media. Brook Larmer of the *New York Times* reports:

> No government in the world pours more resources into patrolling the Web than China's, tracking down unwanted content and supposed miscreants among the online population of 500 million with an army of more than 50,000 censors and vast networks of advanced filtering software. Yet despite these restrictions—or precisely because of them—the Internet is flourishing as the wittiest space in China. . . . The Chinese government . . . appears to suffer from an acute case of humor deficiency. [22]

Bloggers in China resort to a variety of phrases designed to evade the censors. Larmer notes that they "have become masters of comic subterfuge, cloaking their messages in protective layers of irony and satire. . . . Coded language has become part of mainstream culture." The Chinese term *egao* roughly translates as "mischievous mockery," which enables the bloggers to "lampoon the powerful without being overtly rebellious. . . . Better a virtual laugh, after all, than a real protest."

The satirical expressions and commentary are not all fun and games there. People do get arrested or suddenly disappear. There is a "blurry line between the permissible and the punishable." It is a dangerous form of social criticism for Chinese activists. Humor can sometimes be sufficient to disguise other agendas and protect free speakers, but sometimes it is not enough. Blogger Wen Yunchao comments on the mobilizing effect of jokes that mock the abuse of power: "Every time a joke takes off, it chips away at the so-called authority of an authoritarian regime." [23] In some ways, the more effective a Chinese citizen's humor is, the more dangerous it is.

Restrictions on political humor in America are prevented by the First Amendment of the U.S. Constitution—thus the TV networks' late-night comedy shows, especially the Comedy Channel's *The Daily Show* and *The Colbert Report*. No similar programs can be seen in China or other countries with authoritarian governments. As Wen explains, "Whenever censorship grows, so do the opportunities for sarcasm and satire." [24] That's better than bullets and bombs.

One of America's great humorists, Garrison Keillor, prepared a speech in 1994 to give to college graduates at their commencement ceremony. When no one invited him to speak, he published it in newspapers as an opinion piece. He offered this advice: "Get together in a comfortable place with people you like a lot, dance, be romantic, be silly, and see if you can get each other laughing by making fun of your elders. Satire, kids, is your sacred duty as Americans. Be funny. Poke them cows and make them moo."[25] No matter how long ago we might have graduated, it's not too late for us all to follow Keillor's counsel for our own benefit and also for the benefit of those in our social world.

EMPIRICAL QUESTIONS ABOUT HUMOR

There are many important questions about humor that are empirical, which means that their answers must definitively be obtained from controlled and rigorous studies, thus extending our information beyond mere clinical reports and casual impressions. For example, the following ten illustrative empirical questions, in no particular order of priority, clearly require more empirical research to determine whether humor can be legitimately recommended as a known safe and helpful treatment. My own very brief answers, based upon some scientific data and plenty of educated speculation, follow each question:

1. Can humor techniques help patients in pain as well as or better than standard pain medications? [*Yes, but take the medications, too.*]
2. Is there a place for humor in the practice of psychotherapy? [*Yes, and therapists should be explicitly trained to use it.*]
3. What are the potential pitfalls in using humor in professional and personal relationships? [*Rapport and relationships can be damaged, sometimes permanently, by misuses of humor.*]
4. Can humor making extend a terminally ill person's life or improve the quality of the remaining life? [*Humor may not be able to extend life, although a 2010 study of 53,500 individuals in Norway over seven years found that those with a sense of humor were more likely to reach their mid-seventies, after which biology and genetics became more influential in longevity. The participants' gender and subjective estimates of their own health made little difference to their survival.*[26] *Regardless, humor at any age certainly can make whatever life is left more comfortable and pleasurable.*]
5. Which of the alleged physical and physiological benefits of humor and laughter can be documented objectively? [*Short-term lowering of blood pressure and heart rate, pain relief, stress reduction, relaxation, lower risk of heart attack, and positive changes in immune functioning.*]
6. Does the use and encouragement of humor in the workplace directly contribute to improving the profitability of the company? [*Evidence is weak regarding increased profitability, but strong in terms of creating an enjoyable work environment and lowered absenteeism.*]

7. Are people with a keen sense of humor more likely to be elected to public office or to be promoted in a business or university? [*Yes, as evidenced especially by Presidents Kennedy, Ford, and Reagan, Senator Al Franken, and New Jersey Governor Chris Christie; not so clear in the worlds of business or universities. Competence for doing the job, of course, is a primary requisite in all the settings.*]

8. Does the salesperson who uses humor on the job actually generate more sales than colleagues who eschew the use of humor? [*Yes.*] In a related question, does the use of the term "eschew" in ordinary conversation make people laugh or cringe? [*Either could happen.*]

9. Can a genuine sense of humor be taught to anyone who is motivated to improve it? [*Yes, for both adults and children.*]

10. Should humor training be formally offered in educational settings from elementary schools all the way through graduate and professional schools, such as psychology, law, medicine, dentistry, veterinary medicine, business, law enforcement, and governmental affairs? [*Yes, but humorless traditionalists will continue to attempt to block such training during our lifetimes.*[27]]

Of course, there really are limitless empirical questions about humor that are clearly important for society to answer with scientific certainty. Research in all aspects of humor is increasing, fortunately, and its acceptability in the university environment is also increasing. These are welcome changes. We will eventually be able to sort out the established facts of the field from the favorite fantasies of humor's proponents.

Let's not ignore what humor can do for you. As comic actor Steve Carell reveals, "Nothing to me feels as good as laughing incredibly hard."[28] That is a strong recommendation when you consider the likely runners-up on his list. Another memorable claim someone made about the moistening value of great humor: "Sometimes I laugh so hard the tears run down my leg." This funny sentiment now shows up on wall plaques, buttons, and T-shirts. We can be assured that the effective use of humor provides multiple benefits to the humor makers themselves, as well as to those with whom they interact.[29]

So, the primary goal of *Just Kidding* is not to provide stand-up performance tips for the pros or future pros, but to guide and coach regular folks to appreciate and initiate humor for their own benefit. Learning the pitfalls and risks in humor making and how to avoid them can be extraordinarily helpful in improving all varieties of personal and professional relationships. Humor making is a self-help strategy that can promote success in dating and marriage, parenting skills, self-confidence, obtaining employment, work and business relationships, recreational sports, and even receiving better service in restaurants and other commercial enterprises. And, other than the price of this book, it's all free!

We must note one important caution. CNN has reported that people can lose their short-term memory following vigorous sex.[30] Or, as the doctor would say, it sounds like a case of "transient global amnesia" in which blood flow to the brain was restricted due to the strenuous activity of the "interaction." One woman, "suffering" from the syndrome, told how she had cracked a joke about being unable to remember how good the sex was that she had just enjoyed. She then proceeded to tell the joke over and over again, each time as if she had just thought of it. Medical experts should not be stumped in explaining her humorous repetition of her humor. Take all the proper precautions, and don't let this "disease" happen to you!

NOTES

1. www.rd.com/laughs/the-funniest-things-we-found-from-a-to-z.

2. L. Raftery, "Jennifer Aniston Named Sexiest Woman of All Time," *Men's Health*, December 12, 2011, www.menshealth.com/sex-women/hottest-women-all-time.

3. J. Jordan, "Jen Gets Real," *People*, February 21, 2011, www.people.com/people/archive/article/0,,20467604,00.html.

4. T. Hanks, interview on *Sunday Morning*, CBS Broadcast Television Network, June 19, 2011.

5. S. Allen and J. Wollman, *How to Be Funny: Discovering the Comic You* (New York: McGraw-Hill, 1987), 3.

6. C. Davies, *Ethnic Humor around the World: A Comparative Analysis* (Bloomington: Indiana University Press, 1990), 324.

7. P. Provenza and D. Dion, *¡Satiristas! Comedians, Contrarians, Raconteurs, & Vulgarians* (New York: HarperCollins, 2010), 57.

8. R. O'Donnell, *Celebrity Detox (The Fame Game)* (New York: Grand Central Publishing, 2007), 196.

9. W. A. Salameh, "The Pinocchio Complex: Overcoming the Fear of Laughter," *Humor and Health Journal* 5, no. 1 (1996).

10. S. Gaidos, "When Humor Humiliates," *Utne Magazine*, January–February 2010, www.utne.com/Science-Technology/When-Humor-Humiliates.aspx.

11. S. Seskin, A. Shamblin, and G. Dibley, *Don't Laugh at Me* (Berkeley, CA: Tricycle Press/Crown Publishing Group, 2002).

12. "Nancy Giles Talks Coffee," *Sunday Morning*, CBS News, November 23, 2010.

13. www.everydayhealth.com/health-center/humor-therapy.aspx.

14. www.everydayhealth.com/cancer/webcasts/healing-through-humor-transcript-1.aspx.

15. M. G. Weinberger and C. S. Gulas, "The Impact of Humor in Advertising: A Review," *Journal of Advertising* 21, no. 4 (1992): 1–25.

16. Weinberger and Gulas, "The Impact of Humor in Advertising"; R. A. Martin, *The Psychology of Humor: An Integrative Approach* (Burlington, MA: Elsevier, 2007).

17. P. Hobbs, "Lawyers' Use of Humor as Persuasion," *Humor: International Journal of Humor Research* 20 (2007): 123–56.

18. "Chelsea Lately," E! Entertainment Network.

19. Provenza and Dion, *¡Satiristas!*, 3.

20. Davies, *Ethnic Humor around the World*, 322.

21. Davies, *Ethnic Humor around the World*.

22. B. Larmer, "Where an Internet Joke Is Not Just a Joke," *New York Times*, October 26, 2011.

23. Larmer, "Where an Internet Joke Is Not Just a Joke."

24. Larmer, "Where an Internet Joke Is Not Just a Joke."

25. G. Keillor, "A Commencement Address: This Country Needs a Good Laugh," *Wilmington (NC) Star-News*, May 30, 1994.

26. S. Svebak, S. Romundstad, and J. Holmen, "A 7-Year Prospective Study of Sense of Humor and Mortality in an Adult County Population: The HUNT-2 Study," *International Journal of Psychiatry in Medicine* 40, no. 2 (2010): 125–46.

27. L. R. Franzini, "Humor in Therapy: The Case for Training Therapists in Its Uses and Risks," *Journal of General Psychology* 128, no. 2 (2001): 170–93.

28. See http://www.searchquotes.com/quotation/Nothing_to_me_feels_as_good_as_laughing_incredibly_hard./42793.

29. J. B. Nezlek and P. Derks, "Use of Humor as a Coping Mechanism, Psychological Adjustment, and Social Interaction," *Humor: International Journal of Humor Research* 14, no. 4 (2001): 395–413.

30. M. Park, "Sex, Then Amnesia . . . and It's No Soap Opera," CNN.com, November 5, 2009.

TWO

The Nuts and Bolts of Humor

C'est la vie! is the secret motto of humor.
—Michael Marder[1]

Michael Marder is a research professor of philosophy, which seems to be a somewhat oxymoronic job title. He argues that the target of a joke by definition is a "brute fact of life. Humor permits reality to laugh at itself. . . . Laughing at ourselves, at the various crises in which we find ourselves, means laughing at our weakness, the feeling of being overwhelmed by the future."[2] His view of the functions of humor is thus more complex than simply helping us cope with stress or accept the inevitable in life with a lightness of being. We cannot avoid death or manipulate future events other than to the most minimal degree. If nothing else, Marder teaches us that the processes and consequences of humor are so far very incompletely understood.

Humor skills may be the only behavioral characteristic that both men and women seek in their partners in approximately equal amounts. However, Geoffrey Miller, an evolutionary psychologist, points to a different motivation for each gender. He suggests that women prefer funny men to bond with, while men deploy humor to attract a mate and perhaps outwit other men who are their competitors.[3] This distinction may be why men, unlike women, are more likely to use insults and put-down humor, usually targeting other men. And so our species survives and continues to evolve via these complex mechanisms of humor appreciation and attraction. Darwin would agree. You must be good at humor to survive, or at least to attract a mate.

Many health care practitioners, traditional and alternative, claim specific health benefits from humor and laughter, such as lowered blood pressure, increased pain tolerance, improved digestion, more efficient cardiovascular functioning, and the quick release of those feel-good chemicals in the brain called endorphins. The use of humor is now even being recommended for improving success and profitability in the workplace and for therapists to supplement their practice of serious psychotherapy.

For physicians, there are very practical reasons for using humor in their practices. First, their patients' symptoms may improve and they will get the credit for delivering excellent health care. Second, the *Journal of the American Medical Association* has reported that primary-care doctors (general internists and family practitioners) who laugh and use humor have fewer lawsuits filed against them. Laughter and humor were not defined separately in the researchers' ratings of the transcripts of the patient-physician interactions. The content of the conversations did not even matter. Perhaps of equal importance, the study's result did *not* show similar effects for surgeons, the medical specialty area which ordinarily generates the highest number of malpractice claims—thereby confirming the stereotype that surgeons are humorless, highly skilled tradesmen with poor communication skills.[4] Presumably, primary-care doctors are also fairly skilled in their humor making, or an opposite result might ensue.

As if these positive effects of humor were not enough, the World Laughter Tour promotes laughter therapy as a vehicle for eventually bringing about world peace. Steve Wilson, an Ohio psychologist and self-proclaimed "joyologist," launched the World Laughter organization in 1998 after meeting Indian gurus who were advocating laughter in hasya yoga clubs as a road toward health and peace. In conjunction with his Indian colleagues and growing numbers of U.S. supporters, Wilson began offering formal training of certified laughter leaders and the formation of laughter clubs literally throughout the world. This rapidly growing movement is propelled by little more than loads of laughter, physical release, and emotional highs.

Laughter clubs are organized by trained and certified laughter leaders anywhere for any sized group that can meet one or more times. What is unusual is that the group participates in a variety of laughter exercises for which *there is no humor stimulus*. The participants laugh loudly as a group, simply upon instruction to use different laughter sounds and cadences. They, and any observers who may come along (if the group has gathered in a public place such as poolside or the lobby of a hotel), just laugh heartily. Capitalizing on the *laughter contagion effect*,[5] soon everyone within earshot is also laughing.

It is an amazing phenomenon. People in a dire or sober mood, who are preoccupied with their own personal problems, who fear for their business's success or the nation's future or a family member's illness or whatever issue is on their mind, all temporarily forget those stressors and laugh along with everyone present, friends or strangers. All are laughing and all quickly feel good. It's simple, it's bonding, it's stress reducing, it's physically relaxing, it's free, and it's legal!

Indian physician Madan Kataria is regarded as the founder of the international Laughter Clubs movement. The clubs are now found worldwide and touted to be applicable to eliminating strife and bellicosity among nations. Given these high stakes of nothing less than preserving humanity, how can anyone deny the innate value of practicing laughter skills and the effective use of humor?

Just Kidding: Using Humor Effectively (which coincidentally happens to be the book you are reading) is concerned primarily with humor making that is *intentional*: someone is trying to be funny. Someone has made the decision to say or do something that is expected to be perceived as amusing by the listeners and observers. In some situations, though, a better decision might have been *not* to make an attempt at humor.

Humor scholar Paul Lewis has a more specific definition of *intentional humor*—that is, humor that is presented with the purpose of making a point or provoking people to behave or believe in a particular way. He notes that such intentional humor can be either harmless and healing or harmful and destructive. Lewis places humor use in the larger cultural context of contemporary America, which he believes to be under extraordinary threats from pollution, global warming, international terrorism, fundamentalist religious fanaticism, and the possibility of nuclear annihilation.[6] Without denying any of these reality potentials, perhaps we all need the tempering anti-anxiety effects of effective humor use more than ever.

Psychologists Rod Martin and Nicholas Kuiper studied what they called "spontaneous conversational humor" by having adults keep daily diaries of their instances of laughter over three days. Some theorists refer to spontaneous conversational humor as *wit*. Their findings may be somewhat surprising to you. Only about 11 percent of laughter occurred in response to hearing a formal joke. Other studies have found as much as 20 percent of people's laughter occurs following a joke or funny story. Regardless, there is much less than we might have expected.

About 17 percent of laughter was a response to stimuli from the media, such as TV, movies, and magazines. The overwhelming source (72 percent) of the participants' laughter was routine social interactions, such as funny comments made by someone or amusing anecdotes of someone's experiences. Being present in that situation was critical to the humor value of the remarks. If they attempted to retell the stories later to others, the result turned out to be much less humorous.[7] The researchers may have confirmed the familiar adage "You had to be there."

Linguist Neal Norrick classified four kinds of humor that most often appear in social conversations. First, the speaker might repeat a formal prepared *joke* that had been previously heard or read. A second category is the telling of an *anecdote* about a funny experience that was experienced or observed. Third, you might engage in deliberate *wordplay*, such as creating puns or wisecrack responses to stimuli from the conversation. Finally, you might use *irony* in making a statement that is intended to communicate a very different message than its literal meaning.[8] For example, Richard Jeni (among others) is credited with having said, "My mother never saw the irony in calling me a son-of-a-bitch."[9]

SENSE OF HUMOR

The sense of humor construct is defined in a variety of ways by different academic theorists and interested observers. Some definitions are as informal as "You have a great sense of humor if we both agree on what is funny." Humor researchers often define the degree of a person's sense of humor by a specific test score on a paper-and-pencil humor inventory. Others define it within just one experiment by their subjects' humor ratings of cartoon stimuli.

Here is my own imperfect working definition: "A sense of humor is a person's propensity and capacity for being amused and for amusing others." Further, this propensity consists of two major components: *initiation* and *appreciation*. The initiator of humor generates it by writing or repeating to others a joke or a funny observation or a witty line. The appreciator of humor recognizes the statement as intended to be funny, acknowledges that, and enjoys the humor conveyed, usually by smiling and laughing aloud. An appreciator may or may not have advanced to also being an initiator, at least occasionally.

Before becoming a successful *humor initiator*, you must first become a master *humor appreciator*. It doesn't work the other way around. These two major aspects of your sense of humor can be separated in your skill development. Of course, it is preferable to work on them simultaneously. I'll discuss just how to do that shortly. Meanwhile, note that psychologist Eric Bressler's research indicates that women prefer men who are humor initiators (*generators* is his term), while men seek women who are primarily humor appreciators.[10] It would seem that these mate-seeking hints are most suitable to heterosexual couples. As scientists within all disciplines typically conclude, we definitely need more research.

Other much more complex research definitions are also available and tend to be tied to the empirical approaches used in specific humor assessment research studies. To complicate the matter even more, would you believe there are well over one hundred different theories of humor in existence? They range from the writings of the ancient philosophers to the authors of classic literature and then on to laboratory research findings of internal brain imaging scans, changes in vasodilation (blood vessel expansion), or the nature of saliva enzymes being obtained by modern medical scientists. In a compassionate nod to your more practical interests, I will not be describing in this book any of these philosophical theories or empirical definitions of humor or the measured physiological consequences of hearty laughter. There are many other good sources available for anyone to pursue these more technical interests. (See the suggested readings at the end of the book.)

An interesting ethnic distinction regarding professional comedians and humorists is that an overwhelming percentage are Jewish, or at least culturally so, if not avidly religiously so. Theorists have tried to explain their predominance in this field. The consensus seems to be that the Jews have had a long history of persecution and discrimination. Using humor has been an important, perhaps essential, coping mechanism to survive as a culture and a religion over many years. Creating humor is also an intellectual skill, and in the Jewish tradition great weight has always been given to the value of learning and formal education.

Just one example: Viktor Frankl, an Austrian psychiatrist and the founder of logotherapy, was imprisoned in Nazi concentration camps during World War II. In his book *Man's Search for Meaning*, he later reported how helpful humor was for him and others in coping with and ultimately surviving the daily horrors of the camp.[11]

However, we can uncover contradictory advice from the Talmud. The Talmud is the most significant and holiest collection of books describing Jewish law and traditions and for interpreting the Torah, the first five books of the Hebrew scriptures. The Talmud says, "Beware of too much laughter, for it deadens the mind and produces oblivion." As a Gentile, I am confused. Most of us savor laughter and encourage it for everyone, but now a holy book warns of its dangers. What to do?

Rod Martin, in his text *The Psychology of Humor*,[12] has summarized the findings of psychologists Debra Long and Arthur Graesser, who studied the conversational humor from talk shows such as the *Tonight Show*. These kinds of data can be helpful in understanding social conversations, but they are limited because televised talk shows are only somewhat naturalistic. To some degree the hosts' questions are scripted, and the guests often have a planned agenda to promote upcoming movies or other events. Sometimes even the conversational humor is preplanned. Totally out of the blue, the host will ask about some specific incident in the guest's life that is likely to produce a funny story for the audience.

Of course, the funniest humor on these shows is usually that which arises completely spontaneously. One classic humorous event from an old *Tonight Show with Johnny Carson* actually involved very little talking. Actor Ed Ames was demonstrating on stage his tomahawk-throwing skill at a target displaying a man's image. Ames threw the weapon, which landed squarely in (the picture of) the man's groin. No punch line was needed. Ames, Carson, and the audience laughed uproariously for many minutes—it was one of the longest-lasting laughs in TV history. Carson's comic expertise was evident when Ames began to approach the target to remove the tomahawk, which would have ended the laugh. Carson gently grabbed Ames's arm to subtly communicate to let it alone. He did, and the audience's laughter continued much longer.

In their analyses, Long and Graesser identified eleven types of seminaturalistic humor that occurred on the televised entertainment-talk programs they reviewed. I present them here for your information, with the caveat that you need not memorize this list to use humor effectively in your own lives. It is useful simply to understand that there are many categories of humor and what they are. Which ones you favor, and thus use more frequently, will be dependent on your own personality style and the specific situations in which you decide to initiate humor. Some types will not fit well with you, while other types will be more fun to try out and master. Attempting humor is always a bit of a risk. Effective humor making, though, pays off very well for everyone.

Long and Graesser's list of talk show humor categories, the definitions of those types, and some illustrative examples follow:

1. *Irony*, when a statement is made in which the opposite meaning is intended. (For example, in the midst of a lightning and thunderstorm, someone comments on what a beautiful day it is.) Actually, the whole matter can get even more complicated with subtypes of irony such as *Socratic irony* (in a discussion when you pretend ignorance for the purpose of exposing the errors of another person by your adroit questioning) and *dramatic irony* (within a theatrical play, irony that is understood by the audience but not the characters of the play).

2. *Sarcasm*, which is similar to irony, except that the criticism and ridicule are more direct and biting. A good example of sarcasm is the writing of contemporary political humorist Andy Borowitz. Sarcasm can be aggressive and hostile and then reflected in the speaker's harsh tone. (For example, someone might say, "That was certainly a fine speech you gave," when the intent is to disparage, not to compliment.) A more extreme version of sarcasm is *sardonic humor*, which is even more bitter and disdainful. Its name came from a plant on the Mediterranean island of Sardinia, which when eaten allegedly would cause the person to laugh convulsively until death. Despite its negative potency, sardonic humor is very unlikely to be fatal to the target. However, if the target is sufficiently unhappy about being the target of humor, the humorist's life, in turn, could be in some danger.

3. *Satire*, which involves statements or longer routines making fun of social policies and institutions or well-known political figures. The long-running TV hit show *Saturday Night Live* has thrived since 1975 with its satirical sketches and bits involving caricatures of

U.S. presidents and candidates for president, and any provocative, noteworthy items from the daily news.

4. *Overstatement and understatement*, when a person repeats a statement said by another and changes the emphasis, thereby changing its meaning. ("Are you hot?" "Oh, yes, I am *very* hot.")

5. *Self-deprecation*, a type of humor that makes you the target of the joke. This form is highly recommended because it does not threaten other people and tends to make them like you more. Rodney Dangerfield built his whole comic persona based upon the "I don't get no respect" image and became one of the greatest comedians of all time. Self-critical humor usually works very well unless *you* start to believe it, or it is constant and excessive.

6. *Teasing*, a mild form of critical humor compared to sarcasm, often with very playful and fairly transparent sexual overtones. The comments are often directed to the other's personal characteristics. When the male talk show host says to his actress guest eagerly displaying her ample cleavage and long legs, "I like your dress," he really means "I like your lack of dress and would like to see it hanging on my bedpost." Of course, he may be "just kidding."

7. *Replies to rhetorical questions*. By definition the poser of rhetorical questions does not expect an answer. To give an answer creates surprise and can be quite humorous. When discussing televised commercials for prescription medications, someone might ask, "Who wants a four-hour erection, anyway?" Your reply might be very funny—at least it *should* be.

8. *Clever replies to serious questions*. Following a seriously posed question, you *seem* to misconstrue it and answer with humor. This fits nicely into the ebb and flow of a conversation, and the surprise response nearly always produces good humor. In a discussion of the merits of different religions, one advocate spoke well of the values defining Christianity. His conversational partner agreed but expressed regret that "it's never been tried."

9. *Double entendres*, when a statement or word is deliberately taken to have a dual meaning, usually sexual in nature. Many common verbs have in recent times taken on a second meaning, making humorous wordplay with them extremely easy. For example, the verbs to "do," "ball," "enter," "eat," "suck," "swallow," "come," "pull off," and other words are obvious double entendres. I don't want to extend these semantic examples any further in order to avoid perpetuating such language of filth—I mean "love."

10. *Transformation of clichés*, taking well-known phrases and changing them slightly to be humorous take-offs on the original cliché. In another, earlier book on unusual psychological syndromes in a discussion of the clinical problem of trichotillomania, which refers to compulsive hair pulling, I used the chapter title "Hair Today,

Gone Tomorrow." Today it doesn't seem so funny, even to me, but it does illustrate this point of transformations.

11. *Puns*, a form of wordplay in which the sound of a word is the same or nearly the same as another word of a very different meaning. The technical term that linguists apply here is *homophone*. Puns display creativity and intelligence. See the writings of Shakespeare for many examples. Unfortunately, in modern times puns seem to be appreciated only by the punster and are more likely to elicit groans than genuine laughter from the listeners.

My favorite personal anecdote about homophones: On Parents' Night we entered our son's second-grade classroom to meet his teacher for the first time. The teacher had set up a large easel with several questions on newsprint for her class, which was currently studying word forms. One prominent question there was "What is a homophone?" My impulsive and too loud response, before even meeting the new teacher, was "That's easy—it's a same-sexed phone." Despite his psychologist father's shaky introduction to Mrs. Cook, Sam did well in the class and advanced smoothly to the third grade the following year. That humor bomb thankfully did not detonate.

The above list of eleven types of humor heard on late-night TV talk shows is not exhaustive, even though it may be exhausting. It would seem less productive for us to discuss some less common humor forms or even the subtle distinctions between sarcastic and sardonic humor. The main point for producing effective humor is to use the kind of humor most likely to be seen as positive and inclusive to your listeners. Chapters 3, 8, and 9 give additional guidelines for making that choice wisely.

PRACTICAL JOKES

Practical jokes represent a dangerous form of humor making in more ways than one. These are situations necessarily prearranged by the joker, because they usually require planning and contrivances to set up. Practical jokes often involve physical humor, such as devices that malfunction (including wardrobes?) or the target of the joke falling, getting wet, getting hit with a cream pie, or suffering some other (presumably temporary) misfortune.

Practical jokes can sometimes be extremely funny. That outcome is a low probability, however. There is much more likelihood that the elaborate preparation somehow goes awry, some person or device does not perform as planned, the target does not arrive or behave as expected, or the target is exposed to possible injury or humiliation. The audience may then object to the proceedings, feel bad for the victim, and simply not laugh at the joker's results.

One real danger is that the victim may actually be injured or else may become very angry and attempt to retaliate aggressively. If you enjoy TV's *America's Funniest Home Videos*, you likely will enjoy the less cerebral practical jokes, as do most children. The difference is that on the TV show, the falls and shots to the groin are usually accidents, taped when someone happened to have a video camera running. Practical jokes that get taped have to be set up beforehand and, of course, could later be entered into evidence in court in cases designed to determine the civil or criminal liability of the joker.

Comedian Howie Mandel produced and starred in *Howie Do It*, a series broadcast by NBC in early 2009 featuring practical jokes played on unsuspecting targets with the cameras clearly visible to them. Steadily decreasing audience ratings ended the show after three months.

Here are a dozen examples of familiar, but rarely funny, practical jokes:

1. Pulling a chair out from behind someone about to sit down.
2. Anonymously enrolling a religious person in a porn website club or on a sex shop mailing list.
3. Inviting someone with a printed invitation to a formal dinner party or testimonial banquet that does not exist.
4. Secretly cutting holes in strategic places of someone's clothes or underwear.
5. Adding water or sand to a car's gas tank.
6. Arranging for automated crank phone calls to be made to someone's home phone throughout the night.
7. Ordering many pizzas to be delivered to someone's home at unusual hours.
8. Placing false requests for services (landscaping, plumbers, gardening, pastoral counseling, rug cleaning, and assorted repairs) that involve visits to the target's home.
9. Covering all the trees and shrubs around someone's home with (unused) toilet paper.
10. Smearing chocolate icing on the bedsheets, which is what comedian Chelsea Handler did while her boyfriend Ted Harbert was in the bathroom with food poisoning.[13]
11. Hiding a whoopee cushion on the seat of someone's chair to create the sound of escaping flatulence. It is sometimes called a poo-poo cushion or a raspberry cushion. The rubber bag can first be blown up by the joker or via remote control, or it can be self-inflating.
12. Another practical joke that emerged from Chelsea Handler's bag of jokes involved her confiding with great sincerity to a friend that a mutual friend of theirs was, in fact, a transsexual who secretly

was in the middle of the gender reassignment process. Neither friend was aware of the false information being provided by Handler. [14]

As you can see, this partial list of practical jokes reveals a hardly hidden hostility within the joker. The victim is likely to be very unhappy and prone to aggressive retaliation. Prank phone calls sadly have even evolved to the point where such callers are now classified as "touchtone terrorists." The target nearly always will fail to see humor in the practical joke. See Chelsea Handler's practical joke on her then boyfriend (listed above) for a good example of a failed practical joke.

Comedians Howie Mandel and Jimmy Kimmel also admit that they enjoy playing practical jokes in their private lives offstage. A main difference with the practical joke format is that the fun at the end is felt entirely by the joker rather than being shared by the joker and the audience, as in the typical verbal joke format.

Comedian Handler seems to possess an extraordinary preference for carrying out practical jokes by simply lying to someone close to her. Despite her acting skills and proclivity for practical jokes being extremely well known to her family and friends, her victims seem unable to resist her outlandish prevarications. The book *Lies That Chelsea Handler Told Me* is a compilation of her practical jokes, with each chapter written by one of her coworkers or family members. All have suffered huge expenses, time lost, unnecessary worries, and gigantic inconveniences for the personal amusement of Chelsea Handler. Some of her pranks are truly cruel. Her friends, perhaps to the complete astonishment of the rest of the world, seem to accept her practical jokes as simply her "love of fucking with people." [15]

Brad Wollack, one of the *Chelsea Lately* writers, has been Chelsea's favorite practical joke target. His unending forgiveness of her is based on this bizarre analysis: "If Chelsea takes the time and energy out of her insanely hectic life and goes to extraordinary lengths to screw yours up royally, leaving you utterly humiliated and degraded, then you'll know you're good to go. She clearly loves you." [16]

Josh Wolf, another writer on the *Chelsea Lately* show and one of her frequent victims, offers his insights into Chelsea's practical joking in his chapter of the *Lies* book:

> She is painfully honest. She will tell you the truth, even if you don't want to hear it, anytime she feels it needs to be said. At the same time, you can't believe a fucking word she says. . . . If the window is cracked open even a bit for her to fuck with you, she will say and make you believe anything so she can have a good laugh. [17]

Wolf goes on to correctly note that "Chelsea is unique. The joy she gets out of even the little things puts her in a class all her own. Even if she has you believing something for only five seconds, it's fine with her. You can tell someone is truly into practical jokes, just the knowledge that it's going to happen is enough for Chelsea."[18] Her humor is really typical male humor. How could that be? Wolf's explanation: "Because Chelsea is a man. A man with really big tits."[19]

Why would anyone put up with Chelsea Handler's lies and cruel practical joking offstage in her private life? Her hairstylist Amy Meyer, as a result of these outrageous stunts, explains that Chelsea is simply a "sick fuck" but also admits that "Chelsea is infectious. She can be so warm and fun that you want to believe her just to be part of her world."[20] A more persuasive explanation is Handler's own succinct insight: "I need to be amused constantly, so I like to play jokes on people."[21]

I would like to point out that unless you, too, are a very rich, beautiful, and famous person with "really big tits," I recommend eschewing practical jokes. Otherwise, you risk receiving a punch in the nose and the consensus social status of an obnoxious person worthy of severe practical joke retaliation. Frankly, it ain't worth it.

One exception to the usual practical joke scenarios occurred recently when I was listening to a speaker at a national humor conference who got hit with two cream pies simultaneously during his presentation. This is a classic practical joke stunt. Despite the audience's being very pro-humor by definition, their overall reaction was subdued, with very mild to no laughter at all. What was notably different in this case was that the speaker had, in fact, prearranged the cream pie attack on himself by two of his cohorts. For most of us, the comedic effort turned out to be largely unsuccessful and detracted from his message. However, that essentially negative outcome may have been lost on the speaker–practical joker himself, because he later inquired whether anyone had captured the incident on video so that he could obtain a copy for himself. It's a hard way to get a laugh, even when you volunteer to be the victim.

Be advised that most mature adults do not care to observe practical jokes, where injuries could occur, and nearly all adults do not wish to be the victims of practical jokes. Many things can go wrong. Thus, I strongly recommend avoiding this form of humor, and you will at the same time be avoiding humor likely to fail.

PRANKS AND PUNKS

Pranks are similar to practical jokes in that something is done that is intended to be playful and possibly malicious. Pranks sometimes become crimes from the point of view of law enforcement. In contemporary slang, to be *punked* refers to being the victim of a prank—a denotation from the MTV program *Punk'd*, which was based on celebrities being set up as targets of elaborate practical jokes. Politicians and other public speakers who are on the receiving end of protestors throwing cream pies as part of some protest movement are said to have been *punked*. Since the intent in those examples is clearly that of political protest, not humor, we need not discuss these incidents further.

In his act, African American comedian James Hannah makes a distinction between pranks and practical jokes. A practical joke, he claims, is when you put a whoopee cushion on a chair seat to create a funny fart sound when someone unsuspectingly sits on it. That kind of joke is harmless and mildly funny. Hannah points out that a prank, which he favors, is definitely more devious and cruel. His best prank is when he invites a white friend to a party where all the other guests are black. After some quiet conversation between him and his friend, Hannah will jump up and yell out for everyone to hear, "Who you callin' a nigger?" It's a very funny bit and no one gets hurt, most likely.

On the other hand, Toyota Motors was sued for $10 million by a Los Angeles woman, Amber Duick, who felt harassed and terrified by a fictitious man who claimed to know her and planned to come to her home. She required her boyfriend to sleep with a club and a canister of Mace in their bedroom. Her work performance allegedly suffered, and she felt ridiculed when it became known that there was no such man.

Why would Toyota Motors carry out such a prank to sell cars? Toyota had hired a marketing agency (Saatchi & Saatchi) to promote its new Toyota Matrix model in a national advertising campaign. Since the woman had given permission to the car company to receive communications from them, the agency felt justified in assuming that she had agreed to participate in the prank with herself as a victim. They sent her numerous personal e-mails from a nonexistent Englishman, Sebastian Bowler, who claimed to be hiding from the police and would be visiting her soon to "lay low." The messages were tantamount to stalking by e-mail. The agency claimed that it was targeting men under thirty-five who hated advertising.[22] How this prank campaign of sending frightening false communications to a woman would help the sales of Toyota cars to men is a major mystery. This prank, like most practical jokes, was not remotely funny and cost Toyota lots of money.

Other examples of pranks gone awry have proved costly to the government. When Christy Toler, age eighteen, appeared to be kidnapped by two men and forced aboard a shrimp boat in Brunswick, Georgia, witnesses notified authorities. The local police, the U.S. Coast Guard, and rangers with the Georgia Department of Natural Resources found the boat and boarded it. Toler introduced her brother and boyfriend to them, claiming that the whole incident was "just a joke."[23] Again, an expensive and unfunny prank.

In a prank that literally bombed, Elphbert Laforteza, an honors student and star athlete at San Ysidro High School in San Diego, California, built and blew up five bottle bombs on campus during lunch hour on the last school day for seniors. No one was injured. School officials labeled the incident a "very bad prank" by one of the school's best students. If convicted, he faced up to thirteen years in prison and most likely the loss of his Air Force ROTC scholarship to college.[24]

After undergoing a psychological examination that determined he was not an ongoing threat to the community, Laforteza was permitted to plead guilty to two misdemeanor charges related to possessing a destructive device. The felony charge of possessing a destructive device near a school was dismissed entirely, even though the five bombs had actually exploded on his school's campus. Justice can create "funny" decisions. Nevertheless, Laforteza was sentenced to three years of probation and thirty days of public service, and he was required to complete a program at the San Diego Burn Institute. He did lose his ROTC scholarship to a fine university and eventually enrolled in a local community college.[25]

Another high school senior prank that bombed happened in 2011 at Rushville High School in Rushville, Indiana. Tyell Morton sneaked a blow-up doll into the girls' bathroom on campus. That is the extent of his prank. Unfortunately, this good student, who had never been in trouble with the law before, was easily identified by school surveillance cameras. He was arrested and missed his high school graduation while in jail. He faced up to eight years in prison for felony criminal mischief. The expenses resulting from his action totaled around $8,000, which included those from the involvement of the state police bomb squad.[26]

Morton's case drew interest worldwide and with the help of the Internet generated an activist support group—Free Tyell Morton. Legal experts questioned the severity of the charges, given that there were no actual damages. In fact, if he had brought a gun on campus, instead of the plastic doll, he would have faced only three years of incarceration for a Class D felony. Ultimately, the judge approved a diversion agreement in which the criminal charges were dropped and Morton was required to provide eight hours of community service to the Rush County, Indiana, schools. Clearly, the eight hours of service was an attractive alternative to eight years in prison.[27] Not all pranks that bomb actually bring out a real bomb squad.

"Wigger Day" was an unofficial designation for part of the homecoming festivities at a Minnesota high school in 2009 and the basis of a 2011 lawsuit by former student Quera Pruitt. What is "Wigger Day"? The lawsuit defined "wigger" as "a pejorative slang term for a white person who emulates the mannerisms, language and fashions associated with the African-American culture." Some of the students dressed in "racially discriminative ways" in 2008 and 2009 by wearing stereotypical low-slung pants, oversized sports jerseys, baseball hats tilted to the side, and "doo rags" on their heads.

As an African American, Pruitt claims to have been offended by these behaviors and distressed to the point of quitting her school activities of track, cheerleading, and student council. She chose not to participate in the school's Martin Luther King Day activities or the senior prom. The suit alleged that Pruitt "suffered severe and extreme emotional distress including depression, loss of sleep, stress, crying, humiliation, anxiety, and shame." She believed that the Red Wing High School authorities in Red Wing, Minnesota, were aware of the racial discrimination and hostile environment created by Wigger Day and thus tacitly approved of it.[28]

Was changing the traditional dress-up days of homecoming at this high school by some students, perhaps with the tacit permission of school officials, a funny and harmless prank? The answer to that question is easy. On December 9, 2011, U.S. District Judge David Doty ruled that the lawsuit may proceed, denying the school district's request for its dismissal.[29] Was the harm inflicted worth the $75,000 claimed in the lawsuit? The courts will have to decide. Is it worth our attention as yet another example of a humor bomb in public? Yes.

SPECIALIZED HUMOR GENRES

There are a number of humor genres that are out there (in more ways than one). Since they are so specialized and so difficult to display, these forms are best left for the professionals. Let's just examine them briefly here and give an example, so that you will at least be familiar with these genres.

Cringe humor is a style in which the humorist takes on topics that are so socially awkward or embarrassing that the audience feels uncomfortable just listening to it. Frequently the material brings very few laughs, which is a bit strange for comedians to strive for. A good example is a monologue by the late Mike DeStefano discussing his interactions with his wife Frannie while she was dying of AIDS.[30] Mike was also HIV positive, but his early death at age forty-four was attributed to a heart attack.

Mike was a recovered heroin addict, having been addicted at age fifteen, but at the time of his death he had been clean for eleven years. His profane routines sprang from his difficult life of crime and addictions on the streets of the Bronx in New York City. He had no sympathy for the clean comics who rant about the minor hassles of daily living. Mike argued, "I talk from darkness and suffering. That's what needs to be made fun of." His comedy exemplified cringe humor and black humor. His bio on Comedy Central's website describes his approach to humor as "turning real life crap into brilliant comedy."

Black humor is something quite different from humor that is about and from the African American subculture. Black humor is also called *dark humor* because it involves a variety of morbid topics associated with death. It presumes to help individuals maintain some sanity in situations that are realistically hopeless. The term *black humor* was coined by André

Breton in 1935 for instances when laughter is generated from cynical and skeptical descriptions of events. Its intent is to make audiences laugh and feel uncomfortable at the same time. Deceased comedians Sam Kinison, George Carlin, and Richard Pryor frequently performed black humor routines, while living comedians Daniel Tosh and Louis C.K. carry on the tradition.

Paul Lewis described the growth of *killing jokes* in American society, which is illustrative of the disturbing trend of an increasing appreciation of destructive forms of humor. He suggests that this sadistic humor, appearing in so many of our popular slasher films and the routines of some comedians—for example, Andrew Dice Clay—resonates with more and more people.

In his review of Lewis's book *Cracking Up*, Rod Martin defines *killing jokes* as a

> type of humor in which the audience is invited to laugh along with the perpetrator of extreme acts of violence and degradation at the expense of the victim, deriving amusement from images of vulnerability, victimization, and bodily mutilation. Rather than providing comic relief, this type of humor serves as a sort of "comic intensifier," heightening the audience's identification with the attacker and detachment from the victim.[31]

I would suggest that this is not a definition of genuine humor but rather a description of pathological impulses and behavior that serve other abnormal psychological functions. I do not recommend killing jokes. They will not make you more popular with your friends or family.

Blue humor is humor usually peppered with curses and references to sex, nudity, and bodily fluids. It is hardly a rare or unusual genre anymore, except for noncable broadcast network comedy. Lenny Bruce introduced blue humor in his club performances, which violated the obscenity laws of the time and led to a number of arrests. Bruce's language in clubs would go totally unnoticed today. But despite the prominence that he achieved as a performer and his extraordinary influence on generations of comedians who followed him, Lenny Bruce appeared on national TV only six times in his life. Many top contemporary comedians work "clean" or can do so as needed, because it gives them greater opportunities for exposure on network TV—perhaps another lesson taught inadvertently by Lenny Bruce.

All of these specialized genres of humor are difficult even for professionals to perform successfully and are very unlikely to be well received by the friends and family members of amateur humorists. Generally my advice is "Don't try this at home." My goal for you is to be able to use humor more effectively, not more dangerously.

NOTES

1. M. Marder, "Jokes and Their Relation to Crisis," *New York Times Opinionator*, October 16, 2011, http://opinionator.blogs.nytimes.com.

2. Marder, "Jokes and Their Relation to Crisis."

3. R. A. Martin, *The Psychology of Humor: An Integrative Approach* (Burlington, MA: Elsevier, 2007).

4. W. Levinson et al., "Physician-Patient Communication: The Relationship with Malpractice Claims among Primary Care Physicians and Surgeons," *Journal of the American Medical Association* 277, no. 7 (1997): 553–59.

5. R. R. Provine, *Laughter: A Scientific Investigation* (New York: Penguin, 2000).

6. P. Lewis, *Cracking Up: American Humor in a Time of Conflict* (Chicago: University of Chicago Press, 2006).

7. R. A. Martin and N. A. Kuiper, "Daily Occurrence of Laughter: Relationships with Age, Gender, and Type A Personality," *Humor: International Journal of Humor Research* 12, no. 4 (1999): 355–84.

8. N. R. Norrick, "Issues in Conversational Joking," *Journal of Pragmatics* 35, no. 9 (2003): 1333–59.

9. Robert Byrne, *The 2,548 Wittiest Things Anybody Ever Said* (New York: Touch-stone Books/Simon & Schuster, 2012), #611.

10. E. R. Bressler, R. A. Martin, and S. Balshine, "Production and Appreciation of Humor as Sexually Selected Traits," *Evolution and Human Behavior* 27, no. 2 (2006): 121–30.

11. V. E. Frankl, *Man's Search for Meaning* (Boston: Beacon, 2006).

12. Martin, *The Psychology of Humor*.

13. Chelsea's Family, Friends, and Other Victims, *Lies That Chelsea Handler Told Me* (New York: Grand Central Publishing, 2011).

14. Chelsea's Family et al., *Lies That Chelsea Handler Told Me*.

15. J. Wolf, "Go Lakers," in Chelsea's Family et al., *Lies That Chelsea Handler Told Me*, 162.

16. B. Wollack, "My Name Is Brad Wollack and I Am Unattractive," in Chelsea's Family et al., *Lies That Chelsea Handler Told Me*, 131.

17. Wolf, "Go Lakers," 157.

18. Wolf, "Go Lakers," 163.

19. Wolf, "Go Lakers," 162.

20. A. Meyer, "Lies and Other Things I Wish Were Lies," in Chelsea's Family et al., *Lies That Chelsea Handler Told Me*, 228.

21. J. Behar, interview with Chelsea Handler, *Joy Behar Show*, HLN Cable Network, August 31, 2011.

22. "Woman Sues Toyota over 'Terrifying' Prank," *ABC News*, September 28, 2009, http://abcnews.go.com.

23. T. Stepzinski, "Kidnapping to Sea Just a 'Prank,'" *Florida Times-Union*, June 5, 2009.

24. A. Martinez, "Student, 18, Is Charged in Blasts at School," *U-T San Diego*, June 16, 2009, www.utsandiego.com/news/2009/jun/16/1m16charge234843-student-18-charged-blasts-school/?print&page=all.

25. G. Moran, "Lesser Charges for Star Student in Bomb Prank," *U-T San Diego*, August 9, 2009, www.utsandiego.com/news/2009/aug/21/lesser-charges-star-student-bomb-prank/?print&page=all.

26. "Tyell Morton, Indiana Teen, Could Face 8 Years Behind Bars for Blow-Up Doll Senior Prank," *Huffington Post*, June 8, 2011, www.huffingtonpost.com/2011/06/08/tyell-morton-prank_n_873244.html.

27. See www.indystar.com/article/20110822/NEWS02/108220357/Rush-Co-teen-s-sex-doll-prank-case-ends-diversion?odyssey=nav l head.

28. "Woman Sues Former Minnesota High School after Being Offended by 'Wigger Day,'" *ABC News*, July 29, 2009, http://abcnews.go.com/US/woman-sues-high-school-offended-wigger-day/story?id=14233178.

29. www.twincities.com/minnesota/ci_19513255.

30. Monologue available on the Internet at www.themoth.org.

31. R. A. Martin, "Review of Paul Lewis' *Cracking Up: American Humor in a Time of Conflict*," *Humor: International Journal of Humor Research* 24, no. 3 (2011): 357–62, quote on 358.

THREE

Political Correctness and Humor

There are no rules, and political correctness is out in the parking lot where the
spics are breaking into the roasters' cars.
— Lisa Lampanelli on why she loves to do Friars Club roasts[1]

Political correctness (PC) is a value system that is becoming extremely commonplace in American society. It directly affects our choice of words in written and spoken communications, workplace hiring and promotion practices, party invitation lists, the observations we choose to comment on and laugh at, and multiple aspects of our daily lives. Its values are inclusiveness, going to extreme measures to maintain inoffensiveness, and the presumed equality of all genders, ethnic groups, races, religions, sexual orientations, physical and intellectual abilities, and philosophical points of view. On the surface it is hard for anyone to disagree with such egalitarian ideals. Of course, I suspect most people don't really believe in all these values "down deep," but due to increasingly strong social pressures, they certainly feel obligated to honor them in their public behaviors and communications.

How does PC impact humor? It directly affects what kind of humorous remarks and formal jokes we can say in public. It directly affects whether we feel free to laugh at a funny comment or joke, when other people with us might possibly regard it in some fashion as non-PC.

The late professor Bernard Saper, a free-speech advocate and academic, used the verb *insinuate* to describe how PC has influenced humor, "insisting that a joke should be judged solely on the basis of whom it might offend."[2] His unhappiness is hinted at in his description of the problem, in which

> the crybabies, the busybodies, and PC activists . . . risk undermining the vitality and vigor of our pluralistic society. . . . PC tries to become the moral and intellectual standard, the latest fashionable mantra of

intolerant and sanctimonious revisionists and activists who wish to control, stifle, or otherwise censor certain kinds of joke-telling which they consider offensive, demeaning, or tasteless. . . . It has spawned a wave of justifiable back-lash, which has equated it to intellectual censorship, political preaching, inquisitorial bullying, anti–free speech, thought policing, and/or anti–academic freedom.[3]

We all wish that Saper had been willing to take a less wishy-washy stand on the matter, but he likely spoke on behalf of a large constituency.

We noted in the introduction that women are becoming increasingly prominent as professional comics as stand-ups, in TV sitcoms, and in romantic comedy movies. One PC change here is how we label the comics of each gender. Answer: It's the same for any of the genders or transgenders. Just as males and females are now all called "actors," all comics are now called "comedians." The term "comedienne" is now officially non-PC, if you didn't get the memo.

Another complication is that our PC guidelines are constantly changing and may indeed not be the same in other countries. Jim Norton, while attacking the *Today* show's Al Roker's ambivalent defense of broadcaster Don Imus's suspension for the ill-considered "joke" described in chapter 5, argued that "what society deems offensive is a transient thing, that what is offensive today wasn't yesterday, and so on."[4] Norton is correct in that the country's PC standards are not fixed, but they certainly do not change as quickly as day to day. It is very possible to learn what the current guidelines are and then decide whether to violate them or not in your humor making.

Some PC concerns might seem unreasonable, and you may choose to proceed with the humor making. For example, what if you are telling a funny story involving a doctor and you refer to the doctor as "he"? Couldn't the doctor be female? Of course, and that difference might be totally irrelevant to the story or PC issues. Thus, for zealous PC devotees to require the storyteller to insert artificially the phrases "he or she" or "his or her" makes for a cumbersome verbal burden when the sex of the doctor protagonist, in this example, is not key to the humor.

Comedian Kathy Griffin's persona is that she will say or do *anything* to gain publicity for herself and her career. Her humor making has included receiving a televised Pap smear test poolside at a Beverly Hills Hotel (true), joking to the audience at the Golden Globe Awards that ten-year-old actress Dakota Fanning had to enter a drug and alcohol rehab program (not true), appearing topless on a fake cover on the national magazine *Out*'s website with Jesse Tyler Ferguson holding her breasts (true),[5] and attacking Jesus during her televised acceptance speech for having absolutely nothing to do with her show winning the Emmy Award (true).

Her speech was unprecedented in tone and content in this setting. Griffin considered it "hilarious and subversive . . . laugh out loud funny."

She read the speech verbatim as commissioned from professional writer Eric Friedman:

> A lot of people come up here and they thank Jesus for this award. I want you to know that no one had less to do with this award than Jesus. He didn't help me a bit. If it was up to him, Cesar Millan would be up here with that damn dog. So all I can say is suck it, Jesus, this award is my god now!"[6]

Griffin certainly has garnered a tremendous amount of attention for herself with her over-the-top humor making, but she has also paid the steep price of alienating a significant share of the public. Nevertheless, her career in comedy continues to thrive. And if it ever falters, her extraordinary public relations and promotional skills will be in demand forever.

EUPHEMISMS

Americans are socialized from early childhood to use euphemisms to spare the feelings of other people, who are assumed to hold extreme sensitivities about specific topics of human behavior. We teach children to refer to their body parts by silly names like "peepee." Kids learn to refer to bathroom functions as "number 1" or "number 2" and may later adopt these more mature phrases, respectively: "taking a wizz" and "dropping a deuce." Even adults will refer to the bathroom itself as "the little boys' (or girls') room." This tendency to avoid the correct biological terminology for body parts and functions creates a lifetime of oversensitivities and a heavy reliance on euphemisms. Private organizations have been founded with the sole purpose of monitoring "offensive" language and topics in the media and then threatening boycotts of advertisers who sponsor the programs on which the transgressions occur.

Early network TV practices and standards departments attempted, for example, to protect the public viewers' sensibilities by a heavy use of euphemisms. The term "pregnant" could not be used in the 1950s to describe women about to give birth. Instead, they had to refer to the woman as being "with child" or "in the family way." Naturally, you could not tell any jokes about how a woman "got herself knocked up."

Another example of euphemisms in comedy occurs with the labels given to humor that is potentially offensive because of sexuality references. These terms appear in descriptions of programs as euphemistic warnings: *bawdy, blue, explicit, adult, XXX, mature,* and others. The translation is that there will be lots of curse words and descriptions of natural and unusual sexual practices in the show. Come prepared.

Steven Pinker, a noted Harvard cognitive psychologist and linguist, has described "the euphemism treadmill" in several of his books.[7] He points out how perfectly acceptable terms used at one time to describe people or events actually tend to change to unacceptable pejorative terms for the same phenomena. That evolution is akin to a treadmill that keeps going, even after we've had enough. Speaking at an MIT convocation,

> Pinker said linguists had already noted the process with concepts as diverse as toilets ("lavatories, bathrooms, restrooms"), disabilities ("crippled, handicapped, disabled, challenged"), and old folks ("elderly, golden agers, senior citizens"). Thus, "Negro" became "black," which led to "African American"; "Oriental" became "Asian"; "Hispanic" became "Latino." This shows that changing a word is not enough to change attitudes, and indicates how far we have to go in achieving racial progress, he said. "We know we will have achieved equality and mutual respect when terms for ethnic minorities stay put."[8]

A previously popular joke genre for kids used to be the moron jokes (format: "Why did the moron . . . ?"). This setup question was followed by the answer, which indicated a stupid and surprising response by the moron. The proper professional categorization of mentally deficient people decades ago was *moron, idiot,* or *imbecile,* depending on the person's degree of intellectual impairment. Of course, these terms are now considered dated, dehumanizing, and degrading. Euphemisms definitely change over time, whether we like it or not.

Even Pinker's term—"physically challenged"—has now evolved to the currently preferred phrase "differently abled." This concept itself can seem quite amusing to some of us. Even the once acceptable term "special" for those with impaired functioning has lost favor because of Dana Carvey's popular comedic tag line as the Church Lady: "Isn't that *special?*" Surely there will soon be a new PC term to use, once the present ones become totally tainted and stigmatized. Any predictions on what it will be?

Most people don't want to be hurtful to others. When angry, though, many of us might use such terms as "moron" or "maniac" to label bad drivers, abusive spouses, and otherwise inconsiderate men or women. Of course, the most popular epithet today is the nonsexist synonym for rectum.

Tim Shriver, chairman and CEO of the Special Olympics organization, discussed the importance of language and labels with Bill Maher on his HBO program *Real Time.* Although Shriver understands that comedians should have a nearly free rein for their commentary, he adamantly maintained that picking on the most vulnerable in our society is "over the line." He considers it a matter of civil rights, when comedians use words like "retard" or "nigger" or "faggot." Maher noted that we might get comedians to avoid those words, but doing so won't accomplish much toward that goal for the general population.[9]

A survey conducted in August 2011 by the Knowledge Networks organization may partially explain the ongoing popularity of these controversial words. This Associated Press–MTV poll randomly sampled via phone and mail interviews a total of 1,355 teens and young adults ages fourteen to twenty-four. Generally the respondents felt free to use these slurs when texting on their cell phones or posting comments on social media sites such as Facebook. As a result, they seem to be jaded by the words that are so offensive to older generations. The young people were twice as likely to use these biased words to be funny as to express hateful feelings.

The most inflammatory racist slur, the "N-word," affected only a minority of the participants (44 percent), who claimed to be very or extremely offended by its use online or in a text message. Over a quarter (26 percent) claimed they would not be offended at all. Surprisingly, only 60 percent of the African Americans in the study reported they would be offended if the word were being used against someone.

Other ordinarily offensive words like "slut," "retard," and "fag" were judged offensive by roughly a third of the young people overall. Women regarded "slut" as deeply offensive in 41 percent of the cases, but if the word was used against them specifically, the number increased, as might be expected, to a high of 65 percent.

Which group was the most frequent target of slurs? The overweight. But given recent public health statistics, overweight people in America are no longer a minority (currently representing 66 percent of the population). The study found that Muslims and gays are also frequent targets of mean-spirited comments.

Only about a third of the respondents felt that discriminatory words about blacks were meant as hurtful, while two-thirds believed they were used jokingly. About 75 percent of the slur words against women were thought to be intended as funny. Use of the expression "That's so gay" to demean something was not offensive to the majority of the group.[10]

What do these findings suggest regarding the appropriate use of humor? Young people in America hear, see, and use these common discriminatory words so frequently that they are becoming more and more jaded to them. When they are not obviously motivated to be hurtful, their use is not particularly offensive. Hearing professional comedians in clubs and on cable TV nearly 24/7 with no constraints on their language has resulted in the desensitization of words that used to be said only in private settings. Young people freely use any of these slurs multiple times per day while talking, texting, posting comments to and about their "friends" online, reading their texts, and listening to rap music and slam poetry, largely without genuine intent of personal assault. Jokes and friendly teasing incorporating such words follow naturally.

George Carlin appropriated new meanings for the well-known terms "idiot" and "maniac," which he applied to the experience of freeway

driving. B.C. (Before Carlin), a long time ago in psychiatry, these legiti-
mate terms referred respectively to conditions of severe intellectual defi-
ciency or extreme hyperactivity. Carlin's traffic-related redefinitions were
"that when you're drivin', anyone goin' slower than you is an *idiot*, and
anyone goin' faster than you is a *maniac*."[11] This classification is certainly
easier than resorting to expensive psychological testing, MRIs, or PET
scans. Word meanings can and do change. Be careful out there.

This linguistic evolution is also happening with references to sexual
orientation. Since humor about human sexuality in all its forms will be a
comedy staple until the end of time, let's look at an interesting bit about
acceptable language in the homosexual subculture. There are many jokes
about homosexuals that use negative terms such as "queer" and "faggot,"
although *queer* used to mean simply strange or odd. Rather than whine
and fight such non-PC language in relation to homosexuality, the gay
community has accepted these terms and even embraced them. They
have been able to neutralize such harsh words and thereby take away
their power to hurt. It is an interesting social strategy that has been at
least partially successful. Gay men in particular still use these words, but
usually in a neutral or positive light.

The term *queer*, for example, has been appropriated by the gay activist
organization Queer Nation, which campaigns for full and equal social
acceptance for gays and the elimination of homophobia. Mainstream TV
programs, such as the American cable reality show *Queer Eye for the
Straight Guy* and the British series *Queer as Folk*, have successfully taken
on the term for their titles. Interestingly, the preproduction working title
for the latter series was *Queer as Fuck*, which may have been too progres-
sive even for European TV viewers.

If anyone's intention is to hurt someone, whether in ordinary conversation or in humorous performances, it is usually very clear and unam-
biguous. The words used, though, are not the only indicator of the speaker's motivation. Tone and inflections will clearly reveal whether the
speaker is sympathetic or antipathetic to sexual minorities.

Here are some language guidelines to observe, if you are not part of
the gay, lesbian, or transgendered community:

- Should you use terms like "queer," "dyke," "homo," "fag," "bi,"
  "trannie," and others, if your intention is to be mean, aggressive, or
  hostile in your humor? NO. No need for any further discussion on
  that.
- Can you use these terms when clearly joking? Maybe, if there is no
  intent to hurt others by your joking comments.
- Should you always avoid these terms regardless, just to ensure
  staying out of PC trouble? No, that would be unassertive at best,
  and at worst it would be allowing yourself and your humor to be
  censored.

- Learn the current acceptable language for same-sex pairings and their conduct and use the terms correctly. For example, not many straight people are familiar with the term "fag hag." Following some education in gay-related terms, you could use the term correctly to reference a heterosexual woman with many male friends who are gay or bisexual. Comedian Margaret Cho proudly describes herself as a fag hag in her stand-up routines and books, although she is married to a man and has had various lesbian relationships as well.[12] Incidentally, the counterpart term for a straight male with many gay and bisexual friends is "stag hag." An additional motivation for many stag hags is presumably that they can readily meet heterosexual women in gay bars, which these women may frequent just to avoid unwelcome approaches by prowling straight men. To complete your gay classification guidebook, the slang terms for straight males with many lesbian friends include "Dutch boy," "lesbro," and "dyke tyke." Most gays, if I may stereotype for present purposes, have great senses of humor. If you approach humor about them and for them with a perspective of understanding, empathy, and knowledge, it will be well received, even if your own sexual orientation is heterosexual or simply unknown. Who cares? Good humor should be good fun, regardless of its content or anyone's sexual orientation.
- Do not patronize. If people are present and fully capable of defending themselves and their "class," there is no need for you to take offense on their behalf. Comedian Russell Peters claims that it becomes a double insult to that group because you would be implying that they are too dumb to pick up on the slur and defend themselves.[13] Certainly you should be overtly supportive, if the matter emerges in the discussion, but no PC sheriff has deputized you to seek out and correct any politically incorrect offenders.
- Be a good model for others, including your own children, by showing respect for all minorities—racial, sexual, or religious—especially in the context of humor making.
- If you may have offended someone with your amateur humor or in conversation, you *can* apologize—for example, "I'm sorry. I didn't mean to offend. What word/phrase would you prefer me to use?" (The rules for apologizing, if at all, may be different for professional comedians. See the discussion about that topic in chapter 8.)

An example of an acceptable joke about sexual minorities: "Do you know what was the toughest role in all of human history? Being the first homosexual!"

Chapter 6 discusses the dilemma that some racist or sexist or otherwise non-PC jokes can actually be funny. Unfortunately, offensive material can simultaneously be very funny, although it certainly is not always so, of course. One example of a very mildly sexist joke is the answer to the setup question, "How can you tell the sex of a fly?"

> A woman walked into the kitchen to find her husband stalking around
> with a fly swatter.
> "What are you doing?" she asked.
> "Hunting flies," he responded.
> "Oh. Killing any?" she asked.
> "Yep, three males and two females."
> Intrigued, she asked, "How can you tell them apart?"
> He responded, "Three were on a beer can, two were on the phone."

STEREOTYPES AND HUMOR

Many jokes and riddles are based on the stereotypical characteristics of specific groups of people. Example: "Why don't unmarried Baptists ever have sex while standing up?" Answer: "Someone might think they are dancing." This is funny, *if* you know that fundamentalist Baptists do not advocate close dancing because it could become an occasion of sin *and* that this mildly anti-religious theme does not offend *even* devout fundamentalist Baptists. The riddle also places an unmarried couple's dancing as a more serious offense than their having sex. Most Protestant theologians, I would argue, would find that rank ordering of sins to be preposterous (and possibly even funny).

The main issue here is whether jokes based on some stereotype of a group actually serve to perpetuate and strengthen that stereotype and possible discrimination—or whether such jokes tend to result in a desensitization of the listeners' attitudes so that any prejudices are diminished. Insult comic Lisa Lampanelli embraces the idea of making jokes based on stereotyping, which is the essential basis of her act. She argues, "Humor works when it's based in truth."[14]

Humor researchers are studying whether and how disparagement humor affects stereotyping. As with so many socially important topics, the studies' results and theorists are divided. Noted scientist Rod Martin has reviewed the literature available thus far and reports:

> [Some] scholars, such as Paul Lewis, argued that degrading forms of
> sexist and racist humor can serve to legitimize and perpetuate negative
> stereotypes and contribute to a culture of prejudice. Others, like Arthur
> Asa Berger, countered that humor is inherently iconoclastic, [and] is
> valuable for rebelling against norms, rules, and restrictions of all
> kinds. . . . [Still others, such as] John Morreall, suggested that the offen-
> siveness of a joke depends not so much on its content but the manner
> and context in which it is told.[15]

Thus, these three experts seem to have covered all the bases. If humor based on stereotypes was magically banned, then there would be very little humor left in the world. No one wants that. Well, hardly anyone wants that.

Martin's summary of the research studies on this issue led to an interesting conclusion. Listening to disparagement humor had essentially no effect on the attitudes of the audience toward the target group. However, telling such jokes did seem to exacerbate negative feelings toward the target group as *held by the joke teller*.[16] It may have been that the teller already held such views before joking about them, although that factor was not tested. There still seems to be some risk that telling such jokes may subtly communicate a social tolerance for prejudice or discrimination against "them." To guard against that possibility, it is vital for the joke teller to be crystal clear that the message is being delivered in a context of fun and not one of mean-spiritedness.

When we hear a potentially offensive joke or comment, should we assertively speak up and say that what was said is offensive? Should we laugh at it? Are we really racist or sexist or ageist, or whatever, if we do laugh? Does it matter if the offending aspect of the joke directly relates to ourselves or not? Should PC override funny? Does it make a difference whether the speaker is a professional comedian or just an amateur trying to get a laugh from friends? These are all important issues in any discussion of how current PC concerns can affect the use and appreciation of humor.

Lisa Lampanelli asks rhetorically, "What's better? Is it better to say the offensive word with love, or the politically correct term with hate?"[17] Of course, her answer is a vigorous vote for the former. Joy Behar adds, "I think when you are a comedian, sensitivity is the last thing on your list."[18] The late Mitch Hedberg contributed his view: "When it comes to racism, you hear people say, 'I don't care if people are white, black, purple or green.' Hold on now, purple or green? Come on now, you gotta draw the line somewhere!"[19] Hedberg made the concept funny by taking it *ad absurdum*.

The concept of political correctness has given rise to a timely illustration of *metahumor*—that is, humor about the processes of humor. Specifically, there is an annual contest at Texas A&M University calling for the most appropriate definition of a contemporary term. When the term the contestants were asked to define was *political correctness*, the deserving winner wrote, "Political correctness is a doctrine, fostered by a delusional, illogical liberal minority, and rabidly promoted by an unscrupulous mainstream media, which holds forth the proposition that it is entirely possible to pick up a turd by the clean end."[20]

PC AND PROFESSIONAL VERSUS AMATEUR HUMORISTS

As defined in chapter 1, we refer to all nonprofessional comedians as amateurs. Amateurs are just regular folks who intentionally incorporate humor into their personal lives as part of their outgoing personalities and desire to share funny stuff with friends. Let's be undeniably explicit about this question: Are the PC rules different for amateurs? YES!

The PC standards are clearly very different for professional comedians than for social humor makers. Pros have the liberty essentially to say whatever they want, especially in nontelevised concert and club venues. Jim Norton's position is that all those PC sensitivities reflect poorly upon America as "a nation of petulant crybabies."[21] Most comedians, nevertheless, give some consideration to PC issues in their routines because they do not want to be boycotted, banned from appearances, or inundated with lobbying from the many activist special interest groups. Their chief interest is trying to be funny and entertaining without spending a lot of their time and energy fighting PC battles.

Comedian Sarah Silverman does not worry as much as her comic colleagues about using possibly offensive material. She says, "It's OK because I'm the idiot." She addresses socially taboo topics, often endorsing them while in character. Her defense is simply "I don't care if you think I'm racist. I just want you to think I'm thin."[22] Self-deprecation can go a long way in getting people to like you. Physical attractiveness is also extremely helpful.

The late comedian Greg Giraldo used to do a bit making fun of an unusual special interest group—dyslexics. He joked that in the last Winter Olympics luge event (a one- or two-person sled race against the clock), one team featured a handicapped person, a dyslexic. The announcers crowed about this special athlete when, in fact, a dead man could have been strapped in and done just as good a job. The CBS censors at the *Late Show with David Letterman*, ever vigilant about PC matters, would not let Giraldo tell this story. As any good comedian would have, he promptly made their rejection his joke. Discounting the possibility of a groundswell of protests from organized dyslexics, Giraldo rebutted, "What were they going to do about it? Write a letter?"[23]

Dan Crohn, a Jewish comedian, tells a joke about the unique habits of Jews. He follows that with a joke that is clearly classifiable as racist. He follows it immediately with a funny twist on the standard anti-racism cliché: "It's OK. Some of my best friends are . . . [pause] . . . racist."[24] The success of Crohn's joke just constitutes more evidence that race remains an unresolved and sensitive social issue in America and therefore continues to be a rich source for humorous material. Of course, it's better for the professionals to take these social risks than you, who simply wish to capitalize on the beneficial results of adding humor to your life.

Surprisingly, some professionals' persona is to be deliberately and blatantly non-PC. They relish being known as "insult comics." Good examples of successful insult comics are Lisa Lampanelli, Don Rickles, Andrew Dice Clay, the late Sam Kinison, Jeffrey Ross, and Robert Smigel's Triumph, the Insult Comic Dog.

Lampanelli is the most contemporary of this group, and she is both self-deprecating and highly insulting of racial and ethnic minorities in her routines. Jay Leno claims, "Lisa is the most outrageous comic we have ever had on *The Tonight Show*."[25] His show even screens all their booked comedians' five-minute routines in advance. Lampanelli points out an important instructive paradox: "To be an insult comic, you actually have to be nice. You don't go to see someone who is mean if you don't like them. You have to really know that they're just joking around."[26]

Rickles, a comic icon, was the first to popularize the insult comic role. However, he is always careful to semi-apologize to his audience near the end of his act, thereby neutralizing his earlier personalized attacks with some comforting phrases about how we really are all alike and it is so important for all people in this world to come together. Clay, whose popularity has waned precipitously since the 1980s, was probably the most vulgar of all insult comics in history with his sexually explicit and obscene attacks on all targets. Kinison, a former evangelistic preacher, used his formidable speaking skills to produce outrageous and obscene comedy about religion, relationships, and sex.

Jeffrey Ross, the current titleholder of "Roastmaster General" of the Friars Club and Comedy Central Roasts, prides himself that he will say on stage what most people barely dare to think and is willing to take all the possible negative consequences. He "isn't afraid of severe consequences . . . or to die for a laugh. . . . A Roastmaster says, 'Fuck 'em if they can't take a joke.'"[27]

Then there is the insult dog Triumph. No one, human politicians or even contestants at the Westminster Dog Show, has been immune to Triumph's comedic poop, although it may not be fair to blame a puppet dog for his master's (Smigel's) outrageous remarks.

Paul Provenza, host of Showtime's *The Green Room*, asked British comedian Jimmy Carr, "What is the most offensive joke you've ever written?" After a brief pause, Carr related, "If only Africa had more mosquito nets, then every year we could save millions of mosquitoes from dying needlessly of AIDS."[28] The joke broke up the panel of other comedians and the audience, attesting to its funniness.

But was it offensive enough to qualify as Carr's "most offensive joke ever"? I very much doubt it, which confirms that funniness and offensiveness are so subjective that many different individual reactions are likely to occur to any given humor stimulus. We can only give suggested guidelines for you to follow about the most probable outcomes from your jokes or witty observations. Many of the factors at play are discussed further in chapter 8.

Bill Maher deserves special mention in any discussion of PC and humor. He once hosted a lively, liberal-oriented TV discussion show on the ABC network called *Politically Incorrect*. The increasing influence of the PC movement was illustrated by his prompt firing from this job when he joked that the hijackers of the planes that were deliberately crashed into the World Trade Center towers on September 11, 2001, had displayed "courage" in their actions. He noted that their premeditated fanatical mission was obviously going to result in their own deaths as well as making unforgettable political statements. Attributing any positive characteristic to these murderers, such as courage in the face of certain death, was considered clearly over the line of acceptability by the ABC executives, who quickly terminated Maher and his show.

Maher subsequently moved to cable TV, where he hosts *Real Time* on the HBO network with apparently no limits whatsoever on his comic observations or use of obscenities about the people in politics and all parts of our society. Maher is fearless in his skewering. His opinion, as stated on ABC's *The View*, is that "somebody has to be out on the ledge to know where the ledge is."[29]

Maher defines himself as a comedian but different from other comics because he is a "comedian with a point of view." His monologues often consist of quite serious points about politics, perceived wrongs, people's trivial concerns, and the rampant stupidity in the world. *Folio Weekly* of Northeast Florida aptly labels Maher as a "rebel without a pause" whose passion is "milking humor from America's sacred cows."[30] *Rolling Stone* gives him even stronger characterizations as "the last flamethrower" and "TV's greatest loudmouth."[31] Maher is assuredly appreciative. Besides, calling himself a comedian gives him license to say anything, whether he really believes it or not or whether it enrages his listeners or not. After all, he's "just a comedian," not a political scientist or peace negotiator.

British comedian Ricky Gervais argues:

> I always expect some people to be offended. I know I ruffle feathers but some people's feathers need a little ruffling. And remember: just because someone is offended doesn't mean they're in the right. . . . No one has the right to never be offended.
>
> I never actively try to offend though. That's churlish, pointless and frankly too easy. But I believe you should say what you mean. Be honest. No one should ever be offended by truth.[32]

Gervais presents an interesting point, applicable to all social protests.

Amateur humorists use humor in private conversations, live or via e-mail; when delivering a formal speech in a club or banquet setting; when introducing another speaker; as an introduction to their presentation in the workplace; and in a whole host of semiformal and informal social situations. Those occasions can range from those with just you and your spouse to larger gatherings with brand-new friends, old friends, coworkers, extended families, and children of varying ages. PC guidelines should be in effect in all these situations. You need to know them and abide by them and realize when they can even be relaxed and stretched a bit, such as when speaking with spouses, very close friends, and other members of your same group. Your group might be your race, your religion, your age, your gender, your political affiliation, and so on.

PC CONCERNS TO CONSIDER

Are your humorous comments within reasonable PC guidelines? Are your jokes attacking certain groups of people unfairly? Might they be perpetuating negative stereotypes? Is the target of your humor about someone's characteristics that are not readily changeable (such as the person's race, gender, sexual orientation, or body integrity), as opposed to someone's specific behaviors or attitudes?

The general concern in this area of PC is to avoid humor that sounds degrading to any group or that implies that people who are different in some noticeable way from the majority of people are somehow inferior as a result. Your choice of words is critical. Slang and any pejorative adjectives usually must be avoided both directly and indirectly.

During the Christmas season, Jay Leno joked about the PC phenomenon itself: "You have to be careful of political correctness this time of the year. You can't call them 'Santa's elves' anymore. They're 'undocumented little people.'"[33] In a classic Christmas blunder, Macy's department store in San Francisco tried to appease the PC fires by dousing them with high-octane gasoline. Macy's fired Santa Claus! After twenty years of faithful and highly praised service in their store of listening to the Christmas wishes of kids and without a hearing or being read his legal rights, "Santa John" (Toomey) was let go early in December.

Let's look closely at Santa's naughty joke. For years, when an adult came into the store to sit on Santa's lap (is that appropriate behavior, even in San Francisco?), Santa had drawn upon his stock joke. He asked, "Have you been good this year?" If they say yes, he replied, "Gee, that's too bad." If someone asked why he was so jolly, Santa typically explained, "Because I know where all the naughty boys and girls live." These (slightly risqué?) jokes have been made throughout his entire career to guaranteed laughs and with no complaints. For some unknown reason, one couple in 2010 reported this offensive (at least to them) humor. Macy's (over-)reacted, and the unemployment rate worsened.

Despite the negative publicity subsequently, Macy's held firm to its decision. A nearby sports bar, Lefty O'Doul's, soon hired Santa John and the unemployment rate returned to its previous level. Sadly, Mr. Toomey died a few months later after working his last Christmas season at the bar.[34]

Have our society's concerns over PC gone too far? Certainly, if a Santa displays inappropriate physical or verbal behavior, it should not be tolerated. But were these particular humorous comments really over that line? And where should the line be? Are we as a free society willing to indulge one or two citizens with unlimited license to determine where to draw the PC line for a major retail corporation, the content of network TV programming, the local public library's holdings, or the high school biology or health teacher's lesson plans?

Jay Leno's "Headlines" segment on *The Tonight Show* capitalized on the inadvertent humor in a correction notice published by a strip club in Duluth, Minnesota.[35] Club Saratoga felt it necessary to publish a clarification of an earlier help-wanted ad that had been placed without due regard to PC issues. The new notice read, "Our ad requesting Pole Dancers did NOT require applicants to be of Polish descent." It is unclear whom the original ad would have offended—or perhaps they just didn't want to limit the number of job seekers. At least they could not be accused of any sex bias in their announcement.

Caucasian comedian Sean Rouse takes an interesting comic twist in his act on the issue of bias against minorities in humor. He says, "All I know is that every time I've bought crack cocaine, it was from a nonwhite guy!" His observation implies that it is much worse to sell drugs than to use them. Health-conscious capitalists might disagree. Rouse further points out that he never uses the "N-word" on stage or in private because his black girlfriend made him promise not to use it—unless they were making love.[36]

A PC ISSUE OR NOT?

Most jokes targeting a specific group are generated from some negative stereotypical characteristic that is then attributed to everyone of that group. For example, some very common stereotypes are that African Americans are lazy welfare recipients, Jews are rich cheapskates, Hispanics have entered America illegally, Asians are poor drivers and have small penises, slow-speaking Southerners are stupid and mate with close relatives, and so on. We are surely familiar enough with such unfair concepts without providing even more publicity here.

But what if the joke is based on a positive stereotype? Would that joke be offensive just because it is generated from a stereotypical characteristic? There are jokes, for example, based upon the intelligence of the Jews, the academic skills of Asians, the lovemaking of the Italians and the French, and the athletic abilities of African Americans. Incidentally, in the interest of full disclosure, Lisa Lampanelli and I strongly concur that this particular stereotype of Italians does happen to be true.

One example of a joke based on a positive stereotype came from Conan O'Brien: "President Barack Obama delivered a speech to America's schoolchildren in which he encouraged them to work hard and study hard. Then he said, if that doesn't work, grab the seat next to the Asian kid."[37] Are such jokes actually flattering to the group—in this case, those of Asian heritage—or are they also exploiting stereotypes that should *always* be avoided?

Vietnamese American comedian Dat Phan was the first winner on the TV comedy competition show *Last Comic Standing*. When he talks about how he got called into comedy, his humor is both self-deprecating and a twist on the familiar Asian stereotype of very bright students: "I knew comedy was for me when I was the only Asian in high school that failed math. But, you know, when I failed, eight other students around me failed, too."[38] They must have taken Conan O'Brien's advice on methods of rapid educational achievement.

Then there is this racist anti-racism joke that is circulating on the Internet. It typifies the use of the element of surprise to produce the humor:

> I'm standing in a bar in Barcelona, and this little Chinese guy comes in and stands next to me.
> I say to him, "Do you know any of those martial arts things, like kung fu, karate, or jiu-jitsu?"
> He says, "No, why the fluck you ask me dat? Is it coz I Chinee?"
> "No, it's because you're drinking my beer, you slanty-eyed little prick."[39]

Finally, since it is unlikely that the pope will have a chance to read this chapter, let's acknowledge that the rest of us are all fallible humans who will make mistakes by occasionally crossing the PC lines in our humor making. Knowledge of the PC boundaries can help us stop or ignore them, but it then becomes our choice and our responsibility.

All professional comedians bomb from time to time, even though that can in part be unrelated to PC issues. Their joke or their routine may just not have been funny. Amateurs' humor can fail because of their unawareness and disregard of the PC humor guidelines and possibly their failure to deliver their humor efficiently and smoothly. The premises of this book are that both of these limitations can be overcome with greater knowledge and repeated practice.

NOTES

1. L. Lampanelli, *Chocolate, Please: My Adventures in Food, Fat, and Freaks* (New York: It Books/HarperCollins, 2010), 68.

2. B. Saper, "Joking in the Context of Political Correctness," *Humor: International Journal of Humor Research* 8, no. 1 (1995): 65–76, p. 65.

3. Saper, "Joking in the Context of Political Correctness," 67.

4. J. Norton, *I Hate Your Guts* (New York: Simon Spotlight Entertainment, 2008), 110.

5. See www.out.com/out-exclusives/2011/11/14/kathy-griffin-jesse-tyler-ferguson-behind-scenes-out100.

6. K. Griffin, *Official Book Club Selection: A Memoir according to Kathy Griffin* (New York: Ballantine, 2009), 257.

7. S. Pinker, *The Blank Slate: The Modern Denial of Human Nature* (New York: Penguin, 2003).

8. R. J. Sales, "Vest Welcomes Frosh; Prof. Pinker Derides 'Euphemism Treadmill,'" *MIT News*, August 29, 2001.

9. *Real Time with Bill Maher*, Episode 208, HBO, April 1, 2011.

10. C. Cass and J. Agiesta, "Young People Jaded by Slurs Online," *Florida Times-Union*, September 21, 2011.

11. G. Carlin, *Napalm and Silly Putty* (New York: Hyperion, 2001), 4–5.

12. R. Lee, "David Atlanta Mag: Fag Hag for Life," May 13, 2009, www.margaretcho.com/content/2009/05/13/david-atlanta-magfag-hag-for-life.

13. R. Peters, *The Green Room with Paul Provenza*, Showtime Network, Episode 7, Season 2, 2011.

14. Lampanelli, *Chocolate, Please*.

15. R. A. Martin, *The Psychology of Humor: An Integrative Approach* (Burlington, MA: Elsevier, 2007), 140.

16. Martin, *The Psychology of Humor*, 141–42.

17. N. Salamat, "Lisa Lampanelli Stops Being Mean for a Few Minutes to Talk about Comedy," February 3, 2011, http://web.signonsandiego.com/news/2011/feb03/all-hail-the-queen/?ap.

18. J. Behar, *The Joy Behar Show*, HLN Network, October 4, 2011.

19. M. Hedberg, Just for Laughs—2002, "On the Edge" performance, Montreal.

20. "Political Correctness Defined," Right Truth, December 18, 2007, http://right-truth.typepad.com/right_truth/2007/12/a-3.html.

21. Norton, *I Hate Your Guts*, 113.

22. http://en.wikiquote.org/wiki/Sarah_Silverman.

23. G. Giraldo, "Dyslexic Luger," in *Good Day to Cross a River* (Comedy Central Records, 2006).

24. D. Crohn, Sirius XM broadcast, 2011.

25. J. Leno, quoted in L. Lampanelli, *Chocolate, Please: My Adventures in Food, Fat, and Freaks* (New York: It Books/HarperCollins, 2010), back cover.

26. N. Salamat, "Lisa Lampanelli Stops Being Mean for a Few Minutes."

27. J. Ross, *I Only Roast the Ones I Love: How to Bust Balls without Burning Bridges* (New York: Gallery Books, 2009).

28. J. Carr, *The Green Room with Paul Provenza*, Season 2, Episode 8, 2011, Showtime Cable Network.

29. B. Maher, *The View*, November 16, 2011, ABC Network.

30. K. Pound, "Rebel without a Pause," *Folio Weekly*, May 24–30, 2011.

31. R. Sheffield, "The Last Flamethrower," *Rolling Stone*, March 17, 2011, 38.

32. The complete quote can be seen at http://newhumanist.org.uk/2640/repeat-offender-new-humanist-interviews-ricky-gervais.

33. This and similar Leno quotes are found at http://politicalroast.blogspot.com/2010/12/jay-leno-political-jokes-wikileaks.html.

34. K. Fagan, "'Naughty' Joke Gets Santa Claus Fired from Macy's," *San Francisco Chronicle*, December 7, 2010.

35. "Headlines," *The Tonight Show with Jay Leno*, October 10, 2011.

36. S. Rouse, Sirius XM radio broadcast, 2011.

37. Daniel Kurtzman, "The Week's Best Late-Night Jokes," September 11, 2009, http://politicalhumor.about.com/b/2009/09/11/the-weeks-best-late-night-jokes-46.htm.

38. D. Phan, "Asian Stereotypes," January 29, 2004, http://comedians.jokes.com/dat-phan/videos/dat-phan---asian-stereotypes.

39. See www.trapshooters.com/noframes/cfpages/thread.cfm?threadid=272005&Messages=66.

FOUR

Not All Humor Is All Good

If you don't know where you're going, you'll end up somewhere else.
—Yogi Berra[1]

Effective humor is like an effective drug. We can extend this metaphor by noting that it is essential to administer humor in proper doses in the right setting to the right person in order to obtain the best results. In this chapter I will describe the desired results of humor making—that is, positive humor—and also some of the potentially undesirable side effects—that is, the characteristics of negative humor.

CHARACTERISTICS OF POSITIVE HUMOR

Positive humor, which should be our goal in all humor making, is characterized by the following qualities:

- *Relationship enhancing*: When the humor is delivered, the result is an improved and closer emotional relationship between the humor maker and the audience. The size of an audience may range from just one other person to a small group gathering or even millions of TV viewers. A rapport is established and can actually build to a permanent bond.
- *Desirable effects on listeners*: It brings people together and is thus not divisive to subgroups. The listeners feel uplifted and joyful. The speaker notes their response and feels no guilt or regret for what has been said or done. There is no need for inserting any eraser phrases in the dialogue. The "Just kidding" disclaimer is never necessary with humor that is positive.
- *Funny*: It almost goes without saying (but naturally we can't let that happen) that the attempted humor is indeed perceived as funny by

61

the observers and listeners. Funniness is displayed by their genuine smiling and laughter. That is, the positive responses are not "courtesy laughter," which might indeed be appropriate when encouraging a child's first tries at telling riddles or jokes.

- *Internal*: Of course, it is also possible that humor can be appreciated by someone who fails to smile or laugh aloud. The setting, such as being alone at the time in a car or movie theater, might lead to a silent reaction, while the person simultaneously acknowledges the funniness. People are thirty times more likely to laugh when others are present than when alone. Or, psychologically, the listener at that moment may happen to be feeling especially stressed or anxious for some unrelated reason. The humor is understood and appreciated as funny, but the listener may not respond in visible or audible ways.

CHARACTERISTICS OF NEGATIVE HUMOR

Negative humor is humor that is destructive, hostile, cruel, anger driven, belittling, humiliating, relationship destroying, blatantly biased, extreme in its effects, unpleasant to nearly all listeners in addition to the butts of the joke, and simply outrageous in its disregard for its consequences and lack of boundaries. Despite such an endless list of pejoratives, negative humor could also be funny to some degree. Its price is too high, though. We want to condemn negative humor and object to it in whatever ways possible. How? By not supporting it by buying tickets, books, CDs, videos, or any other productions from its perpetrators. The strongest nonsupport, of course, is achieved by simply not laughing or applauding.

In his final years, even the brilliant comedian George Carlin presented large doses of negative humor. His typical rants about injustices and stupidity in our society were preceded by extremely hostile setups (for example, "Here's another group of people that should be tied up and beaten and set on fire in a Porta-Potty"). Another example of unrelenting angry humor from a professional comes from comedian Jim Norton's book, relevantly titled *I Hate Your Guts*, which aptly begins with a profane quote from George Carlin. To his credit, Norton does include a bit of self-deprecation in his book. However, his description of his own writing as "some light-hearted humor" is a strong candidate for the award for the Understatement of the Decade. Perhaps it is irony?

Audiences seem to tire quickly of unrelenting hostile humor even from established professionals. Your family and friends are guaranteed to respond negatively even more rapidly if angry rants and sarcasm become your preferred type of humor. It simply comes across as intentionally cruel and soon becomes too hard to laugh at or forgive.

Humor scholar Paul Lewis introduces a different spin to the discussion of negative results of humor. He points out that humor is not a benign influence and can result in audiences' relaxation of their critical thinking skills and the promotion of their nonserious mind-set. While we may agree that these effects might occur, in Lewis's view the ultimate danger from negative humor is that citizens will then become more accepting and apathetic about the many real threats facing our country: pollution, divisive politics, terrorism, and more.[2] This degree of spin approaches grandiosity.

A NEW HUMOR RULE

The best strategy is to not reward negative humor or its proponents in any way. Rather, we can support and model positive humor making with our audiences, small or large, thereby reciprocally inhibiting the negative humor. We could call this the *principle of humorous reciprocal inhibition.* Positive humor drives out negative humor by exclusion.

FAILED HUMOR

Failed humor is different from negative humor. In failed humor the speaker was trying to be funny, but the humor didn't work, for whatever reason. The next chapter contains many examples of failed humor by politicians and celebrities and others who made the news, when their clear intent was to say or do something funny. It also happens occasionally to professional comedians. So it is no surprise to see examples of failed humor from sports stars, TV interviewers, and just average citizens.

Indeed, humor may backfire, leading to a range of serious negative consequences. In the mildest form, you just don't get a laugh or you suffer some slight embarrassment. In its most extreme form, a bad joke has actually been known to result in the murder of the joker. For example, in Jacksonville, Florida, two gay male partners gave a female friend a ride home from a local bar where they all had been drinking. One man joked that the woman liked the other man, presumably in a romantic way. This innocuous joking comment clearly questioned the man's sexual orientation, his lifestyle, and his commitment to their relationship. That seemingly trivial bad joke so enraged the target that he shot and killed the joker on the spot. He received a life sentence for his fatal retaliation.[3]

Second only to actual death is the threat of death. As of mid-2011, at least nine actors, writers, and professional comedians have received death threats in response to their humor making. I suspect there are even more. Nonhumorist authors who have been threatened, such as Salman Rushdie, are not included in this select list: talk show host and comedian

David Letterman; the writers and creators of *South Park*, Trey Parker and Matt Stone; actor and screenwriter Kevin Smith; comedian Kevin Nealon; and comic actors Russell Brand, Alexi Sayle, Sacha Baron Cohen, and Ricky Gervais.[4] Some clarification of this list is in order, however. Nealon was threatened with death for *not* being funny, and the threat to Gervais was made by singer-actress Jennifer Lopez, who claimed she was "just kidding."

The threat to Letterman was declared the most serious, since it had been made on the website of the jihadist terrorist organization Al Qaeda. In June 2011 Letterman had joked about the reported death of Mohammad Ilyas Kashmiri, the suspected leader of a Kashmiri militant group. There had never been confirmation that the terrorist had even been killed. Over two months later on the group's website, Letterman, as "a lowly Jew," was threatened with having his tongue cut out and then being killed. CBS and the non-Jewish comedian notified the U.S. authorities of the threat, but he proceeded immediately to joke about it on his show, "accusing" his rival comedian Jay Leno of being the source of the threat, while presenting his "Top Ten List of Thoughts That Went through My Mind after Hearing about the Threat."

Comedian Ian Edwards of MTV's *Punk'd* claims his life has also been threatened because of jokes that he made in his stand-up act. Sometime after a show, a man hunted him down by phone and alleged that Edwards's banter with his wife during the club performance had caused the breakup of their marriage and he, her husband, was planning to have Edwards killed for that. Edwards did not even remember the interaction, but he does admit to breaking up several other couples' relationships in his lifetime via some noncomedic performances.[5] As of this writing, Edwards remains alive and reasonably well.

Of course, most failed humor is not so tragic or dramatic. Humor that hurts still can lead to personal estrangements, the loss of jobs or election votes, or the public embarrassment of politicians or professional comedians, as well as regular folks. Public figures, with the aid of their PR aides, usually have to offer formal public apologies to undo their humor errors. Some examples of these humor bombs by well-known people are presented in the next chapter.

Sunda Croonquist, a veteran professional comedian, suffered the indignity of being sued in the U.S. District Court in New Jersey by her own family members. Her mother-in-law, her own daughter, and her daughter's husband accused her of spreading defamatory and racist lies as part of her stand-up act in clubs and on TV. Ruth Zafrin, the mother-in-law "victim," had never even bothered to complain directly to the comedian about these jokes prior to filing the suit.[6]

Croonquist enjoys a unique multicultural heritage, which she mines successfully for her routines. As the daughter of an African American mother and a European musician, the comedian describes herself as a "half-black, half-Swedish" woman who married into a humorless Jewish family. (Her family description may well be oxymoronic.) Interestingly, she had been reared in the Catholic religion but converted to Judaism before she even met her Jewish husband, which became part of her defense that she is not anti-Jewish. She even keeps a kosher home. This real-life *All in the Family* case, with all its internal conflicts, was further complicated in that Croonquist's husband, Mark Zafrin, was a partner in the law firm that represented the comic against his own mother and the other family members.

Woman's Day magazine included the Croonquist case in its list of the Most Laughable Lawsuits of the year because of the ridiculous reasons that people went to court.[7] And this was not Family Court! The good news is that the federal court judge dismissed the lawsuit in May 2010, although family harmony may not have been totally restored.[8]

The best news for other comedians and all amateur humorists is that the ruling specified that jokes and humorous comments are considered protected speech by the First Amendment to the U.S. Constitution. However, there is no constitutional protection from being offended by humor. Most complainers forget that. The funny lines are just opinions of the speaker, not necessarily factual. Behavioral quirks, semi-delusional beliefs, and the malapropisms of our own family members can continue to be one of the richest sources of humor for us all to draw upon. Don't argue with the judge!

TABOO TOPICS AND HUMOR LIMITS

Bathroom humor is not confined to preteen children. Perhaps playing his "I am a professional comedian" card, Louis C.K. in a televised discussion of comedy offered his views on the funniness of farts: "A fart is funny. It comes out of your ass. It smells like poop. It makes a toot noise. That's hilarious." To adults, Louis? He went on: "You don't have to be smart to laugh at farts, but you have to be stupid not to."[9] Mr. C.K. has created his own unusual test of intelligence. Future psychologists will have to be trained accordingly in our graduate school programs.

Some topics, particularly historical tragedies, are often regarded as taboo topics for humor. Prominent examples of topics that I recommend for amateurs to avoid include the Holocaust; the Challenger rocket explosion; the crucifixion of Christ; the 9/11 attacks; the Columbine or Norwegian massacres; AIDS; the shooting of U.S. Representative Gabby Giffords; Hurricane Katrina; the 2011 Japanese triple disaster of an earthquake, nuclear plant meltdown, and tsunami; public figures known to have a terminal illness; any publicly known cases of child or animal abuse (which technically includes bestiality); or unusual sexual disorders, such as necrophilia.

Just what is the difference between a psychiatric disorder and simply a person's rare erotic interest or preference, if no one is coerced or gets hurt? In fact, all of these topics have been subjects of humor, albeit with varying degrees of success and social acceptance. For example, at some career risk while on stage, comedian Mark Normand has made jokes about pedophilia. He suggests we shouldn't automatically condemn it when some smart kids may be doing it just for the candy.[10] His funny comment is similar to taking a liberal view of prostitution, seeing it as just a viable employment vehicle for uneducated people, primarily women, to make good money in tough economic times without having to dance with a cold pole or create any consequent income tax problems (except in Nevada). You certainly do meet lots of interesting people in that line of work. Of course, I'm sure that Normand was "just kidding" about the pedophilia.

"THE ARISTOCRATS"

For over a century a classic inside joke, originating in the heyday of vaudeville, has been passed down to professional comedians. It was reportedly late-night TV legend Johnny Carson's favorite joke. That joke, technically a postmodern anti-joke, is now available to the general public through the documentary movie *The Aristocrats: 100 Comedians, One Very Dirty Joke* (2005), produced by magician-comedian Penn Jillette and director-comedian Paul Provenza.[11]

The movie features many comedians and actors telling and analyzing the joke. For students of humor, the film is instructive and funny. For those with any social sensitivity to word choices in language, it could be fatal. The joke itself consists of a brief setup; the main body of the joke, which is of variable content and length, subject only to the fertile imaginations of the tellers; and then the brief punch line.

The setup is simply that a family, consisting of a husband, wife, two children, and their dog, enters the office of a talent agent and asks that he book their act. The talent agent asks, "What is your act?" The joke teller then proceeds to describe the act, which is generated totally from each comic's warped unconscious psyche. Thus, the "variable content and length" of this joke consists of describing the most vile, filthy, and disgusting incestuous human and animal behaviors imaginable, physically possible or not, and involving all known bodily fluids. (I fear that I may have understated this aspect.) *Nothing* is left out. Some tellers go on for many minutes, since, when telling this joke, there are no language or time limits. Eventually, the teller quotes the talent agent, who asks, "OK, what is the name of your act?" The answer is the punch line: "The Aristocrats."

Shockingly, at the end of the documentary these words appear on the screen: "Now that you know the joke, keep it alive. Spread the word. All you have to do is remember one word." That advice may not be such a good idea. Some people will surely find the joke funny, but most likely the majority of people will not appreciate it. Then you would not have achieved our goal of "using humor effectively."

The Aristocrats documentary, as you might guess, did not achieve great commercial success. Nevertheless, it was nominated for the Grand Jury Prize at the well-respected Sundance Film Festival. Of course, in less liberal states than Utah, this documentary could gain the attention of other grand juries.

Comedian Gilbert Gottfried is one of the most profane working comics. He has both won and lost big-time by breaking taboos. He lost his job of making voiceover commercials for the Aflac Insurance Company by making a few in-bad-taste jokes about the 2011 Japanese natural disasters on his Twitter account.[12] However, Gottfried also has been credited for "saving" the Friars Club Roast of *Playboy* founding publisher Hugh Hefner, which happened to have long been scheduled in New York for about two and a half weeks after the 9/11 attacks. There had been considerable concern about whether to go through with the event so close in time and geography to the World Trade Center catastrophes. The roast did go on, but haltingly. Gottfried seemed to decide on the spur of the moment to tell the one joke that violates all the taboos that his perverse mind could generate—"The Aristocrats." The joke "killed," with the other comedians rolling on the floor laughing, while "Hef" himself appeared a bit befuddled at the events surrounding the joke.[13]

Gilbert Gottfried's case is one example of an unfair (in my view) negative consequence to tasteless humor. Gottfried is widely known as a blue comedian whose jokes and language are as raunchy and obscene as anyone else's in the business. This persona existed long before the occurrence of the triple tragedy in Japan. Gottfried did make some poor-taste jokes about the combined Japanese nuclear plant meltdown, earthquake, and tsunami. It so happened that his professional work at the time also included serving as the voice of the iconic Aflac duck in some animated commercials for that insurance company. Many people probably were unaware of the identity of the voiceover artist for the ad. There was, in fact, no connection whatsoever between Gottfried's jokes and the commercials or the company, other than the fact that it was the same person speaking.

Despite public support from Howard Stern and comedian Joan Rivers and his formal apologetic statement for his "attempt at humor regarding the tragedy in Japan," Gottfried was promptly fired. Joan Rivers's unsuccessful defense claimed, "That's what comedians do! We react to tragedy by making jokes to help people in tough times feel better through laughter." Gottfried, having no other recourse, then openly advised other comedians to "observe everything I do and do the opposite."[14] Unfortunately, that is very good advice.

Roseanne Barr is also no stranger to public controversy. On July 26, 1990, before a San Diego Padres baseball game, she gave what *Time* magazine has proclaimed to be the worst public rendition of "The Star-Spangled Banner" in history. The Bleacher Reports website concurred with *Time's* number one ranking for Barr's singing, over the only slightly less horrible versions of the anthem performed elsewhere by Carl Lewis, R. Kelly, and Steven Tyler, in that order.[15]

In addition to the fans' booing, which erupted immediately, she actually received death threats later from unhappy "patriots." Originally it was reported that she had thought it would be funny to sing off key intentionally and to mimic baseball players by scratching and spitting. More recently, though, Barr has explained that she actually is a good singer, but had erroneously started the anthem in a key that was too high for her to stay with throughout. Thus, her poor singing was unintentional, but the scratching and spitting were not. Regardless, she was wrong about her mimicry being funny. But unlike some other professional singers in this role at a public event, she at least remembered all the words to the song.

Roseanne's persona and philosophy of humor almost guarantee that she will be offending some portion of the public within earshot. It doesn't bother her. She boasts, "I always get in professional trouble. . . . I'm a comic. I have to spit in their eyes. . . . They don't ever invite me back again. That's how it is."[16] At least she doesn't try to spit in their ears.

Outspoken talk show host and comedian Chelsea Handler admits that even she has limits to her comedic attacks. She won't attack celebrities or friends whom she respects and who conduct themselves with dignity. She adds, "I don't want to make fun of people's children who aren't good-looking, or if someone has a disease, I don't want to make fun of that." She prefers targets who are stars that "bring the crazy on themselves," such as Paula Abdul and David Hasselhoff.[17] There should be no shortage of material for her.

Russell Brand is a no-holds-barred, bawdy British actor, comedian, and "reformed womanizer," according to *USA Today*. But this Brand also has limits. In a more reflective moment, he explains, "Authenticity and integrity are vital components in creating comedy that people can identify with. I wouldn't say anything that would embarrass her [his then wife Katy Perry] or compromise us."[18] Is this a new maturity? Sensitivity? Fear of loss? Inebriation? Just a lie? Take your pick.

Professional comedians must continually push the good-taste envelope to get noticed and to be funnier than their competitors. With the increasing artistic freedoms available on cable TV and the antiquated obscenity laws unenforced for comedy clubs in America, comics are becoming more and more outrageous in their language and the topics they pick to discuss in their acts. Is there any topic too blue or too sensitive to be joked about in public?

Two examples from the Comedy Channel's roast of comedian Joan Rivers certainly danced around the borders of bad taste.[19] Joan's husband, Edgar Rosenberg, had committed suicide twenty-two years previously. A roaster asked Joan, "Any messages for Edgar? Carl Reiner [an elderly comedian-author present on the dais that night] will be seeing him soon." Robin Quivers, an African American radio and TV personality, was also on the dais. Another roaster pointed out, "Robin Quivers is here because someone later will need turndown service." In this special setting of a formal roast, it was deemed fair game to make fun of the honoree's husband's death and to make a racist joke about one of the participating stars. There are no limits at celebrity roasts. Nothing is cut unless it's not funny.

Jim Norton believes, "A good comic disrupts the ideology of everyone in the audience. He disses everybody's beliefs."[20] Of course, the philosophy of "a good comic" is not necessarily the recommended path for regular folks who'd simply like to add more humor to their everyday lives for greater interpersonal effectiveness. It is so much safer to avoid attacking personal beliefs and to increase the degree of self-deprecation in your personal humor.

Comedian Rob Mailloux claims that even abortion jokes and Holocaust jokes are now acceptable for the professionals, but any story implying the injury of an animal is still taboo. Even bestiality jokes will work, if the behavior is classified as an act of love rather than one of animal cruelty. Mailloux's material, though, has gotten him banned from various Canadian comedy clubs.[21]

The late comedian Sam Kinison epitomized extremism in comedy. A friend of Sam's once told him that he had read a news story about a very bizarre clinical case in California that was extremely interesting but definitely too weird and too gross to ever be made into a joke. Sam instantly took up the challenge and asked him what the case was about. His friend reluctantly admitted, "Homosexual necrophilia." Kinison soon added this story to his act and made it hilarious.

Very little, if anything, is truly off limits in professional comedy. George Carlin agreed: "I think you can make a joke about anything. It all depends on how the joke is constructed. It depends on what the exaggeration is."[22] Most humor theorists point to the equation of "tragedy + time = potential for funny." This equation is so well known that when a joke on a sensitive topic falls flat, professional comedians will often use the recovery line "Too soon?" A heckler yelled out the same thing after one of Gottfried's jokes at the Hefner roast about an airplane "stopping" at the Empire State Building, just two and a half weeks after the 9/11 World Trade Center crashes.[23]

Chris Rock joins the free-swinging comedians under the banner of "Nothing Is Off Limits" in comedy. His view is as follows: "You don't want to hurt people—unless they hurt people. . . . I'll talk about anything."[24] And he does so in very funny ways, with a liberal use of the N-word and other profanities. He tackles topics that non–African Americans might not be able to get away with.

Robin Williams's career has long been the benchmark of outrageous improvisational comedy. However, his recent heart surgery for an aortic valve replacement, his divorce after nineteen years of marriage and subsequent new marriage, and various stints in rehab facilities for his alcohol and drug dependencies have changed his on-stage persona. He now admits, "There are boundaries. . . . Everything is not fair game, especially about my family."

Williams suggests a good practical test for determining whether you should make a joke about something or somebody: "Are you OK with the consequences of what you say? And do you have the [guts] to stand behind it?"[25] For the professional comedian, those consequences might be hearing "boos" in response, having people walk out of your show, ticketholders demanding refunds, receiving hate mail, cancellation of future TV bookings and concert dates, and the subsequent economic and professional status losses. For the amateur humorists, the losses are more likely to be social than financial. Friends and potential friends will be turned off by someone who constantly tries to tell offensive jokes or makes off-color comments as poor and immature ways to draw attention.

Some professional comics, though, can attack these taboo topics successfully. For example, Ralphie May, a white Southern comedian, is a great mimic of African American dialect and humor forms. He becomes adamant about his hatred of racism. He then does several very funny bits about interacting with blacks in movies and restaurants. His audiences, well aware of the latest PC standards, initially tend to become restless and subdued. May then reassures his nervous audience that it is really OK and not to worry because he carries a "brother card" in his back pocket. He probably does.

May fearlessly jumps into the murky and treacherous PC waters after his performances by brazenly selling T-shirts that prominently display the initials "H.N.I.C." (Head Nigger In Charge). He points out that black people can buy the shirts for half the price and white people can get them too, if they very nicely ask a black person to make the purchase for them. May believes he is contributing to the social fight against racism. His is certainly a provocative position worthy of some serious discussion.

Comedian Sarah Silverman has boldly taken on major taboo topics such as AIDS, 9/11, rape, abortions, the Holocaust, and the children of Britney Spears, whom she labeled "adorable mistakes" to a national TV audience.[26] Children of celebrities and politicians are usually off-limits for comedy (cf. Chelsea Clinton), at least until they reach adulthood. Yet Silverman won't do fat jokes about women, a seemingly much tamer topic.[27] Who knows how much her joking about taboos has limited Silverman's career? She does very well as it is, but it is logically impossible to say that she could or could not be an even bigger star.

Silverman, whose humor has been described by Associated Press as "cute, obnoxious, and depraved," explains, "I just want to be funny, and the things that make me laugh tend to be toward the taboo side. I try not to imply anything deep. But, if something's inferred from it, all the better. . . . A lot of dumb stuff can be seen as smart if a smart person chooses to find it thought-provoking, and glean something from it." [28] Silverman is very aware that she has no control over what people conclude from hearing her jokes. "Some people are going to enjoy your jokes in a very horrific way." [29] Perhaps this is an oxymoron from her, but most likely a truism as well.

Following the tragedies on 9/11, the U.S. Department of Homeland Security in 2002 introduced a five-level color-coded terror alert system. This system immediately prompted near-universal ridicule. Conan O'Brien joked, "Champagne-fuchsia means we're being attacked by Martha Stewart." Jay Leno contributed, "They added a plaid in case we were ever attacked by Scotland." [30] The general public never knew exactly what to do or not do in response to these various alerts. The widespread joking and ridicule about the color system resulted in its vigorous "benign neglect" and ultimately a revision.

Comedian Jim Norton contributes a thoughtful discussion point when he notes that actors are treated differently than comedians in terms of how the public holds them accountable: "Actors can play any role and it's OK, but comedians can offend with their humor." [31] What is different, though, is that when an actor speaks on stage or in a movie, the audience knows that the words really come from the author or screenwriter. When comedians speak, their message is presumed to be their personal beliefs and unique "take" with their observations.

Audience members, though, should be aware that what comedians say may or may not be what they *really* believe. Even Andrew Dice Clay in interviews strives to distinguish his obscene comedy performances from his behaviors in his personal life. The problem is that audiences tend to accept and believe what the comedian is saying from the stage. That is part of establishing rapport with the audience. However, who really knows how much of any comedian's comments are truthful? Depending on the particular comedian and the bit in question, I am certain that the answer is somewhere between 0 percent and 100 percent. Your percentage may vary.

There are definitely jokes out there about all of the taboo topics mentioned above. Some of them appeared on the Internet or among friends almost immediately upon the occurrence of the tragic events. However, instant joke writing does not ensure social acceptability or demonstrations of compassion for disaster victims, their loved ones, or empathic members of society in general. Professional comedians can frequently, but not always, get away with jokes on these very sensitive topics. Our best advice for amateurs: "Don't try this at home."

THE RIDICULE EFFECT

Politicians are especially vulnerable to instances of failed humor or unintentional humor at their own expense. They must constantly seek votes and financial support for the next election. Consequently, their "misstatements" can be quite costly to them. If there is a pattern of remarks that sound silly or stupid, they soon will become subject to the Ridicule Effect. Thomas Jefferson long ago noted, "Ridicule is the only weapon which can be used against unintelligible propositions."[32] His advice remains useful today.

The Ridicule Effect occurs when someone's statement or belief system is so off the charts that most people, whether professional comedians, conversationalists at the water cooler or around the dinner table, or folks on Facebook, begin to openly make fun of the statement and the speaker. That person's credibility and viability as a leader become diminished immediately. Politicians and government policies, such as the color-coded terror alert system, become neutralized and are no longer taken seriously.

Recent prominent victims of the Ridicule Effect include Howard Dean, Michael Brown, and Dan Quayle. Howard Dean was unique in that he became subject to the Ridicule Effect without even speaking. His downfall was an exuberant yodel/yell in celebration of his third-place finish in the Iowa caucus for the Democratic nomination for president in January 2004. Dean had been leading the polls until then and was showing great joy and excitement in his effort to rally his supporters in the face of the disappointing results. If you look back at his unplanned speech, Dean's enthusiastic outburst was actually quite tame and reasonable—certainly not ridiculous. Unfortunately, it allowed the media (with which he already had an antagonistic relationship) to criticize him unrelentingly to the point of ridicule. Jon Stewart and others dubbed the event Dean's "I Have a Scream" speech.[33] He soon dropped out of contention for the nomination, partially due to becoming a victim of the Ridicule Effect.

Michael Brown, the head of FEMA (Federal Emergency Management Agency) during the Hurricane Katrina disaster in New Orleans, was a lawyer whose previous experience was that of heading up an Arabian horse association. The mere mention of his name today connotes managerial incompetence, and he has never regained public acceptance. President's Bush's attempt to be supportive with his compliment, "Brownie, you're doing a heckuva job," won an award from Global Language Monitor as the most memorable "Bushism" of 2005.[34] The phrase has remained a permanent line of classic comedy.

Former Vice President Dan Quayle became subject to the Ridicule Effect by, among a series of other misstatements, misspelling "potato" by adding an "e" to the end of the word during a spelling bee on June 15, 1992, at a Trenton, New Jersey, elementary school—which was exacerbated by his inability to recognize his error. Even the twelve-year-old student whom Quayle had wrongly corrected later referred to the vice president as an "idiot."[35] The late-night comics feasted on this blunder, and in less than five months, the first President Bush and his poor-spelling running mate were voted out of office.

These three men largely brought public ridicule upon themselves. Sigmund Freud suggested that as an expression of aggression, you could intentionally use ridicule as a vehicle to hurt or limit the effectiveness of the target person. He pointed out, "One can make a person comic in order to make him contemptible, to deprive him of his claim to dignity and authority."[36] Thus, you can suffer from the Ridicule Effect via your own hand or at the hands and mouths of others.

The ridicule continues, with Quayle still considered America's favorite dumb politician, although the second President Bush became a strong competitor for the title. An amazon.com search for "Bushisms" yields fifty-eight different entries for collections of George W. Bush's classic misstatements, sometimes euphemistically referred to as his "accidental wit and wisdom."

Some of the best of the Bushisms include the following:

"I'm the master of low expectations."
"There's an old saying in Tennessee—I know it's in Texas—probably in Tennessee—that says, fool me once, shame on—shame on you. Fool me—you can't get fooled again."
"Is our children learning?"
"I appreciate the fact that you really snatched defeat out of the jaws of those who were trying to defeat us in Iraq." (Bush to Lieutenant General Ray Odierno)
"I think if you know what you believe, it makes it a lot easier to answer questions. I can't answer your question."[37]

By volume alone, "W" certainly deserves world-class status for English-language malapropism. Former comedian and now U.S. senator Al Franken cautions us, "But don't be fooled. He's less stupid than you think."[38] Any ridicule for the president's innumerable and verified verbal errors may have been somewhat thwarted by Bush's appealing folksy and genial persona. He was indeed elected and reelected president of the United States, albeit in close and disputed elections.

As an upcoming popular political figure, 2008 vice presidential nominee Sarah Palin came dangerously close to disqualifying herself as a serious presidential candidate by not being able to give a coherent answer to Katie Couric's softball interview question about what newspapers and magazines she reads. After pausing briefly for apparent reflection, Palin responded, "All of 'em, any of 'em that have been in front of me over all these years."[39] Ms. Palin has now accumulated enough misstatements to have a desk calendar of 366 "Palinisms" published for 2012, which is a leap year.

Publishing two ghostwritten books within two years may have partially restored Palin's literary credibility, at least among her most devoted fans. However, the ridiculing jokes about her apparently limited knowledge of history and geography, her down-home folksy style, and her lack of gravitas continue to be a serious concern among Palin's supporters. Adding to their dismay is the 2010 publication of Jacob Weisberg's book *Palinisms*: "The best Palinisms of all result when the huntress encounters something she wasn't hunting for—that is, when Sarah Palin comes into contact with most anything to do with domestic, foreign, or economic policy."[40] Weisberg's collection contains the following verbatim classic comments from Sarah Palin:

> "If God had not intended us to eat animals, how come He made them out of meat?" (This serious observation from her first published book is likely to alienate any potential voter who is vegetarian or has an IQ greater than 75.)
>
> "Nuclear weaponry, of course, would be the be-all, end-all of just too many people in too many parts of the planet." (Note that this position misstatement came from an aspiring leader of the world's number one nuclear superpower.)
>
> "Obviously we gotta [sic] stand with our North Korean allies." (This was stated on Glenn Beck's TV show, which led to his quick correction to her memory of U.S.-Korea history.)

Sarah Palin's unique use of language has resulted in one curious award. Her neologism *refudiate* was designated by the New Oxford American Dictionary as the official 2010 Word of the Year.

To be fair, the Bushisms (and now the Palinisms) were usually not intended by the speaker to be funny, but they were indeed funny and quickly led to ridicule. Editor Weisberg points out an interesting difference between the comments of Bush and Palin: "Bushisms, which I collected for many years, often hinged on a single grammatical or factual error. Palinisms, by contrast, consist of a unitary stream of patriotic, populist blather. It's like Fox News without the punctuation. It is so devoid of content that it hardly deserves the adjective 'truthy.'"[41] Public speakers must always be cognizant of how their remarks will be interpreted. They can often create backfiring humor, while trying to be serious.

One humor theorist, Michael Billig, considers all humor to be ridicule. He sees it as a vehicle to resist change and favor the current power holders, because ridicule can keep people behaving in accordance with the conventional norms of social life by our laughing at them. Professor Billig argues that ridicule plays a disciplinary function in all cultures to maintain control.[42] This consequence surely does occur frequently, but this equation hardly is explanatory of all humor.

When public figures become public jokes subject to widespread ridicule, their credibility is typically significantly diminished. The effect tends to be permanent, with the person forever regarded as "damaged goods." Politicians would be better served if they let their speechwriters prepare their humor for them. All they need to do is keep smiling and practice sounding sincere.

SHOULD YOU BECOME A CURMUDGEON?

Jon Winokur has compiled over a thousand outrageous and irreverently funny quotations from world-class curmudgeons in his book *The Portable Curmudgeon.* Younger readers may not be familiar with the characteristics of a curmudgeon, while older readers might find it an enticing persona and lifestyle. In fact, its tendencies may subtly creep up on people as they age. Let's examine this fascinating option for humor making and its multiple risks and rewards.

What is a curmudgeon? One synonym is *grouch.* It is more complicated than that, of course, because we are concerned with people who are intentionally funny, not just grouchy. Generally professional comics and amateur humorists signal their humor making by smiling simultaneously or otherwise indicating that humor is coming. There are exceptions among the pros, such as Steven Wright and the late Mitch Hedberg.

Although Winokur's book is portable, his description of the curmudgeon is complete and compelling. Most often curmudgeons are described as males, but there is no reason why women cannot join this group with full honors. Political correctness has not yet reached all frontiers.

Winokur's description is as follows:

> Dictionaries define *curmudgeon* as a churlish, irascible fellow; a cantankerous old codger. . . . A curmudgeon's reputation for malevolence is undeserved. They're neither warped nor evil at heart. They don't hate mankind, just mankind's excesses. They're just as sensitive and softhearted as the next guy, but they hide their vulnerability beneath a crust of misanthropy. They ease the pain by turning hurt into humor. They snarl at pretense and bite at hypocrisy out of a healthy sense of outrage. They lack maudlinism because it devalues genuine sentiment. They hurl polemical thunderbolts at middle-class values and pop culture in order to preserve their sanity. Nature, having failed to equip them with a serviceable denial mechanism, has endowed them with astute perception and sly wit. Offense is their only defense. Their weapons are irony, satire, sarcasm, ridicule. Their targets are pretense, pomposity, conformity, incompetence. . . .

Curmudgeons are mockers and debunkers whose bitterness is a symptom rather than a disease. They can't compromise their standards and can't manage the suspension of disbelief necessary for feigned cheerfulness. Their awareness is a curse; they're constantly ticked off because they're constantly aware of so much to be ticked off about, and they wish things were better . . . . They have the temerity to comment on the human condition without apology. They not only refuse to applaud mediocrity, they howl it down with morose glee. Their versions of the truth unsettle us, and we hold it against them, even though they soften it with humor.[43]

Winokur strives to give solace to all closet curmudgeons. He argues that "there's no shame in chronic alienation, that curmudgeonry is a perfectly valid response to an increasingly exasperating world."[44] He does admit to being in a bad mood since 1971.

A Sampling of America's Greatest (At Least Most Famous) Curmudgeons

W. C. Fields: "I am free of all prejudices. I hate everyone equally."
Truman Capote: "It's a scientific fact that if you stay in California you lose one point of your IQ every year."
Groucho Marx: "She got her good looks from her father. He's a plastic surgeon."
Mark Twain: "If Christ were here now, there is one thing he would not be—a Christian."
Calvin Trillin: "Health food makes me sick."
James Thurber: "You can fool too many of the people too much of the time."
Oscar Levant: "I don't drink. I don't like it—it makes me feel good."
George S. Kaufman in a review of a play: "There was laughter in the back of the theater, leading to the belief that someone was telling jokes back there."
Gore Vidal: "I'm a born again atheist."
Woody Allen: "Life is divided into the horrible and the miserable."

As you can see, these curmudgeons' comments are pithy, provocative, and perceptive. Of course, they will not likely obtain immediate or universal agreement from their audiences. Let's review the positives and negatives of your adopting a curmudgeon's persona.

Possible positive results:

- You will be seen by others as intelligent, witty, clever, and a host of other desirable characteristics, but not necessarily sexy.
- You may be seen as irascible, principled, funny, and worthy of others' friendship.
- You may be quoted by others in admiring ways to their friends.

- It can be great personal fun to indulge yourself and express your curmudgeonly opinions widely.
- You may even have some impact on the world by affecting others' behaviors, attitudes, and values, if they adopt your point of view.

Possible negative results:

- The positive results listed above are only possible, not necessarily probable or certain.
- You may be quoted by others in critical ways.
- You may turn off family and friends by seemingly sounding so negative and cynical that nothing is ever good.
- Your curmudgeonly persona may produce a quick dismissal of any potentially positive contributions to your discussions, conversations, or meetings with others.
- Others may admire your intellect but would not choose you to be their personal friend or lover.

Given these pros and cons to the curmudgeon lifestyle, what to do? Are you willing to take the risks for the potential rewards? Certainly, one does not have to "go all in" and make it a lifestyle choice. You can dabble with an occasional curmudgeonly comment while perhaps indulging yourself privately by devouring the writings and interviews with known great curmudgeons.

Many curmudgeons are foreign-born writers whose works you can read and enjoy for a lifetime: George Bernard Shaw, François Voltaire, James Joyce, Leo Tolstoy, Quentin Crisp, Alexandre Dumas (senior and junior), Honoré de Balzac, Bertolt Brecht, Friedrich Nietzsche, and innumerable others.

One final caution: There seems to be a clear developmental trend in humans, perhaps especially so in men, toward taking on curmudgeonly values with age. Is this an inevitable outcome? Not necessarily. You can develop it or stifle it. You definitely have a choice as to what degree you want to display those values and opinions. As funny as they might be to you, you need to know that their positive reception is likely to be something less than 100 percent of your audience.

In June 2011 feisty Jack McKeon returned to major league baseball by accepting the job as the manager of the Florida Marlins team. At age eighty he became the second-oldest manager in baseball history. Given Jack's well-known persona as a curmudgeon, a pundit immediately pointed out that McKeon spent the first day yelling at his players "to get the hell off my lawn." Curmudgeons can be comic targets, too.

NOTES

1. www.goodreads.com/author/quotes/79014.Yogi_Berra.

2. R. A. Martin, "Review of Paul Lewis' *Cracking Up: American Humor in a Time of Conflict*," *Humor: International Journal of Humor Research* 24, no. 3 (2011): 357–62.

3. P. Pinkham, "Man Gets Life Sentence in Roommate's Shooting," *Florida Times-Union*, May 9, 2009.

4. "David Letterman Death Threat: 7 Other Comedians Who Have Been Targeted," August 17, 2011, www.huffingtonpost.com.

5. I. Edwards, interview on Sirius XM radio broadcast, 2011.

6. A. Roker, interview with Sunda Croonquist, *Today Show*, NBC Television Network, August 26, 2009.

7. A. Gekas, "9 Most Laughable Lawsuits," www.womansday.com/life/9-most-laughable-lawsuits-110630.

8. J. Rogers, "Judge Tosses 'Mother-in-Lawsuit' vs. Comedian," Associated Press, May 4, 2010.

9. J. Stewart, interview with Louis C.K., *The Daily Show*, Comedy Network, June 28, 2011.

10. M. Normand, January 3, 2011, www.youtube.com/watch?v=bord-rlANYo.

11. *The Aristocrats: 100 Comedians, One Very Dirty Joke*, produced by P. Jillette and P. Provenza (2005), DVD.

12. CNN Wire Staff, "Comedian Gilbert Gottfried Fired as Voice of Aflac Duck," March 15, 2011.

13. G. Gottfried, 2001, www.youtube.com/watch?v=7VE2VVbpZ7w; J. Ross, *I Only Roast the Ones I Love: How to Bust Balls without Burning Bridges* (New York: Gallery Books, 2009), 146–49.

14. L. Powers, "Howard Stern, Joan Rivers Defend Gilbert Gottfried," *Hollywood Reporter*, March 15, 2011, www.hollywoodreporter.com/news/howard-stern-joan-rivers-defend-167799.

15. http://bleacherreport.com/articles/751210-worst-national-anthem-performances-of-all-time.

16. R. Barr, *The Green Room with Paul Provenza*, Showtime Network, June 18, 2011.

17. G. J. Carter, "Chelsea Handler Gets a 'Bang' out of Her Future," *USA Today*, April 26, 2010.

18. O. Barker, "Russell Brand Bares His Talkative Self," *USA Today*, June 3, 2010.

19. Roast of Joan Rivers, Comedy Central Cable Network, August 6, 2009.

20. *Jim Norton Show*, Sirius XM radio broadcast, July 24, 2010.

21. S. Davidson, "Rob Mailloux: Burning Bridges . . . and DVDs," *The (Toronto) Grid*, June 11, 2011, www.thegridto.com/culture/arts/rob-mailloux-burning-bridges%E2%80%A6-and-dvds.

22. G. Carlin, "George Carlin—Parental Advisory: Explicit Lyrics CD," 1990, www.iceboxman.com/carlin/pael.php.

23. Ross, *I Only Roast the Ones I Love*, 147.

24. C. Rock, "Talking Funny," HBO Cable Network, April 22, 2011.

25. D. Freydkin, "Robin Williams' New Life on the Slow Track," *USA Weekend*, June 4–6, 2010.

26. F. Moore, "Daring to Be Sarah Silverman," *Florida Times-Union*, October 10, 2007.

27. K. Lopez, "Comic Sarah Silverman Shares Stories of a 'Bedwetter,'" *USA Today*, April 20, 2010.

28. F. Moore, "Daring to Be Sarah Silverman," *Florida Times-Union*, October 10, 2007.

29. K. Lopez, "Comic Sarah Silverman Shares Stories of a 'Bedwetter,'" *USA Today*, April 20, 2010.

30. J. Schwartz, "U.S. to Drop Color-Coded Terror Alerts," *New York Times*, November 25, 2010.

31. J. Norton, interview on Sirius XM radio, 2011.

32. www.goodreads.com/quotes/show/39508.

33. "Howard Dean's 'I Have a Scream Speech': The Making of a Media Event," 2010, http://ratchetup.typepad.com/eyes/2004/03/howard_deans_i_.html.

34. A. Spiegelman, "President Bush's 'Brownie' Quote Wins Award," *Common Dreams*, December 30, 2005, www.commondreams.org/headlines05/1230-01.htm.

35. P. Mickle, "1992: Gaffe with an 'E' at the End," *Trentonian*, www.capitalcentury.com/1992.html.

36. www.bartleby.com/279/7.html.

37. J. Weisberg, ed., *Still More George W. Bushisms* (New York: Touchstone Books/ Simon & Schuster, 2007).

38. A. Franken, "Foreword," in *Still More George W. Bushisms*, edited by J. Weisberg (New York: Touchstone Books/Simon & Schuster, 2007).

39. J. Weisberg, ed., *Palinisms: The Accidental Wit and Wisdom of Sarah Palin* (New York and Boston: Mariner Books/Houghton Mifflin, 2010).

40. Weisberg, *Palinisms*.

41. J. Weisberg, "Introduction," in *Palinisms: The Accidental Wit and Wisdom of Sarah Palin* (New York and Boston: Mariner Books/Houghton Mifflin, 2010).

42. M. Billig, *Laughter and Ridicule: Towards a Social Critique of Humour* (London: Sage, 2005).

43. J. Winokur, *The Portable Curmudgeon* (New York: Penguin, 1992), 1–2.

44. Winokur, *The Portable Curmudgeon*, 6.

FIVE

Public Bombings

No matter what goes wrong, there's always someone who knew it would.
—Evans and Bjorn's Law[1]

Why try to improve your humor making and be more effective in its use? Humor sometimes fails. It bombs, and when that metaphorical bombing occurs in public, it can be nearly as disastrous as a weapon of war. The results can range from embarrassment to humiliation and ridicule. Often a public apology is called for when the failed humor came from the mouths of celebrities or politicians. Luckily for them, such highly paid people usually can hire public relations consultants to craft their apologies to help minimize the damage. It would be so much better if they, and all of us, were less likely to set off those humor bombs, thus making our use of humor as effective as intended.

This chapter describes many examples of failed humor by both well-known and not-so-well-known people. It is important and instructive to present these examples of negative modeling. They teach us what *not* to say in our humor making. Social acceptability is a delicate variable to assess, and so is deciding what is tasteful, appropriate humor. That depends on a host of factors that make it impossible to present rigid guidelines. Any guidelines must be relative to the context of the proposed humor.

Are humor bombs really a big deal for the average person who isn't trying to make a living from comic performing? YES. Inappropriate humor, cruel remarks, tasteless jokes, unfunny innuendos, hurtful "just kidding" comments—all can create serious negative consequences. No one enjoys being the butt of jokes—at least not for very long. Yes, just as with the disruptive child in a classroom, it does gain you some attention, but ultimately that attention is short lived and not positive.

Human resource experts tell us that the number one reason people leave their jobs is because they are unhappy. This becomes one of the bases for incorporating humor into the corporate culture. The business world, especially in the largest organizations, has traditionally discouraged humor and laughter. Consider the phrases "business-like," "getting down to business," "business oriented" and others, which all connote characteristics such as being sober, serious, hard-driving, aggressive, single minded, and HUMORLESS. Humor is seen (falsely, we must emphasize) as a distraction to the company's main missions of efficiency and profitability.

What bad outcomes could happen due to the misuse of humor? Here are some possibilities related only to the workplace: You may be denied an interview for a job based on a humor bomb in your cover letter or your resumé. If you gain the interview, you may be disregarded as a viable contender for the position. Once hired, you may not be taken as a serious worker and your suggestions in meetings or in memos to superiors may be summarily dismissed. Sales may not be closed, coworkers may complain of harassment by you, and promotions may be delayed or nonexistent. In the workplace, smiling and friendliness are certainly helpful in establishing cordial relationships with coworkers and those above or below you on the organization chart. However, taking up work time telling formal jokes or sending funny e-mails, especially those with potentially offensive content, represents the kinds of humor making most prone to bombing.

On a personal level, due to inappropriate humor, friendships don't get established or ongoing ones can become threatened. If you see someone in a bar or at a party whom you are interested in as a possible friend or date, humor can work like a magic key to intimacy—or it can result in the quickest turnoff on record. Even long-term relationships with spouses or family members can be jeopardized with frequent inappropriate humor attempts. The inappropriateness is typically due to overtly hostile humor or salacious content unsuitable for that group. Not only is the immediate reaction negative, but the failed humor may also create an ongoing and festering personal irritation with the aspiring "humorist."

Buddy Hackett's advice was simple: "Don't hurt anybody." He explained that even if your friend is offended by your humorous attack, he may not say anything about it. Hackett's buddy, insult comic Jeffrey Ross, reports that Buddy believed that "most people will never bother to tell you that they're upset. Instead you'll just quietly lose them as a friend."[2] Would any laugh be worth it?

Lisa Lampanelli is a regular roaster on the Comedy Channel. In all hyperbole she points out, "Being roasted is the highest form of flattery. . . . That's the biggest honor in the world."[3] Other than this special format of roasting someone you really care about, most humor attacks occur unintentionally. Speakers are ordinarily trying to be funny without hurting. Their errors are their unawareness of the audience's sensitivities, their disregard of social consensus for acceptability, and their willingness to be hurtful as a side effect of their remarks.

Even formal roasts by professionals have their limits. Not all of the Friars Club roast's jokes get broadcast on TV. Self-proclaimed Roastmaster General Jeffrey Ross subtitled his book on roasting techniques *How to Bust Balls without Burning Bridges*. Of course, the boundaries still get stretched just about as far as the roasters' imaginations can carry them, with few bridges surviving.

Some people, even those with a keen sense of humor, seem unable to interact with others without immediately expressing every thought that appears in their mind. This impulsivity is a dangerous trait. Larry David's role on the HBO hit show *Curb Your Enthusiasm* is a good example of this characteristic, even though not all of Larry's thoughts are intended to be humorous. He becomes outraged at the most picayune social behaviors by others, makes a blunt comment to the offender, and soon creates a confrontation. These common scenes are easy for the audience to identify with, but most well-socialized people would ignore such trivial slights. Not Larry. And that is what makes it all very funny. In defining his comedic perspective, Joy Behar quotes Larry as saying, "The more people I can offend, the better."[4] But what if you or a close friend behaved in real life, especially with regard to humor making, as Larry David does on his show? That wouldn't be so funny.

In all of these instances we can enjoy others' missteps, indulging in some *Schadenfreude*, and learn what kinds of humor-making blunders to avoid from their negative examples. Professional comedians all occasionally bomb, so it is little surprise that other public figures also frequently make humor blunders.

RACISM AND HOMOPHOBIA IN STAND-UP COMEDY

Are there any boundaries at all for stand-up comedians performing before paid audiences in clubs? Should there be? As comedian and writer Elayne Boosler reminds us, "Words won't kill you unless they are 'Ready, aim, fire!'"[5]

Comic actor Michael Richards, whose greatest fame came from his role of Kramer on the giant TV hit *Seinfeld*, committed professional suicide with his racist rant at The Laugh Factory comedy club in Los Angeles in late 2006. His meltdown was captured on video and naturally is now widely available on the Internet.[6]

Richards had been heckled that night by some club patrons prior to his loss of control on stage. Heckling, though, goes with the territory for stand-up comedians. Most of them learn to deal with it effectively early in their careers and can quickly defuse the tension. It demonstrates who is in charge without provoking more emotion or rebuttal. For example, when people were talking during his performance, Eddie Brill was more subtle in dealing with the distracting behaviors by calmly pointing out, "It sucks when you come out for a chat and they build a comedy club around you." A low-key response usually will return control to the comedian without creating a confrontation.

Unfortunately, Michael Richards became extremely angry and was at a loss for an effective response. Rather, he "lost it" big-time that night. He later apologized to those heckling individuals and other patrons, partially at the public behest of Jerry Seinfeld, but he has not yet been fully forgiven by the general public.

Paul Mooney is a senior African American comedian, highly respected by his peers in the world of comedy. He credits the meltdown of his friend Richards for being the precipitating stimulus for his own campaign to eliminate the N-word from all comedy routines. He accepted Richards's apology as unquestionably sincere: "It fucked with him and scared him, and he was *really* sorry." Mooney added, "*Everybody's* responsible for it and has to *take* responsibility for it before we can change any of this. . . . I knew I was a *part* of it."[7]

Elayne Boosler (among very few other comic professionals) was also sympathetic to Richards's plight. She certainly does not condone the use of the N-word by stand-up comedians, seeing it as a substitute for actual comedy. She explained, "He's not racist. He was simply in the zone. Comedy clubs are like Indian reservations. They are their own country. I don't think he should have apologized."[8]

However, if you watch Richards's performance that night, he was definitely *not* "in the zone" of performing flawlessly and funny. His "zone," in fact, was a racist tirade that shocked all listeners, coming as a result of some fairly mild heckling. Heckling a working comedian is certainly in bad taste and discourteous to other audience members. But Richards's response was extreme and totally unfunny. Humor bombs can be career threatening.

Michael Richards may have inadvertently founded the Homophobic Comedians Club, but new members Filipino American comedian Jo Koy and African American comedian Tracy Morgan have joined as well. Some female fans in the front row at one of Koy's shows could see that Koy's fly was open and pointed to it. Then a man shouted, "I saw it." While the "it" reference is ambiguous, Koy then singled out the man and called him a "fucking faggot." Koy issued an apology on Twitter the next day, regretting his "poor choice of words" and stating explicitly, "Homophobia is not funny."[9]

Morgan had mentioned in his stand-up act on June 3, 2011, in Nashville that if his son turned out to be gay, he would "pull out a knife and stab that little nigger."[10] Morgan thus was able to offend two groups simultaneously within a single sentence in his threatened homicide. Even more surprising is that, as members of racial minorities themselves, Koy and Morgan did not have sufficient empathy to refrain from making cruel comments about another minority group. Verbal tirades against any ethnic, religious, racial, or sexual-orientation group are never effective uses of humor.

Audience members of both shows were somewhat divided over whether the comedians' anti-gay rants on stage were even intended to be funny or not. Regardless, many patrons were offended and publicized their distress immediately on Facebook and other Internet sites. The resultant publicity prompted acting colleague and comedian Tina Fey to defend her friend Morgan, albeit rather weakly, by noting that "the Tracy Morgan I know, who is not a hateful man . . . is generally much too sleepy and self-centered to ever hurt another person."[11]

Both Koy and Morgan issued public apologies for their gratuitously offensive remarks. Morgan stimulated a minor Tweeter battle involving Louis C.K., who supported him; Chris Rock, who at first supported him before backpedaling; and Wanda Sykes, who had condemned Morgan's comments from the beginning.[12]

Shortly after his controversial performance, Morgan met with a group of homeless lesbian and gay teenagers in Brooklyn to apologize in person and presumably undergo some self-imposed sensitivity training. He also met in Nashville with the man, Kevin Rogers, who had complained of the insults on Facebook. Rogers and Morgan had a public discussion of the issues, which ended with Rogers accepting Morgan's apologies as sincere and their engaging in a genuine mutual hug.[13]

An anti-gay tirade on stage north of the U.S. border has generated a new controversy related to the apology question: Should nightclub comedians be held legally accountable for their jokes or their "takedowns" of hecklers? Could their comments be considered hate speech, which would then be a criminal violation?

Canadian comic Guy Earle was heckled by two "uncloseted" lesbians while he was emceeing an open-mic comedy night at a Vancouver restaurant. When the women kissed passionately at their front-row table and called him a "fucking asshole," Earle responded with a homophobic rant that by his own admission included many extreme and "offensive comments."

It never has been clear who actually started it all. The interaction eventually became physical, in that Earle accused the women of throwing water on him twice and they accused him of breaking a pair of sunglasses. In a later interview Earle admitted to being an "asshole" and "half drunk at the time." He explicitly apologized for breaking the glasses but was very clear that he apologized for nothing that he had said that night. Earle argues that he does not hate anyone because of their sex or sexual orientation, but he really does hate hecklers.

This minor incident, involving what columnist Morley Walker of the *Winnipeg Free Press* called a "talentless amateur" comedian, occurred in May 2007 but remains of continuing interest as a possible very important legal precedent. Earle was called before the British Columbia Human Rights Tribunal, the province's watchdog group, where he was accused of making sexist and homophobic insults toward Lorna Pardy and her girlfriend. They subsequently claimed to suffer from generalized anxiety disorder, panic attacks, and posttraumatic stress disorder. The matter was not resolved until 2011 and may yet go on to Canada's Supreme Court, if it agrees to hear Earle's appeal. It remains uncertain whether this tribunal even had proper jurisdiction to intervene in this matter. Nevertheless, Earle was ordered to pay the couple $15,000 (Canadian) and the restaurant owner was to add an additional $7,500 (Canadian).[14] In essence, a comedian was convicted and fined for comments made to hecklers during his act.

Was this fair? This case became a classic conflict between a paid performer's right of free expression versus his audience's right to be free of another's discriminatory speech and behavior. Is the traditional verbal jousting between comedians and their hecklers the same thing as illegal "hate speech"? Other local comedians admitted to toning down their own comments on stage due to fears of suffering similar consequences. News reporters described the "chilling effect" of the verdict and the resultant self-censorship "sugarcoating" by performers. Could this happen in the United States, with its many insult comics and televised raunchy roasts?

What if the comedian deliberately makes "you are gay" jokes about another well-known celebrity rather than impulsively lashing out at anonymous audience members? The late late-night TV host Johnny Carson once made a series of jokes implying that Wayne Newton was gay. While Newton is a singer with an unusually high singing voice, he is also a large strong man with "a long and unforgiving memory," by his own account. Without recognition of the irony in his self-description, Newton insisted that he "would not turn the other cheek."

Mr. Newton "paid a visit" to Mr. Carson to confront him about the jokes and to "reach an understanding," not unlike other similar meetings that often take place in his hometown of Las Vegas. Newton explained, "I'm here to find out what your problem is . . . because the kind of humor you're doing about me, pal, nobody does. I'll knock you on your ass."[15] The offensive jokes stopped. Newton, also known as Mr. Las Vegas, continues to live there happily with his second wife and daughter.

ARE APOLOGIES IN ORDER?

Comedians are paid to be funny, and they work very hard to achieve that with every joke or observation made on stage. Some comics specialize in satirical and political humor. We discuss in chapters 3 and 9 how the standards of acceptability are different for professionals than for other well-known people, such as actors, politicians, athletes, and for regular folks. If hardly any topic is taboo for comedy, should professional comedians *ever* apologize for the nature or content of any of their jokes?

African American comedian Katt Williams found himself in a public controversy in September 2011 when an Arizona civil rights activist complained that Williams's response to a heckler at his show was anti-Mexican "borderline hate speech." Although his publicist apologized for him, Williams publicly disavowed it, saying he was merely defending the country he loves, America, after a single guy in his audience shouted, "Fuck America!" He very clearly pointed out, "Mexicans are my friends. . . . It was a whole crowd of Mexican Americans." If he had in fact retaliated against the entire audience instead of just the one man who Williams "suggested" was a landscaper, "I wouldn't have been able to get out of there alive—with all due respect." That explanation, provided in his later CNN interview, might itself seem somewhat incendiary.

Let's look closely at the joke Williams made in the comedy club. He had just pointed out that whites have often told black Americans to go back to Africa. His joke followed: "If Mexican Americans love Mexico, could they give it to the blacks? Because we can't go back to Africa—because of the flies."

The African American CNN interviewer T. J. Holmes kept trying to get Williams to apologize for his comments in his act. Williams held firm to the party line for most comedians: "I'm not allowed to [apologize] as a stand-up. The only thing that I tell is uncensored thoughts. So, I'm only telling them uncensored. . . . That's for the Tracy Morgans of the world."[16] Are comedians becoming more outrageous or is the public becoming more sensitive?

Late-night TV host David Letterman made a joke about former vice presidential candidate Sarah Palin's daughter. The offending reference was to her daughter being "knocked up" by New York Yankee Alex Rodriguez. Actually, his comment was about Bristol, who wasn't named but is indeed an unwed mother. However, the Palin family argued that the target of the joke had been their younger daughter Willow. Sarah Palin even referred to the joke as "sexually perverted." Regardless, Letterman agreed that the joke was "coarse," "bad," and "can't be defended." He took responsibility for the misunderstanding about which daughter he had referred to. In view of the public support of Palin's complaint, Letterman felt he should "do the right thing" and made a formal apology statement for his remark on his national program.[17] Such an apology was practically unprecedented for comedians.

Later that year comedian and TV talk show personality Joy Behar also made a public apology under some coercion. On *The View* discussion show, Behar had made a joke about Rachel Uchitel, one of Tiger Woods's mistresses. In her joke Behar referred to Uchitel as a "hooker"; Uchitel then hired celebrity lawyer Gloria Allred to defend her damaged reputation. In an effort to thwart a defamation lawsuit against her and ABC, Behar quite mildly offered, "I apologize for any misimpression the joke may have created."[18]

Rosie O'Donnell also created controversy while on Barbara Walters's *The View* program. As part of a discussion of a previous guest's apparent drunkenness, O'Donnell noted that people were talking about it all over the world, including China. In a misguided attempt to be funny, she then gave her imitation of a faux Chinese–accented speaker, including throwing in the words *ching* and *chong*. Many complaints were received by Ms. Walters and the network about O'Donnell's allegedly insensitive mockery. Nevertheless, she had no plans to apologize until she happened to ask a personal friend who was of Chinese origin if she had been offended by the joke. Her friend admitted that she had felt hurt by it. This one person's reaction was enough for O'Donnell to issue a public apology for her joke, which was never ill intended.[19]

On her own TV show Joy Behar discussed the issue of apologies with her guest, comedian Chelsea Handler. Behar asked Handler if she felt that she should apologize to Angelina Jolie for calling her during a stand-up performance "an f—ing home wrecker and the C-word." Not surprisingly, the two comedians adopted opposite positions. Handler replied, "If you apologize once, you can never say anything again." Behar rebutted by saying, "All comedians have to apologize at some point." Handler disagreed: "No, I haven't and I won't. I'd rather quit. I have enough money."[20]

It creates an interesting discussion point for all of us: Should comedians ever apologize for something said during their professional performances? What will be the long-term consequences for future comics or any satirical performances or writing if professional comedians are frequently asked or expected to apologize in case something in their routines might have possibly offended someone? Do they not have rights of free speech, even if their remarks or jokes may be hurtful? Can and should comedians ever be sued for anything they might have said during performances?

Roseanne Barr claims that stand-up comedy is the last bastion for free speech: "It makes the sacred and the profane totally line up. No taboos is the ability to make the world's most horrific things funny."[21] Chelsea Handler proudly tries to make fun of all minorities with the provision to "make sure I focus on a fair amount of time, so that one group can't get madder than the next."[22]

Of course, free speech is limited legally for everyone by prohibitions on inciting riots or creating danger—for example, by shouting "Fire!" in a crowded comedy club. However, yelling "Fire the comedian!" is obviously an example of naturally protected speech and sometimes may be a good idea. Even professional comedians differ on whether it is acceptable and desirable to apologize under certain circumstances. Among others, though, Handler, Kathy Griffin, Jeffrey Ross, Lewis Black, and the late Buddy Hackett have all explicitly argued that if your humor is ever attacked or criticized, "*never apologize.*"

Never apologizing *may* be good advice for the professionals, but I do not recommend it for regular folks who would like to use more humor effectively. If you think you may have offended your listener(s) with a joke or comment meant to be humorous, it is much better to acknowledge that by saying "I'm sorry. I didn't mean to offend you." No need for the standard eraser phrases, such as "Just kidding" or "No offense." They sound hollow and insincere and therefore do not do the job of assuaging the feelings of your listeners and maintaining your relationship.

Professional broadcasters, even though not comedians, are especially prone to apologizing unnecessarily. One example occurred when a caller, trying to answer a trivia quiz question, phoned a National Public Radio program with his answer: "Henry Kissinger." The host replied, "No, but I wonder who's *kissing her* now." Admittedly his retort for the wrong answer was not very funny, but when concluding the quiz later, the host offered, "We apologize for the joke earlier." Why did he feel the need to apologize for this humor effort? It could not have offended anyone, including Dr. Kissinger, and bad humor can frequently elicit a sympathetic chuckle. Too many apologies dilute the effectiveness of any genuine apology that might be given later.

Kathy Griffin's stand-up act consists primarily of tales of her humorous interactions with other celebrities, who naturally come out in second place in her point of view. Belittling the famous by name on stage is Griffin's *shtick*, known to all. At times, well-known people have even told her to never pick on them on stage. Of course, their attempts at intimidation practically guarantee that their names will get mentioned in her act.

Lisa Lampanelli is a strong admirer of her comic colleague Kathy Griffin, and concurs in her uniquely gentle way: "Celebrities think they're so above us that they can't be made fun of. . . . Kill 'em all."[23]

In 2005 Griffin was hired by the E! cable channel to do very brief interviews of celebrities on their way in to the Golden Globe awards and make observations. To spice up the evening for herself and her audience, Griffin created a bit by starting "a rumor that the most unlikely celebrity you could imagine had gone to rehab for drug and alcohol abuse." Then, in her interviews, she would ask other Golden Globe attendees for their comments on that celebrity's woes. Whom did she pick to be the star of this fiction? She ruled out references to Britney Spears and Lindsey Lohan because such a story about them would be too believable. She chose ten-year-old actress Dakota Fanning, who obviously was an adorable talented child, acclaimed by everyone as "impeccably mannered." Griffin asked a variety of celebrities on live TV for their comments on the tragedy of Fanning's addictions. All of them realized that it was a joke question and responded accordingly.

However, the legal and PR representatives of the network and the innocent Ms. Fanning unfortunately did not appreciate the humor. It so happened that she had a major motion picture coming out shortly involving both Tom Cruise and Steven Spielberg. Director Spielberg was reportedly "furious," fearing loss of box office revenue because of the child's alleged need for rehabilitation for multiple substances abuse.

Griffin's response to the request for an apology was as follows: "Okay, here's my statement: 'You'd have to be a complete fucking moron to think I was serious. The end.' How's that?" When told that her statement was not really an apology, she added, "Well, that's the best I've got. I'm standing by it." Kathy Griffin, whose own publicity-seeking drive is unparalleled, was truly overjoyed that a major cable channel, the most famous movie director in the world, and a renowned and beloved child actress (or her representatives) all were even aware of her existence, let alone actually fearful of her widespread public influence via this joke interview question. And she did not apologize any further. [24]

However, San Diego Superior Court Judge DeAnn Salcido was forced to resign her position after the Commission on Judicial Performance filed thirty-nine formal misconduct charges against her. The charges consisted of her making disparaging, unflattering, and improper comments that belittled defendants, attorneys, and court staffs. One example from the formal complaint: "After placing Rodolf Rodriguez on probation, you [Salcido] made the following remark: 'What that means is don't come before the court on another case . . . 'cause you will definitely be scr— and we don't offer Vaseline for that.'" [25] Salcido's defense was that she tried to use humor and less formality in her unorthodox approach to cases. The "rest of the story," as the late broadcaster Paul Harvey would say, is that Judge Salcido's courtroom was being monitored by TV producers who were considering her for starring in a new judicial reality show. Consequently, the judge was trying to be humorous, lively, and entertaining in her real-life auditions. She is no longer a judge anywhere.

In 2007, nationally syndicated talk show host Don Imus made comments about the Rutgers University women's basketball team who played in the NCAA championships. He referred to the players as "rough girls" with tattoos and said some were "nappy-headed hos." [26] These descriptions set off a firestorm of protests and charges of racism against Imus, who was publicly called a dried-up fossil and "deranged druggie." Imus was suspended by his network despite his defense that people shouldn't worry about "some idiot comment meant to be amusing." His professional image has never recovered completely.

The White House Correspondents' Association annual dinner is a gathering of major media figures with the president of the United States. A number of speakers engage in a roast-like interactive event with the president. Presidents vary in their ability to take a joke and to deliver a joke in rebuttal. The event is traditionally a fairly hilarious evening, and all presidents participate in the good fun. A well-known comedian is chosen each year to be the host and deliver a lengthy monologue. Some are more successful than others in this very visible setting.

For example, at the 2006 dinner, Stephen Colbert's biting satirical roast of President George W. Bush and other prominent guests, including Supreme Court justices, was especially noteworthy as perhaps the greatest bomb in Colbert's career. He remained in character throughout the evening as an extremely political and socially conservative commentator in strong support of Bush's policies. Of course, he proceeded to paint those policies with a broad brush of laughable irrationality and stupidity.

Colbert's performance was extraordinarily unfunny and not well received by those Republican dignitaries in attendance. Interestingly, his comments were not any more hostile than those of other hosts at this dinner in the years before and after. While satirical, they simply seemed to be consistent with criticisms usually made by Bush's political opponents. Robin Williams has suggested that the Republicans who had invited Colbert to be the host for the evening may have actually fallen for his persona and inadvertently believed that he, too, was politically a right-wing Republican. If true, that is really funny!

Satirist Colbert implied that he and President Bush are "not brainiacs on the nerd patrol" and hate actual books because they are "all fact, no heart." He addressed Bush's low approval ratings at the time: "Now, I know there are some polls out there saying this man has a 32 percent approval rating. But guys like us, we don't pay attention to the polls. We know that polls are just a collection of statistics that reflect what people are thinking in reality. And reality has a well-known liberal bias. . . . Sir, pay no attention to the people who say 'the glass is half empty' because 32 percent means it's two-thirds empty. There's still some liquid in that glass, is my point. But I wouldn't drink it. The last third is usually backwash."

Colbert complimented the president for being "steady" with this backhanded remark: "Events can change; this man's beliefs never will. He believes the same thing Wednesday as he did Monday. No matter what happened Tuesday." This comment is funny and more typical for comedians at these dinners. It illustrates much more effective humor than most of the remainder of Colbert's sixteen-minute monologue.

Another brief example of "support" by Colbert that surely President Bush would have been happy not to hear can be seen in this excerpt: "I stand by this man. I stand by this man because he stands for things. Not only *for* things, he stands *on* things. Things like aircraft carriers, and rubble, and recently flooded city squares. And that sends a strong message: that no matter what happens to America, she will always rebound—with the most powerfully staged photo ops in the world."

Finally, Colbert showed a clip of his own eight-and-a-half-minute fake "audition tape," allegedly promoting himself for the position of presidential press secretary. This tape consumed 35 percent of Colbert's monologue time of just over twenty-four minutes. President Bush appeared to be listening to the live and recorded presentations but remained completely expressionless throughout. If he ever laughed, it was not captured by the TV cameras. At the end of the excruciating performance, Bush quietly said, "Well done," as the two shook hands.[27]

Despite this setting of the annual White House Correspondents' dinner, which customarily calls for humor at the expense of the sitting president, Colbert seemed to have stepped over the imaginary line of bad taste. He also used bad judgment to satirically attack the jurists of the nation's highest court, the media, and assorted other celebrities present, such as Senator John McCain and the Reverend Jesse Jackson.

Despite the widespread bad reviews for his performance at the dinner and his misreading the audience of over 2,500 VIPs, some fellow comedians nonetheless were quite impressed with Colbert's satirical work that night. Robin Williams called him "brave," and Paul Provenza heralded his "unbelievable courage and fearlessness" for entering the lion's den alone, armed with nothing but his transparent anti-Bush message via humor.[28] Colbert has regained most of his own temporarily lowered approval ratings and rightly remains a very popular comedian and TV star.

Comedian Wanda Sykes hosted the dinner in 2009 during President Obama's first year in office and also created considerable controversy with her humor. Fox News host Greta Van Susteren complained that Sykes "viciously hammered" conservative commentator Rush Limbaugh when she called him "the 20th hijacker" in the 9/11 attack on the two World Trade Center towers in New York. She had joked that Limbaugh had simply missed his flight because he was so strung out on OxyContin.[29] Sykes's comment came during the time when Limbaugh had publicly admitted to legal and health trouble because of his addiction to painkillers.

Sykes also pointed out at the dinner that Limbaugh on his radio show had expressed the view that he hoped Obama and the country would fail. She suggested this point of view is treasonous, not unlike the speeches of Osama bin Laden: "I hope his kidneys fail. How about that? He needs a good waterboardin'. That's what he needs."[30]

Were her comments fair and fitting for a man whose own broadcast career is based on publicly criticizing political figures on his extremely popular radio program? President Obama's press secretary, Robert Gibbs, when asked, diplomatically pointed out that "there are a lot of topics that are better left for serious reflection rather than comedy. I think there's no doubt that 9/11 is part of that."[31] Note that Gibbs's careful statement did not defend Limbaugh but rather addressed just the topic of 9/11.

Sykes's jokes about Obama himself were quite gentle. A more valid criticism of her comedy that night is that her most biting humor revealed her partisanship because it was directed toward Republican targets not present at the dinner: former president George W. Bush, former vice president Dick Cheney, radio talk show hosts Sean Hannity and Rush Limbaugh, and the most recent Republican national ticket of John McCain and Sarah Palin.

Neither Colbert nor Sykes ever apologized. Should they have? Their comments may have been hurtful on a personal level and somewhat funny as attacks on icons. Yet the setting of the White House Correspondents' Association dinner was one known by long tradition to be that of an evening of satirical fun for everyone. After all, they were hired as professional comedians with established reputations for outspokenness (to understate it) to host the affair and perform in the spirit of a roast of the sitting president.

Even some typically attention-craving egocentric celebrities clearly come off as bad sports when they frown and become hostile in retaliation to being made fun of in public. The prime example of that kind of reaction is Donald Trump. Check out the Internet video of Trump listening to emcee Seth Myers's humorous jabs at the 2011 White House Correspondents dinner. Myers's work that night received quite positive reviews overall as he trod the border successfully between funny biting humor and cruel personal sarcasm.[32]

Everyone can "misspeak" at times, but attempting to use humor thoughtlessly is especially risky and can lead to disastrous consequences. Dick Cavett, veteran comedic writer and polished performer, warns us all that humor is "treacherous quicksand."[33] Popular TV and movie comedian-writer Tina Fey accepts that "bombing is painful, but it doesn't kill you."[34] Despite the occasional death threats to professional comedians, bad humor is rarely fatal. Bombing is an inevitable part of humor making, even for the best of them.

Literal bombing is a real possibility in modern society by terrorists offended by political cartoons. In 2005 a Danish newspaper printed twelve editorial cartoons depicting images of the Prophet Muhammad. A paper in Norway reprinted the cartoons, and ultimately they appeared in the periodicals of over fifty countries. Protests, violent clashes, arson, and other negative backlashes quickly followed there, and also in many other countries, by those who felt that publishing the cartoons blasphemed the faith of devout Muslims throughout the world.[35] Over one hundred deaths were ultimately attributed to the reactions to the publications. Humor really can result in death threats and death itself.

As recently as November 2011, the Paris offices of a satirical French magazine *Charlie Hedbro* were firebombed and destroyed just prior to the publication of the issue in which the periodical had jokingly asked Muhammad to be its special editor-in-chief "to fittingly celebrate the victory of the Islamist Ennahda party in Tunisia." That issue's cover page had depicted Muhammad (a grave offense itself, according to Islamic law) with the caption, "100 lashes if you don't die of laughter."[36] Joking and a sense of humor can indeed be fatal, if not displayed discreetly and effectively.

We all must strive for positive results from our humor. Certainly, being aware of our audience's current social sensitivities and the potential for misunderstanding can be immensely helpful in delivering humor effectively. What is PC and what is not and to what degree you want to abide by those PC standards become part of your decisions when humor making.

Should complaints or problems still result from a failed public attempt at humor, it is paramount for the offender to know how to make a prompt and sincere apology (or at least be able to *sound* sincere).

POLITICIANS

Politicians inevitably produce many gaffes in their public comments. Late-night comedians consider them to be prayers answered. Some of our elected and appointed officials' remarks become unintentionally funny because they happen to be stupid, illogical, or malapropos. We are more concerned here about their allegedly joking comments that bomb. The perpetrator specifically claims to be attempting to be humorous. Of course, we have to sort out whether the perpetrators really were humor making or whether they were trying to escape responsibility for some ridiculous and hurtful comments.

James Watt, secretary of the interior under President Ronald Reagan, presumably to tout the diversity of an affirmative action panel he had appointed, jokingly told a meeting of the U.S. Chamber of Commerce in 1983 that his staff included "a black, a woman, two Jews, and a cripple. And we have talent."[37] It was unclear whether the "talent" was represented by those on this list or was present in addition to them. Do you think that the black, the woman, the two Jews, and the "cripple" found Watt's summary either funny or inclusive?

This mocking of affirmative action was not Watt's only humor bombing. First Lady Nancy Reagan, a fan of the Beach Boys, was prompted to apologize for Watt after he had banned them from a July 4 performance on the National Mall in Washington, D.C., because they were likely to attract drug users, alcohol abusers, and criminals. His blunders became so common that the White House staff jokingly presented Secretary Watt with a plaster cast of a foot with a hole in it, where presumably he had symbolically shot himself. Watt resigned eighteen days after his speech to the Chamber of Commerce.

President Obama has often received bipartisan praise for his speech-making skills. However, as a guest on NBC's *The Tonight Show*, he tried to be self-deprecatingly funny (and failed) by comparing his well-known low bowling scores to those of the Special Olympians.[38] Presidents and presidential candidates must be acutely aware of this country's increasingly rigid PC standards. Clearly, Obama did not mean to make fun of the handicapped individuals who participate in the valuable Special Olympics programs and contests. Yet he received considerable negative publicity for his bungled humor making, prompting a public apology.

Senator John McCain (R-AZ), in good humor, sang "Bomb, bomb Iran" on April 19, 2007, at a presidential campaign rally in South Carolina. He later explained to ABC News that he "was just trying to add a little humor to the event."[39] Was this an effective way to appear young, vibrant, and humorous to the electorate? I think not. Bombing another country unilaterally would certainly lead to some "collateral damage" of dead Iranian citizens, which is hardly a joking matter or an appealing campaign strategy.

Gerry Ritz, Canada's federal agriculture minister, made jokes about a fatal outbreak of listeria, a rare bacterial infection acquired from eating contaminated food such as meats and cheeses. While briefing scientists and government officials on the disease, Ritz joked, "This is like a death by a thousand cuts—or should I say cold cuts." When informed of a new death recorded, he added spontaneously, "Please tell me it's Wayne Easter [a political opposition member of Parliament at the time]." Ritz apologized later for his claimed stress-induced "tasteless and completely inappropriate offhand comments."[40]

While not exactly attempting to be funny, Congresswoman Michele Bachmann (R-MN), candidate for the 2012 Republican presidential nomination, exuberantly asked her campaign audience in South Carolina on August 16, 2011, to wish Elvis Presley a happy birthday.[41] Unfortunately, Elvis had died on August 16, 1977, having been born on the date of January 8.

Rick Santorum (R-PA), former senator and also aspirant to his party's 2012 presidential nomination, gave a lecture on Islam at the University of Nebraska. He pointed out in a serious tone, "The Qur'an is perfect just the way it is. That's why it is only written in Islamic."[42] The person elected president of the United States in 2012 will most likely have to deal with Islamic fundamentalist terrorists. Perhaps a President Santorum would attack them with confusing malapropos and thereby render them militarily ineffectual by his muddled messages.

In a primary debate by candidates being considered to oppose incumbent Massachusetts Senator Scott Brown, Elizabeth Warren pointed out that Brown had posed nude for the June 1982 issue of *Cosmopolitan* magazine while in law school at Boston College. When she was asked how she had paid for her college tuition, she noted that she did so while keeping her clothes on. When asked for comment on Warren's remark, Brown glibly replied, "Thank God." His humorous retort sounded sexist to many observers, which prompted him to clarify to the media that he was "just joking."[43]

While campaigning for his party's nomination for president, multimillionaire Mitt Romney jokingly pointed out to his audience in Tampa, Florida, that he too was presently unemployed.[44] However, his joke bombed and only revealed his cluelessness about the genuine hardships facing Floridians who had been without work for a long time.

Politicians all know that being perceived as having a good sense of humor can result in more votes on Election Day. What most of them do not know is that they should rely strictly on their speechwriters for their jokes. Comedian and writer Dick Cavett offers this constructive advice to the typically overly serious politicians: "A laugh never hurts and is worth a thousand straight lines."[45] But politicians, please listen to your writers and leave the funny ad libs to the pros.

One exception is "plain-speaking" New Jersey Governor Chris Christie, whose sense of humor is one of his popular appeals. When comedians began making fun of his weight, Christie cleverly defused that topic by simply acknowledging his problem of eating too much and saying he felt guilty about endangering his health. After his candid public admission, the comedians were disarmed, at least temporarily.

Athletes, coaches, and sports announcers have all made far more than their share of humor blunders. They prove repeatedly that their best skills are on the field or court, not in comedy. Professional football player Chad Ochocinco, a pass receiver for the Cincinnati Bengals at the time, was fined $20,000 for his on-field joke about trying to bribe a referee. In a grand public gesture, he borrowed a $1 bill from a sideline worker and offered it as a way to induce the officials to stand by a challenged call, since it favored his team.[46] Ochocinco carried a long-standing reputation as a jokester for such antics as legally changing his surname from "Johnson" (a name already reeking of potential humor) to reflect his football jersey number in Spanish. No one, except perhaps NFL executives, could have mistaken Ochocinco's humorous televised joking for a genuine bribery attempt.

Bruce Pearl, head coach of the University of Tennessee basketball team at the time, was speaking at a charity fund-raising event. In discussing the difficulty of creating a unified team from a very diverse group of young men, Pearl resorted to using humor to make his point: "I've got to put these guys from different worlds together, right? I've got guys from Chicago, Detroit. I'm talking about the 'hood! And I've got guys from Grainger County, where they wear the hood!" Grainger County, Tennessee, was the home of one of his new freshman players. Presumably its citizens did not appreciated being associated with the Ku Klux Klan. The recruit's father quickly and graciously accepted the coach's apology, saying he took the comments as a joke. [47]

ESPN broadcaster Bob Griese was reprimanded and briefly suspended by his employer for his on-air "racist remarks" about NASCAR star driver Juan Pablo Montoya. During the TV broadcast of a college football game, a promo featuring the top five NASCAR drivers was shown, but it did not include Montoya. When Griese's colleague Chris Spielman asked where the Colombian driver Montoya was, Griese replied, "Out having a taco." [48] We might debate how serious the unplanned "humor" offense was, even by current PC standards. Was it truly racist and mean-spirited? Montoya was extremely gracious in his response to the PC furor, making his own jokes about going out with his wife for dinner and ordering tacos. [49]

Ohio State University President Gordon Gee made a sports-related bad joke in 2011. He mocked other university football teams, such as Texas Christian University and Boise State University, who allegedly don't play as tough a schedule as does Ohio State. Gee pointed out, "We do not play the Little Sisters of the Poor." The Little Sisters became offended, although they do not even field a football team. Administrator Mother Cecilia forgave President Gee after he visited them and toured their facility for the elderly in northwest Ohio. Gee enthusiastically shouted, "My penance is over!" [50] We can agree that he handled this delicate situation well and hope that he has gone forth to sin no more.

We all claim to appreciate good humor, regardless of the setting. We all have certain boundaries for what we consider acceptable humor in public. Noted broadcaster and social commentator Bill Moyers and many other speakers and educators have reminded us that humor makes any medicine go down better. Perhaps since he was speaking on NPR, Moyers commented in a culinary context, "Truth goes down easier when it's marinated with humor." [51]

Of course, just regular people also produce humor that bombs. For example, a man married for two years to a "wonderful, pretty" woman whom he still loved found himself being sued for divorce for making one joking comment in front of her family. He described his wife's sister, Zoe, as "supermodel gorgeous," but denies even the slightest attraction to her. At a family gathering ironically held on April 29, 2011, to watch the British royal wedding of Prince William and Kate Middleton, our protagonist made an unfortunate ill-timed remark. During a group discussion of which sister was more attractive, the bride Kate or her sister Pippa, he reports, "That's when I made the biggest mistake of my life. I joked that my brother-in-law was lucky he nabbed Zoe first, or I would have snatched her up. I don't know why I said it. I didn't even mean it."

The evening ended badly. His wife was silent for the rest of the party and when they returned home, she refused to accept her husband's repeated and sincere apologies. She packed up her clothes and announced that their marriage was over. True to her word, very soon thereafter she served him with divorce papers. From his point of view, their "wonderful marriage" was lost due to that one comment in which he claimed to be "just kidding."[52]

We should not rule out the possibility that his wife had been harboring additional unvoiced complaints long before that party. However, the ineffective use of humor today could indeed land you back in the singles marketplace by Tuesday. We are not dealing with trifling matters here.

NOTES

1. www.info.bw/~jacana/Murphology.htm.
2. J. Ross, *I Only Roast the Ones I Love: How to Bust Balls without Burning Bridges* (New York: Gallery Books, 2009), 273–74.
3. N. Salamat, "Lisa Lampanelli Stops Being Mean for a Few Minutes to Talk about Comedy," February 3, 2011, http://web.signonsandiego.com/news/2011/feb03/all-hail-the-queen/?ap.
4. J. Behar, interview with Ricky Gervais, *Joy Behar Show*, HLN Cable Network, December 2, 2011.
5. E. Boosler, "Now That the Smoke Has Cleared," *Huffpost* Politics, December 13, 2006, www.huffingtonpost.com/elayne-boosler/now-that-the-smoke-has-cl_b_36272.html.
6. www.youtube.com/watch?v=G5Q1rOG2rf0.
7. P. Mooney, in P. Provenza and D. Dion, *¡Satiristas! Comedians, Contrarians, Raconteurs, & Vulgarians* (New York: HarperCollins, 2010), 43–44 (italics in original).
8. Boosler, "Now That the Smoke Has Cleared."
9. J. H. Ubalde, "Fil-Am Comedian Slammed for Homophobic Remark in Show," *Interaksyon*, June 18, 2011, www.interasksyon.com.
10. "Tracy Morgan: I'll Kill My Son If He Acts Gay," June 10, 2011, www.tmz.com/2011/06/10/tracy-morgan-homophobic-act-rant-comedy-gay-threats-kill-son-30-rock.
11. "Tina Fey Scolds but Protects Tracy Morgan after Anti-Gay Rant," June 11, 2011, www.theatlanticwire.com/entertainment/2011/06/tina-fey-apologizes-tracy-morgan/38733.
12. C. Robbins, "Chris Rock Backpedals after His Defense of Tracy Morgan's Offensive Routine," June 12, 2011, http://gothamist.com/2011/06/12/chris_rock_backpedals_after_his_def.php.
13. "Tracy Morgan Apologizes to Kevin Rogers, Gay Community for Homophobic Rant," *HuffPost* Entertainment, August 21, 2011, www.huffingtonpost.com/2011/06/21/tracy-morgan-apologizes-kevin-rogers-gay_n_881440.html.
14. E. Levant, "Canada's Kangaroo Courts Strike a Rocky Mountain Low," *Toronto Sun*, April 24, 2011, www.torontosun.com/2011/04/21/canadas-kangaroo-courts-strike-a-rocky-mountain-low.
15. "Richard Schlesinger's Interview with Wayne Newton," *Sunday Morning*, CBS News, March 14, 2010.

16. "Kat [*sic*] Williams Unapologetic about Rant," CNN News, September 3, 2011, www.cnn.com/video/#/video/bestoftv/2011/09/03/exp.kattWilliamsResponds.

17. D. Bauder, "Sarah Palin Accepts David Letterman's Apology," June 16, 2009, http://wire.jacksonville.com.

18. "Joy Behar Apologies [*sic*] on 'The View' for Remark about Rachel Uchitel," *Access Hollywood*, December 14, 2009, www.nbcnewyork.com/entertainment/celebrity/Joy_Behar_Apologies_On__The_View__For_Remark_About_Rachel_Uchitel-79250297.html.

19. R. O'Donnell, *Celebrity Detox (The Fame Game)* (New York: Grand Central Publishing, 2007).

20. J. Behar, interview with Chelsea Handler, *Joy Behar Show*, HLN Cable Network, August 31, 2011.

21. R. Barr, *I Am Comic* (film by Jordan Brady), Showtime Cable Network, December 18, 2011.

22. Behar, interview with Chelsea Handler.

23. Salamat, "Lisa Lampanelli Stops Being Mean for a Few Minutes."

24. K. Griffin, *Official Book Club Selection: A Memoir according to Kathy Griffin* (New York: Ballantine, 2009), 257.

25. M. Rothfield, "Judge's Attempts at Humor Leave Judicial Commission Stone-Faced," *Wall Street Journal Blogs*, September 24, 2010; G. Moran, "Misconduct Charges against Judge Detailed," September 27, 2010, http://signonsandiego.printthis.clickability.com.

26. "Imus Called Women's Basketball Team 'Nappy-Headed Hos,'" Media Matters for America, April 4, 2007, http://mediamatters.org/research/200704040011.

27. http://video.google.com/videoplay?docid=-869183917758574879#.

28. P. Provenza and D. Dion, *¡Satiristas! Comedians, Contrarians, Raconteurs, & Vulgarians* (New York: HarperCollins, 2010), 11–12.

29. "Did Wanda Sykes Go Too Far at the White House Correspondents' Dinner?," *On the Record*, Fox News, May 12, 2009.

30. www.whitehousecorrespondentsweekendinsider.com/tag/wanda-sykes.

31. A. Burns, "Robert Gibbs on Wanda Sykes: 9/11 Is Not 'Comedy,'" May 11, 2009, www.politico.com/news/stories/0509/22369.html.

32. www.youtube.com/watch?v=7YGITlxfT6s.

33. D. Cavett, *Talk Show: Confrontations, Pointed Commentary, and Off-Screen Secrets* (New York: Time Books/Henry Holt, 2010), 74.

34. T. Fey, *Bossypants* (New York: Little, Brown, 2011), 123.

35. P. Belien, "Jihad against Danish Newspaper," *Brussels Journal*, October 22, 2005.

36. H. Samuel, "French Satirical Newspaper Firebombed after Prophet Mohammed Announcement," *The Telegraph*, November 2, 2011, www.telegraph.co.uk.

37. www.nndb.com/people/010/000023938.

38. V. Salazar, "A Gutter Ball," *USA Today*, September 18, 2009.

39. D. Edwards and R. Brynaert, "Unplugged McCain Sings 'Bomb Bomb Bomb, Bomb Bomb Iran,'" *The Raw Story*, April 19, 2007, http://rawstory.com/news/2007/McCain_unplugged_Bomb_bomb_bomb_bomb_0419.html.

40. R. Cassingham, "Politically Incorrect," *This Is True* blog, September 28, 2008, www.thisistrue.com/blog-nice_work_if_you_can_get_it.html.

41. See www.huffingtonpost.com/2011/08/16/michele-bachmanns-elvis-birthday_n_928454.html.

42. F. Shakir, "Santorum Ignorantly Refers to Language of Qur'an as 'Islamic,'" *Think Progress*, February 18, 2009, http://thinkprogress.org/politics/2009/02/18/36232/santorum-on-islam.

43. "Pelosi: Senator Brown Clueless about Women," *Florida Times-Union*, October 10, 2011.

44. J. Zeleny, "Romney: 'I'm Also Unemployed,'" *New York Times*, June 16, 2001, http://thecaucus.blogs.nytimes.com/2011/06/16/romney-im-also-unemployed.

45. D. Cavett, "Candidate, Improve Your Appearance!," *New York Times Opinionator*, March 28, 2008, http://opinionator.blogs.nytimes.com/2008/03/28/candidate-improve-your-appearance/?pagemode=print.

46. N. Canepa, "Fining Ochocinco over Bribery Jest Is a Joke," November 14, 2009, http://signonsandiego.printthis.clickability.com.

47. "Tenn. Coach Apologizes for KKK Joke at Fundraiser," Associated Press, September 25, 2009, http://signonsandiego.printthis.clickability.com.

48. http://php.terra.com/English/templates/print_article.php?id=OCI23062.

49. J. Fryer, Associated Press, October 30, 2009, www.metronews.ca/ArticlePrint/355624?language=en.

50. "Buckeyes' Gee Tries to Atone for Comment," *Florida Times-Union*, August 18, 2011.

51. B. Moyers, interview on National Public Radio, May 23, 2011.

52. M. Sugar and K. Mitchell, "One Comment Said in Jest and His Marriage Is Over," Annie's Mailbox, *Florida Times-Union*, July 30, 2011.

SIX

Effective Humor Pitfalls

A cheap laugh sacrifices good will. No matter how funny the joke is or how much the audience chuckles, if someone has been offended, the effort ultimately fails. . . . If in doubt, leave it out.
—Larry Wilde, comedian and humor author[1]

Humor that is racist, sexist, ageist, obscene, and otherwise politically incorrect can at times be as funny as it is offensive. This is the great dilemma for both amateur and professional humor makers. Psychologically, any resulting laughter rewards the humorist for delivering that type of humor. Laughter of other people is the greatest reward possible for the efforts of humor makers—even more so than loads of money or sex (at least in public). The late George Burns wrote, "There is nothing that feels as good as . . . hearing the laughter and applause of an audience."[2] After ninety-three years in show business and living until age one hundred, Burns's evaluation of the best sources of pleasure must be valid. Creating hearty laughter in your audience is better than a good cigar, even when it's lit.

The downside of inappropriate humor is that it usually is offensive to an increasingly large proportion of the population. In turn, it generates negative publicity and attitudes that can be detrimental to your friendships or career. The irony is that while the language standards on cable TV and in comedy clubs have been significantly lowered, the general population in the United States seems to be clearly moving toward more conservative attitudes and values in accord with the increasingly influential PC movement.

The complications on this issue come from the fact that what is judged to be appropriate or not, and what is funny or not, are all highly subjective conclusions. It is a good example of "different jokes for different folks." Some people have a very large window for appropriateness and

101

funniness, while the windows of other people can be as tiny as peepholes. As discussed in chapter 8, nothing is funny to all people. If you observe the reactions of the audiences of the best comedians in the business, rarely will you see every single person in the room laughing at the same time or equally heartily. For less skilled humor makers, the percentage of listeners who are laughing can go down fast when the appropriateness of the jokes is in question.

People naturally enjoy different forms of humor. Some folks like the more cerebral forms, which capitalize on illogical assumptions or irrational conclusions. This group also tends to favor humor that is based on intellectual wordplay. Others like the more physical forms of joking, in which someone gets hit or falls unexpectedly. Some people adamantly hate obscene humor, while others prefer the profane. Some generally like extremist humor, while others enjoy only the tamest types of humor. Some audiences love high-intensity controversy and banter, while others prefer only safe, noncontroversial topics. Some comedians specialize in ethnic humor, with most of their jokes coming from their specific subculture, such as African American, Hispanic, Jewish, Italian American, Irish American, gay, and so on. Their audiences are usually representative of that same subculture to a large degree, but certainly not entirely so. Do you like politically based humor or humor that is simultaneously trying to deliver a social criticism message? Some people do, but not everybody. Some comedians pride themselves on delivering only "clean" humor or humor from within a particular religious perspective—for example, Christian humor.

The many variations of humor content and styles explain why professionals usually focus on just one or two of these approaches in their acts. Coming from the same subculture as the comedian can make the humor especially successful because of the audience's greater recognition and identification with the attitudes and values portrayed. If you happen to be from a different subculture, comedy shows with a definite ethnic perspective can be a great educational experience in learning about and accepting cultural differences in humor and other aspects of that group's general experiences. There is truly something for everybody in the world of humor, if you are open to it.

To the extent that any of these factors is important to you, before buying a ticket for a club show or comedy concert you can easily research the descriptions of the comedians' perspectives and even listen to humor samples from previous performances of the stars of the upcoming show. I certainly am not interested in getting you to change your humor preferences in one direction or the other. I am only suggesting that to avoid disappointment or distress, you can and should become informed about the many choices of comedians and humor styles available out there before buying your ticket. Of course, it wouldn't hurt to see someone "new and different" occasionally to see if your own humor appreciation arena might be expanded.

What does this all mean, though, for nonprofessionals who are trying to develop and apply humor skills in their personal lives? *All of the rules and guidelines for using humor effectively apply equally to amateurs and professionals.* The same issues, such as the strongly subjective judgment of appropriateness and the established principles for determining funniness, are just as relevant for everyone using humor. Lengthier discussions on various strategies to increase your personal funniness appear in chapters 8 and 9.

Let's look at some forms of humor that might be especially likely to traverse the usual boundaries of propriety.

Rough humor is dark, harsh, and very near or even over the border of appropriateness. To the degree that it crosses that line for all or most of your audience, you will not be using your humor effectively. Comic writer Tina Fey offers an example of a "rough" joke, which (in my view) is inappropriate for most audiences and yet is quite funny: "A pedophile walks through the woods with a child. The child says, 'These woods are scary.' The pedophile says, 'Tell me about it. I have to walk back through here alone.'"[3]

Examination question: Does the humor in the preceding sentence offend you, even a little? If so, your distress illustrates just how sensitive this topic is and how dangerous it is to try to turn it into acceptable humor. It clearly shows why Fey's joke is both fey and rough.

Pedophilia is a serious subject. It is criminal behavior and is abusive of a child by definition, regardless of how loving, affectionate, and emotionally giving the adult may be. Of course, there is an element of sexuality always included in this relationship, which can range from innocent picture taking to touching to full-fledged sexual contact or sadistic murder.

Comedian Bill Burr fearlessly discusses pedophilia in his stage act. He jokingly complains how tough things are these days for pedophiles: "In the old days all the pedophiles had to do was rent an ice cream truck. Nowadays parents won't let their kids play outside without the parents being there, especially after dark. They keep the kids inside and just keep on feeding them to the point of obesity. As a result, these kids become totally 'unfuckable!'"[4] Funny to you?

The issue here is this: When does a joke or comment about child molestation or animal abuse or murder become funny enough to overcome its offensive qualities? Much humor of all types involves attacking sacred cows, breaking taboos, capitalizing on known group stereotypes, and suggesting violations of moral and social standards. Should you self-censor or be censored by others for a particular joke or remark? That is the crux of the dilemma for all of us who must make the decision to go ahead with the joke or not.

Part of the equation is whether the humor making is truly mean-spirited or not. "Kidding on the square" occurs when someone makes a comedic point that they actually believe to be true. It allows the speaker to make fun while also making a serious point that is critical of the person or institution that serves as the butt of the joke. If the target protests, the joker can easily reply with one of the standard eraser phrases, such as "just kidding" or "no offense intended" or "present company excluded."

Why exclude present company? For example, if the joke is clearly anti-Semitic and Jews are known to be present, why should they be asked to not be offended? At the very least, speakers should own their comments and take the chance that they are sufficiently funny and well intended to be able to say such things without meekly following up with any of those insincere eraser phrases.

ARE COMEDIANS VALID SOCIAL CRITICS?

Just how much of comedians' jokes and observations really represent their true beliefs can be very difficult to discern. It presents an inherently interesting question: If a joke is racist or sexist, for example, can we fairly conclude that the humor-making speaker, professional or not, is racist or sexist? What about the audience's reactions? Are you racist or sexist if you laugh in response, even a little? What if you just smile?

All speakers strive hard to establish emotional and intellectual rapport with their audiences in order to communicate successfully. They may even preface their remarks with "This is a true story" to add credibility and to help ensure that connection. That statement itself may or may not be true. Are the jokes that follow really truths and reflective of their values (and yours)? Maybe. Maybe not. Maybe somewhat.

Thus, it is likely that professionals' humor reflects their own real views somewhere between 0 and 100 percent. For amateur humorists, my best estimate is that their percentage of "beliefs reflected in humor" may, on average, be higher than that for the pros. The pros' careers are based more on being funny than on expressing particular points within their social groups. Thus, professionals tend to be willing to say anything if they think it will draw laughs. That is their major criterion for humor, above any concern about how possibly conflicting points of view fit with their audiences. Clearly, this conclusion represents my opinion on an issue that needs more good data. In contrast, there is the opinion of comedian Lizz Winstead, who bluntly states, "I say it because I believe it. We all have to deal with the shit that comes to us from saying what we say. . . . But the second it comes out of our mouth, it's no longer in our control about how it's supposed to be interpreted. People can hate it."[5]

Does a general joke about pedophilia, for example, necessarily reveal the jokester's personal sexual interests or yours? Not necessarily. Can the joke be funny without the listener feeling that they must endorse the practice in order to laugh and enjoy it? I think so. Do the audiences' reactions vary depending on whether they are in a public setting or sitting alone reading or watching late-night TV? Yes, usually.

When others are present, your laughter at any comic material seems to imply your agreement with the content. However, the phrase "seems to imply" does not necessarily carry the same meaning as "Yes, me too. We definitely agree on that." One test of this hypothesis is this: Are you able to laugh heartily at something funny when it is *your own* identified group (race, religion, national origin, gender, age group, sexual orientation, political party, favorite sports team or hobby, vehicle choice, neighborhood, private club, and so on) that is the target of the humor? Or do you quickly shut down your personal laugh machine and retreat emotionally (become silent or upset) or physically (walk away) because of an internal upsurge of negative reactions, suggesting that you and your group may have been offended somehow by that particular joke or humorous comment?

When humor making has been well intended—that is, the jokes were delivered solely for their humor value and were indeed funny—it is far and away better to enjoy the humor with everyone else. Everyone loves a good sport. No one and no group has immunity from being made fun of by insiders or outsiders.

Psychologist and humor chronicler Bernard Saper wrote:

> Humor is not pretty, and most jokes can be found to offend one or another individual, institution, group, or idea. American humor exaggerates and ridicules the stereotypes, myths, and mores of our culture. Gross or demeaning, put-down jokes are the favorite of millions of Americans. Very little of such humor is meant to hurt or destroy the butts.[6]

When the motivation for someone's joking is clearly *not* hateful or in horrendously bad taste, then why not laugh along? It is usually quite easy to tell what the spirit surrounding the humor really is. However, when you are in doubt, it is assertive and psychologically healthy to make your uncertainty or dismay known to the speaker. It can begin an important dialogue.

When speaking with someone informally in person or even by e-mail or texting, it is best to mention your concerns immediately. When viewing a professional comedian's performance, especially in small comedy clubs, it is often possible to speak with the comedian right after the show. At that time they usually are selling your interest in their future shows along with their CDs, DVDs, T-shirts, and books.

If the comedian is already a major star performing in a giant arena or theater, you can more easily make contact by writing an e-mail message via their website or book publisher. All performers welcome well-reasoned critiques and feedback about the content of their work. Hint number one: They especially appreciate unqualified praise. Hint number two: No one seems to appreciate hate mail or death threats. Neither of the outreaches mentioned in the second hint will usually lead to constructive conversations. Remember, you read that here first!

ESTABLISHING RAPPORT

When the speaker has been able to establish rapport with the audience, it creates more leeway in the boundaries of acceptable humor. If you are speaking with a friend, as opposed to someone you have just met, certain topics and attitudes will be permissible in your humor making. Well-known and beloved professional comedians are often given the good rapport card before they utter a word at their performances.

For example, Jerry Seinfeld merely needs to walk on the stage and say, "Good evening" and his audience laughs. He is not even intending to be funny yet, but his reputation as a nice guy who makes funny and "clean" observations that are common to all of our daily lives provides him with a receptive audience very willing to laugh easily. Seinfeld has earned the good fortune to be given this instant rapport card, not to mention his indisputably gigantic personal fortune in cash. Of course, if he did not become funny very soon or if he came on stage impaired in some way, that rapport card would have a very early expiration date (within ten minutes).

Unknown comics must work to establish rapport with the audience at the outset in their acts. They quickly employ such techniques as displaying a friendly familiarity with the audience's hometown and their likely shared personal values. The ensuing jokes and observations are then much more likely to be perceived as funny and enjoyed by that audience.

Sometimes it can be difficult to establish a high level of rapport, and sometimes, shockingly, even some professional comedians don't seem to have a clue on how to do it. Examples of big mistakes made in trying to build a positive relationship with the audience, which I have heard personally by (over)paid comedians: (1) After a token amount of applause after his introduction, the unknown comic responded, "Well, that was a shitty welcome!" (2) Another comic's first words were "What's happening, bitches?" (3) A female comic was greeted with loud cheers and applause, to which she instantly responded, "Aw, shut up!" These three professionals created an uphill battle for themselves to fight from the first few seconds of their appearances.

Who could have ever recommended to them that those lines would be good openers for a comedian? By definition, it is very difficult to make friends instantly with a group of strangers and then make them laugh. That is a tough assignment under the best of circumstances. Needless to say, I do not recommend beginning your new humor-based relationship with angry insults of your listeners. Well-delivered humor should bring you together, not immediately create a divide that must be overcome.

HUMOR AND SEXUAL HARASSMENT

American businesses, schools and universities, and government offices are especially attentive to issues of sexual harassment in the workplace. Laws are now in place to bolster what previously had been vague institutional policies or guidelines. PC concerns influence the language that is to be used in formal documents and informal speech, hiring and promotion policies, and the appropriateness of ethnic jokes. The issues of harassment and possibly creating a hostile workplace are even more serious as potential violations of civil law. Anyone found guilty of sexual harassment could be sued, fined, expelled, demoted, or fired as punishment.

The great dilemma currently is that the use of sexually related humor has become intertwined with offensive sexual harassment. Historically one major social function of this category of humor is to test the sexual waters, so to speak, in order to determine whether another person may have a romantic interest in you. Making a very slightly off-color joke or humorous remark or even giving a clear compliment to someone about their clothes or physical attractiveness has been a standard part of flirtatious social conversations between mature adults for many years. We are not talking about gross jokes, disgusting images, or insulting propositions. Incidentally, this discussion applies equally to inquiries between either opposite-sex or same-sex individuals.

In general terms, light sexually toned repartee allows each person to assess any possible interest in the other one, while being free to drop the matter without feeling great embarrassment or rejection if the interest is not reciprocated. Societal sensitivities have definitely changed in recent years. It can be difficult to know what to do or say that will be received graciously. What previously was considered a reasonable conversational interchange using socially appropriate language could potentially become the basis for sexual harassment charges these days. How, then, can one show an initial romantic interest in another person using humor without such legal risks?

One guideline is to consider the *setting*. If you first meet someone as a workplace colleague, the safest strategy is to not pursue the topic there. There are lots of good reasons not to date anyone at work ever, but realistically people spend many hours of their day at work and some workplaces present many opportunities to meet terrific potential partners. Simply being friendly, without engaging in obtrusively blatant flirting at work, could most likely lead to a safe exchange of contact information, which, in turn, could allow the relationship to be pursued at a later time and another place.

Sexual harassment involves creating a hostile work involvement in any of a variety of ways. It could mean the explicit threatening of a loss of some kind or promising a favor of some kind in exchange for sexual contact very broadly defined. One individual will have proposed a reasonably clear *quid pro quo.*

Let's consider this example: A person in a superior position in the organization requests a dinner date with someone in an inferior position of status in that organization. Having dinner is not a sexual invitation per se, and nothing has been said explicitly about any contingencies related to the offer. However, if such a request is made repeatedly with one party's consistent refusal, the possibility that this is valid harassment emerges. Of course, any combination of genders could qualify as perpetrator and victim in this example.

Our interest in *Just Kidding* is primarily when the experience of sexual harassment is said to involve humor. Sometimes humor is part of the alleged harassment, but many times it is not. Often there is a differential in power or status between the individuals, but that is not a requirement for a valid case. Usually the offending behavior requires repetition, clear and documentable occurrences, and then (usually) specific reasonable attempts having been made to resolve the concerns within the organization before any formal legal machinations should begin.

Brown University in Providence, Rhode Island, has been a leader in establishing formal definitions and guidelines related to sexual harassment in the university setting. The university even has an administrator on call twenty-four hours a day to receive complaints. A number of other educational institutions have modeled their own policies after Brown's.

The Brown University Sexual Harassment Policy, dated September 2010, which is specifically applicable to humor, states, "The unwelcome use of sexually degrading language, jokes or innuendos" is considered explicit sexual harassment. Further, the policy notes very clearly that any form of "sexual harassment need not be intentional" in determining whether a violation has occurred. What is relevant is whether "a reasonable person could have determined the alleged behavior to be sexual." The good news is that the policy has been revised as of November 2011; the bad news is that jokes and innuendos are still listed as examples of unintentional sexual harassment.[7]

Unfortunately, the ambiguity in defining just who is a "reasonable person" and the lack of specification of the context in which a possible offense takes place makes it especially difficult to pursue the matter legally. Aren't these very different scenarios: a college student on a talent night program told a particular sexually charged joke to a gathering of a hundred fellow students; a paid professional comedian told the same joke to a large diverse audience in the university auditorium; or someone told the joke to just one other person in the student lounge while out on a social date? Are any or all, or even none, of these cases possible illustrations of sexual harassment?

Concerns about the "epidemic" of sexual harassment have now reached middle and high school students. A major online survey on the topic was commissioned by the American Association of University Women, in which 1,002 girls and 963 boys were asked about their experiences in the 2010–2011 school year. Our interest, of course, is primarily on how humor became a part of the harassment process.

While the study addressed some important social issues facing young students today, it did contain some procedural flaws, including the use of extremely broad definitions for types of sexual harassment, which probably inflated the data on the frequencies of occurrences. Further, it was the researchers who determined whether harassment had occurred, not the students themselves.

According to the final report, one-third of the students encountered "unwelcome sexual comments, jokes, and gestures," which easily registered as the most common form of sexual harassment.[8] It is misleading, though, to lump all these different types of behaviors together. While most of the students ignored harassing behaviors directed at them, about one-third tried to defend themselves to the perpetrators or turn the matter into a joke. Ignoring and making a joke about the offending actions are two very different behavioral responses.

Joking became both a vehicle of sexual harassment and a potential method of coping with harassment by victims. The reports from this study unfortunately make it very difficult to tease out just how inappropriate humor contributed to the incidents and how effectively the humor worked to ease the pain of those who were targeted.

On the positive side, the survey questions included cyberbullying incidents. E-mail, texting, and social media are new and very popular communication modalities that obviously had not been assessed in earlier years' surveys. Further, this research has drawn attention to what unquestionably is a serious and increasingly common problem at the secondary school level, not just in our universities and workplaces.

Future work in this area needs to do the following: (1) refine the categories of problem behaviors in specific terms; (2) tally the students' own experiences and judgments of offensiveness or not; (3) develop valid measures of the intent of the perpetrator and the degree of the questionable conduct; and (4) parse out which behaviors are simply normative for middle and high schoolers as they develop their socialization skills, and which of their behaviors are indeed harassing and illegal.

Sexual harassment by adults in the workplace continues to be a current and extremely sensitive topic. What previously had been normative office behavior has definitely changed in recent years to become clearly unacceptable behavior and possibly a violation of law. Humor frequently plays a role in such charges. It should be helpful for us to review the many ways in which aspects of humor could be part of a person's perception of sexual harassment. Knowing where the danger zones are can help you avoid them and save lawyers' fees, your reputation, and your job.

Here are some behaviors that could potentially be construed as examples of *sexual harassment involving humor* in the workplace:

- Telling jokes involving or even hinting of sexuality, very broadly defined.
- Sending e-mails of cartoons or jokes clearly involving or hinting of sexuality.
- Making any joking comment about your own or another person's sex life.
- Making any joking verbal observations about another person's body parts or attractive attire.
- Posting sexually explicit pictures, cartoons, or jokes in your work area or on your office door.
- Sending sexually related humorous greeting cards or giving sexually related gifts.
- Jokingly imputing a sexual reason to someone who comes to work looking fatigued or frazzled.
- Accusing someone of not having a sense of humor when a sexually related joke produces only scowls and no laughter.
- Initiating sexually based teasing in the office by commenting on someone's clothes or physical appearance.

Surely this list, while a bit lengthy, is certainly not complete. It mostly describes creating a hostile work environment by promoting and creating joking references to sexuality. Descriptions of sexual activity, even without a hint of humor, might also qualify as sexual harassment. Everyone seems to have a different threshold for defining offensive behavior in this realm, which enhances the ambiguity. This form of harassment need not involve a *quid pro quo*. When tempted to engage in any of the above behaviors or anything else that should have been included on our list, the best advice is simple: *"Don't do it!"*

You may be a genuinely nice person with a terrific sense of humor, but there is no need to prove it while on the job or you may not be on the job for long. Any laughs obtained there by any remotely potentially questionable material are just not worth it and could be very costly to you. Be aware of these "new rules," even if they were not made up by Bill Maher.

Professional comedian Craig Shart tells of being informed by a club owner to do "only family-appropriate material" when performing at her club. How was he to know if his jokes were acceptable? "Look at her face and if she's frowning, it wasn't appropriate."[9] Presumably we all should attend to such visual feedback for guidance on our humor.

Humor in the office may really be funny, but when it is sexually related, it is also really likely to fail. Save your sex jokes for private conversations, dinner dates, close friends and family, and anyone who is likely to be appreciative and not likely to call a harassment lawyer (if that's not a redundancy).

Remember, though, that *anything*, including sexual harassment, can be made funny. Comedienne (her title) Mel Fine reports, "I quit a job once because of sexual harassment. There was nowhere near enough of it going on to keep me around. I got needs."[10]

TAKING THE PISS

"Taking the piss" is a curious international expression referring to banter, a back-and-forth form of repartee involving various humorous strategies designed to deflate someone's ego. Humor theorists may call it "jocular abuse." You probably know it as a form of teasing. Years ago the practice was often called "scoring" on someone or "scorching" someone. The exchanges can get very personal and superficially critical, but the overall context remains one of good-spirited camaraderie.

University of Auckland researchers Barbara Plester and Janet Sayers studied the functions of "taking the piss" in three similar New Zealand information technology (IT) companies. This kind of industry presented an ideal setting for their study because the employees were typically very bright, verbal, and already enjoyed a high base rate for banter. Their workplaces were not noisy and so were conducive to easy conversations, both serious and joking. It became the group norm to laugh at a barbed joke directed toward you and for the target to "take it." Usually the barb focused on the demographics, behavioral traits, habits, dress, or other specific characteristics of the target person.

U.S. companies and traditional business school teachings clearly would not encourage such joking behaviors in American workplaces. They tend to emphasize its probable negative effects, while remaining disinterested in any possible positive aspects. Can we learn from and apply successful business practices from companies abroad? American businesses rarely seek or adapt strategies from other countries, sometimes to their own disadvantage. People might tend to regard "taking the piss" banter as just another vehicle to provide some relief from work activities without having to go outside the building to smoke.

The New Zealand findings of Plester and Sayers were surprisingly mixed. Some employees, who had not yet been socialized into the in-group, found "taking the piss" to be unpleasant, exclusionary, and even personally insulting. Overall, though, most of these young and creative employees enjoyed the interactive atmosphere of high-level quips and barbs. It's always more fun to be in the in-group.

Based on their interviews and observations, Plester and Sayers identified six positive functions of encouraging "taking the piss" in a company's corporate culture. The phrase itself is funny, especially when you consider doing it in (or on?) a conservative American company.

The benefits found by the researchers in these New Zealand IT companies are presented below. Note that any given bantering statement might fulfill more than one function simultaneously:

1. Making a barbed point about something serious.
2. Boredom busting, particularly at their regular weekly meetings.
3. Facilitating the socialization process of inducting new workers into the in-group and thereby their becoming possible future targets of the banter.
4. Celebrating differences within the group (e.g., the extremes of age, height, and weight, along with any gender and racial differences).
5. Displaying a unique corporate culture and its shared norms, such as these joking patterns.
6. Defining a person's present organizational status and then moving to lessen status differences over time.

While "taking the piss" was a continuous practice and enjoyed by most of the employees in these particular IT companies, even there the appreciation was not universal.[11] It might be difficult to import such an organizational practice to American companies, where long-standing power hierarchies are firm and clear. Most U.S. office policies remain very conservative in attitudes, dress, and acceptable behaviors for their employees. If you are laughing at work, it is usually assumed that you must not be sufficiently focused and "businesslike" in your approach.

Further, the presence of the PC value system is solidly entrenched these days in most U.S. businesses. "Taking the piss" bantering might easily trigger charges of sexual harassment or of establishing a hostile work environment. Perhaps some subversive cadre of highly paid employment lawyers is covertly responsible for any efforts to import such a new humor-intense corporate culture into America. Their full-time employment of filing and defending harassment lawsuits would be virtually guaranteed.

THE DARWIN AWARDS AND HUMOR

The Darwin Awards are published annually and consist of a rank-ordered list of true anecdotes in which a person's outrageously stupid behavior results in death. In most cases, the person was not necessarily trying to be funny, but their experiences become a rich source of humor for the readers.

The name of the awards comes from biologist Charles Darwin's famous theory of evolution, which presumes that these deaths contribute to the survival of the human species by eliminating any (more) reproduction from the protagonists. As their website succinctly puts it, "The Darwin Awards commemorate those who improve our gene pool by removing themselves from it." The website lists the candidates and their tales of qualification from each year beginning in 1995. The number one award winner each year is the story receiving the most votes from readers.[12]

I recommend reading these compilations of stupidity as part of my general recommendation to immerse yourself in all expressions of humor by all means possible. Enjoy the many humor sources on the Internet: jokes, riddles, cartoons, quotes, the annual Darwin Awards, video re-broadcasts of late-night talk shows, comedy specials, and the several YouTube videos that are actually funny.

STUPID PEOPLE VERSUS MENTALLY "DISADVANTAGED" PEOPLE

Stupid people do stupid things, and they are entirely appropriate to be joke targets. The Darwin Awards are good examples of that principle. When people who have at least average amounts of native intelligence make poor choices and do or say ridiculous things, it is funny and fair to laugh at them. The daily news is full of stories exemplifying their absurd behaviors, especially those that do not result in death.

People's crazy antics could result in arrests, injuries, and great embarrassments. For example, there is a graphic photo circulating on the Internet of the physical results when a patriotic man decided to insert a firecracker into his rectum and light it. It was painfully funny and gruesome to view, but undoubtedly more painful to him. There are better ways to celebrate the Fourth of July, such as watching a parade and attending a picnic.

In contrast, many times foolish behaviors are shown by people with limited intellectual capacity. The results may be a bit amusing, but it is unfair to laugh at the misfortunes of those less capable of exercising full responsibility in their choices. Further, your laughing at them would likely not be well received by any friends and family who observed your inappropriate laughter in such instances. Why? To laugh in that situation is cruel.

This basic principle of failed humor is applicable here: When relatively intelligent people do stupid things, their stupidity is funny. When people of relatively limited intellect do stupid things, it becomes more sad than funny.

A related example arises when a restaurant or hotel in a foreign country tries to create a menu or an informational sign in English. Some bizarre errors can occur. The inept translations often inadvertently create illogical or obscene semantics that can seem funny to native English speakers. The sign writers with their limited language abilities are trying to be helpful to their English-speaking customers and tourists. Yet late-night TV shows and daily calendar publishers try to capitalize on the potential humor in their errors. Before laughing too heartily, I'd suggest asking yourself how well you would do if you were asked to write a menu in Mandarin Chinese or Thai. Would that be equally funny?

HOW TO INCREASE THE CHANCES YOUR HUMOR WILL FAIL

Perhaps we have been focusing too much on the positive aspects of creating effective humor. A brief foray into *non*-recommended practices may be informative. Here are some tips that make it likely your humor making will fail.

- Try telling jokes or making funny comments when you are high on drugs or alcohol. Your impairment becomes a lubricant for inappropriate speech and poor decision making about your humor choices.
- Disregard all PC concerns. Review chapter 3 for specific issues and then ignore them vigorously.
- Use your X-rated material for audiences filled with elderly people, children, church members and the clergy, and any distinguished citizens of the community.
- Repeat well-known canned jokes and long stories from the Internet or famous comedians.
- Start telling a joke without being certain that you actually know all its parts and the punch line.
- Do immature humor for your persona and your audience, such as dropping your pants or using unnecessary obscenities.
- If at a party, make fun publicly of your hosts and their food and drinks.
- Tell satirical jokes targeting specific politicians or religions whose followers are likely to be represented in the group present.
- Attempt potentially dangerous or disgusting practical jokes in front of the group.
- If not specifically asked to perform, act to take over the group's attention by telling jokes, singing, speaking loudly and intrusively, and displaying other blatantly narcissistic behaviors more likely to annoy than amuse others.
- In social conversations, where humor might be injected appropriately, do not listen to others' comments, but just wait to seize an opportunity to jump in with something that is intended to be funny but is actually out of context.
- Minimize self-deprecating humor.
- Maximize aggressive and sexually based humor.

- Use specific individuals who are not present as the butts of your harshest jokes.

This list is definitely not complete, but enough about my experiences for now.

NEGATIVE EFFECTS FROM GOOD HUMOR

When funny things produce negative consequences, that humor can be considered as having failed. We hear a lot about how humor is positive and can have so many benefits of health and happiness. We should add, though, that there can be some negative effects coming from good humor. That is, despite the funniness created, misinterpretations and unwanted inferences may be drawn from a zealot's excessive and too exuberant humor making.

The unanticipated negative possibilities that we have observed resulting from well-intended jocularity include the following:

- The audience perceives that the speaker is insensitive to certain groups because of the jokester's seemingly blatant violation of PC standards.
- The audience presumes that the speaker is cruel and hostile toward the targets of the humor.
- The humor makers use comedy to distance themselves emotionally from other people and from emotionally sensitive topics, such as love, death, fears, and various personal needs.
- The excessively "on" humorist treats everything so lightly that it can become extremely difficult to be taken seriously when discussing another topic of importance. We might call this "laughing wolf."
- Perhaps a subtype of the syndrome above is the class of therapy patients who engage in "pathological humor." That is, these patients treat everything possible as a joke, and thus the joking becomes a mechanism for avoiding therapeutic forays into dealing with their real problems. Such individuals typically display other avoidant behaviors as well, such as missing appointments, failing to complete homework assignments, and belittling the entire enterprise of psychotherapy. This pattern is not unlike that of people who use humor (perhaps funny stuff) as an emotional wall to avoid psychological intimacy with their spouse or lover—but rarely both of them.
- Good humor at a prolonged and intense level can appear to be a subtle way of indirectly putting down other people, who are "obviously" not as smart, witty, verbally quick, or perceptually observant about the bizarre and irrational things that go on in this world.

- Sarcastic humor, when directed at specific individuals, can stimulate threatened lawsuits against the comedian for slander or personal defamation.
- Humor can be used to extend and strengthen status differences in relationships—for example, males over females, bosses over lower-level employees, and even parents over children. Even if it's funny, the humor can solidify the power differential and create distressful negative emotions in those who are the butts.
- Lower-status individuals can also use humor to their own benefit, relative to the higher-status persons. They might use humor as a deliberate ingratiation tactic to gain specific favors or general approval, especially if the speaker's insincerity remains hidden. Such strategies are not recommended because they are patently manipulative and could backfire with severe negative results if discovered.
- Several research studies have shown that aggressive teasing, also known as verbal bullying, can have negative effects on the observers of that teasing as well as on the direct targets themselves. Presumably those who see the teasing feel that they also might be at risk for the same treatment, even when there is no other evidence that they would be. Psychologists Leslie Janes and James Olson have labeled this phenomenon the "jeer pressure effect." Their research has shown that people who have observed the ridicule of others have become more conforming and fearful of failing than those who observed self-ridicule or none at all.[13]
- The *jeer pressure effect* could also extend to comedy club patrons who observe other customers, usually in the front seats near the stage, being singled out for attention and ridicule by the professional comedians. Customers sitting further away, even though they are much less likely to be seen and picked on, are likely to feel some noticeable discomfort themselves as a result. Is fear of public humiliation and ridicule a real psychological disorder or rather an adaptive style of functioning? Is this fear underdeveloped in many of our politicians?

Thus, in a sense, when the humor has actually been funny and successful, it may also have failed because of such potentially negative outcomes. No one wants trouble. The goal for all amateur and professional humorists is to create laughter and to enjoy the energizing good feelings together. When that doesn't happen, even when the humor is clever and well delivered, there has been some detectable degree of failure.

NOTES

1. L. Wilde, *The Larry Wilde Treasury of Laughter* (Half Moon Bay, CA: Jester Press, 1992), 9.

2. G. Burns and D. Fisher, *All My Best Friends,* large print ed. (Boston: Hall, 1991), 15.

3. T. Fey, *Bossypants* (New York: Little, Brown, 2011), 221.

4. www.bestcomedyonline.net/video-routines/bill-burr-pedophiles-routine.

5. L. Winstead, *The Green Room with Paul Provenza,* August 25, 2011, Showtime Cable Network.

6. B. Saper, "Joking in the Context of Political Correctness," *Humor: International Journal of Humor Research* 8, no. 1 (1995): 65–76, esp. 69.

7. www.brown.edu/Administration/diversity/documents/SexualHarassmentPolicy.pdf.

8. D. Crary, "Teen Bullies Crossing into Sexual Harassment," *Florida Times-Union,* November 7, 2011.

9. C. Shart, interview on Sirius XM radio, 2011.

10. M. Fine, Internet biography.

11. B. A. Plester and J. Sayers, "'Taking the Piss': Functions of Banter in the IT Industry," *Humor: International Journal of Humor Research* 20, no. 2 (2007): 157–87.

12. www.darwinawards.com.

13. L. M. Janes and J. M. Olson, "Jeer Pressure: The Behavioral Effects of Observing Ridicule of Others," *Personality and Social Psychology Bulletin,* 26, no. 4 (2000): 474–85.

SEVEN

Spontaneous Humor versus Spontaneous Sex

Brevity is the soul of wit.

—William Shakespeare, from *Hamlet*

Wit is the brevity of levity.

—Henny Youngman[1]

Spontaneous humor or spontaneous sex? Both! Spontaneity can make any activity more fun because it is unplanned and surprising. It can also backfire because of the definition of "impulsivity," which is essentially the same concept but with a more negative connotation than "spontaneity." Both terms mean an act with little forethought or preparation, often resulting in unintended consequences. I'll allow your imagination to conjure up spontaneity's potential applications to sexuality while we discuss examples of its effects on humor making.

Spontaneous humor is generally known as "wit." The term *wit* has evolved from earlier meanings, which emphasized a person's attempts to elicit laughter from others by aggressive cleverness and intellectual wordplay within a context of sarcasm and antipathy. Today, though, wit is best thought of as a much more appealing form of humor, which remains intellectual and clever and is most likely to appear suddenly and unpredictably in conversations. It requires rapid perception skills and usually a general feeling of verbal felicity, although wit can also be the motivator of sharp hostile barbs. Wit is frequently displayed as a powerful tool for individuals engaging in spontaneous and lively repartee. In his more formal definition, Mark Twain wrote, "Wit is the sudden marriage of ideas which, before their union, were not perceived to have any relation."[2]

Demonstrating wit is an admirable ability because it is not simply a matter of reciting a canned joke or some previously rehearsed or written material. The witty speaker truly is resorting to spontaneous innovative humor making that arises from within the immediate situation. Witty remarks, like all forms of humor, can fall within or outside the confines of social appropriateness for the group. That is its danger, because of the element of impulsivity characterizing witty comments.

WIT VERSUS HUMOR

Charles S. Brooks, an early twentieth-century essayist, described the differences between wit and humor, at least in his view. His distinction clearly favors the concept of humor over his conception of wit and the kinds of people displaying each element:

> I am quite positive that of the two, humor is the more comfortable and more livable quality. Humorous persons, if their gift is genuine and not a mere shine upon the surface, are always agreeable companions and they sit through the evening best. They have pleasant mouths turned up at the corners. . . . But the mouth of a merely witty man is hard and sour until the moment of its discharge. Nor is the flash from a witty man always comforting, whereas a humorous man radiates a general pleasure and is like another candle in the room. I admire wit, but I have no real liking for it. . . .
>
> Wit is a lean creature with sharp inquiring nose, whereas humor has a kindly eye and comfortable girth. Wit, if it be necessary, uses malice to score a point—like a cat it is quick to jump—but humor keeps the peace in an easy chair. Wit has a better voice in a solo, but humor comes into the chorus best. Wit is as sharp as a stroke of lightning, whereas humor is diffuse like sunlight. Wit keeps the season's fashions and is precise in the phrases and judgments of the day, but humor is concerned with homely eternal things. Wit wears silk, but humor in homespun endures the wind. Wit sets a snare, whereas humor goes off whistling without a victim in its mind. Wit is sharper company at table, but humor serves better in mischance and in the rain. When it tumbles, wit is sour, but humor goes uncomplaining without its dinner. Humor laughs at another's jest and holds its sides, while wit sits wrapped in study for a lively answer.[3]

Brooks's descriptions are certainly intriguing and unique, but that doesn't necessarily make them valid. They are definitely worthy of your thoughtful consideration. Personally, I see wittiness to be a highly desirable personality trait and an important humor-making skill. The question is this: How can we build it up in people so that it can be used in positive ways and thus make everyone's lives and interactions more enjoyable?

Unfortunately, it is very difficult, perhaps even impossible, to train people *directly* to be witty. Spontaneous humor can be developed indirectly, though, by diligently performing humor exercises and by practicing verbal skills, such as picking up on double or triple meanings of words from street signs or billboards and from the comments of other people in conversations.

General speechmaking tips are especially apropos when learning to deliver humor. Beginners tend to be nervous, which is normal and expected, but "nerves" typically lead to errors in verbal delivery that practically negate the intended humorous effects. Obviously, you want your material to be heard and well received. In fact, it *must* be heard to be well received. Funny stuff won't seem funny if your audience cannot follow it without strain or confusion. Speak clearly and with energy. Be careful not to slur or mumble your words. Pacing is also critical to maintain interest in the setup—and then a tiny pause before the punch line.

The most common error is speaking too fast for the audience to comprehend your message. Rushing a joke comes from knowing it well. Slowing to a reasonable pace, while simultaneously displaying your enthusiasm for the task, comes with frequent practice. There really are no shortcuts, no pills or potions to take, or even online courses to substitute for serious practicing, ideally with a humor coach for feedback.

It is critical to be able to respond quickly to setups and unpredicted potential humor stimuli. It is vital to be knowledgeable about the variable meanings of words and their contexts. The best way to learn that is just to read voraciously. Any content will suffice. No need to pore over the dictionary or thick joke books for this purpose. Thick jokes are rarely funny, anyway. Reading in our society, however, appears to be a dying interest—at least, reading anything longer than 140 characters.

One example of spontaneous humor occurs in this story: Some residential communities feature the prominent traffic sign that reads, "SLOW CHILDREN PLAYING." Is that sign giving good advice to drive more slowly, or is it proclaiming that the neighborhood contains children who happen to be intellectually retarded (or "differently abled")? Why would anyone want to advertise that there are slow children living there? If they are too slow moving, these children probably couldn't get out of the way of vehicles. Seeing such a sign and immediately pointing out its multiple meanings would be an illustration of wit.

Despite Charles Brooks's bias against wit in his definitions, wittiness is most often the specific characteristic that people are seeking when they advertise for or announce that they favor friends with a "good sense of humor." They really are not looking for someone to stand up in front of the room and tell jokes for fifty minutes (or even five minutes). They are not looking for someone who will surprise them with a cream pie in the face or show up for a date wearing a rubber red nose and a fright wig (unless they are going to a Halloween party).

We strongly encourage everyone to expose themselves . . . (pause for laughter here) . . . to *all* forms of humor in order to facilitate the crooked thinking and perceptions that, in turn, can stimulate the skills of wit. That is, go to current funny movies in the theater; rent classic comedies for home viewing; watch TV sitcoms; visit your local comedy clubs; attend concerts of major contemporary comedians; subscribe to magazines that feature lots of humor, such as *Playboy* (only for the cartoons and jokes, of course) and *Reader's Digest* or other humor-specialty publications, before they go out of print; read biographies and tell-all books by well-known comedians and humorists; review the increasing number of how-to books on comedy techniques as well as the humor classics of literature by authors such as Thurber, Benchley, Twain, and Wilde (Oscar or Larry); check out the many humor sources on the Internet (performance videos, joke websites); subscribe to the free joke-of-the-day services; and consider joining an acting class or a local improv group for some practical humor training. Actually, it is only helpful to join the group as an active participant, rather than merely considering doing so.

As Steve Allen cogently urged, "Immerse yourself in humor."[4] When you see and hear lots of humor in its various forms, you cannot help being influenced to think frequently in ways that maximize the humor potential of everyday events that are common to us all. Jerry Seinfeld is one of the best at picking out the funny from things that we all experience as merely mundane events in our daily lives.

Reading many joke books can be very helpful. Your reading should not be for their specific content—that is, to memorize some jokes for you to retell later. The purpose of this reading is more to familiarize yourself with the rhythm of jokes, the best words to use to elicit laughter in others, and the different styles of humor delivery. Do you want to deliver most of your humor with a harsh sarcastic edge or within a clear context of felicity? A positive reception is more likely with the latter, especially when the humor is part of important personal relationships rather than a formal comedic performance.

Humor expert and experienced comedian Larry Wilde discusses the value of the *illusion of spontaneity*. Professional comedians rehearse constantly to ensure that their timing is flawless and relaxed. Listeners believe that their words are being spoken for the first time, and hence their humor seems to be spontaneous. This is the secret. Practice your humor so much that your funny comments are errorless and seem spontaneous. Your listeners will praise your wittiness as much as the content of what was said.[5]

Of course, the more truly spontaneous the delivery, the less preparation time has been devoted to it. Thus, your preparation can range from just a few seconds of mental rehearsal to presenting something that has been written and thought about for weeks or longer. This principle is most applicable to amateur humorists. The professionals prepare and practice their material so well that it just appears to be spontaneous. Of course, any genuine humorous ad libs are spontaneous and witty.

Professional coaching can't be beat to assist you in honing your humor delivery skills, even though you may have no ambition to become a paid comedian. Using humor effectively and in what seems to be a spontaneous way can be learned from good instruction, information from coaches and books, modeling by the experts, diligent practice followed by constructive corrective feedback, and then more practice—the more, the better.

FREUD'S VIEWS OF HUMOR AND WIT

Sigmund Freud's psychoanalytic theory of personality has been more influential in the thinking of psychotherapists and in affecting our overall culture than any other single psychological approach. His views dominated the world of psychotherapy for many decades in the twentieth century. The widespread acceptance of Freudian concepts is also revealed in society's expressions of our art, literature, language, values, childrearing methods, beliefs about the causes of overt behavior, and the symbolic importance of dreams—and, yes, even our humor.

Other personality theorists have emerged over the years and tweaked Freud's original theories, first developed in the early 1900s, to create their own perspectives. Only in modern times has psychoanalysis been vigorously challenged by some very different alternative approaches. The current therapy zeitgeist is dominated by the more empirical methods of biological psychiatry and cognitive behavioral psychology. Psychoanalysts still exist in the world, but due to the results of many scientific studies that have not been very supportive of their approach and the lack of insurance company reimbursements for their prolonged treatment protocols, traditional Freudian analysts seem doomed to extinction.

Our particular interest here, of course, is the effect of Freud's theory on humor. His theory's influence will remain strong throughout our general culture for generations to come. It is absolutely no coincidence that most of our humor appears in the arenas of sexuality, aggression, and bathroom functions. These areas coincide with the most important stages of humans' psychological development, according to Freud. Whether you love or hate those topics of humor, there is a Freudian-based explanation for your feelings. Basically, the theory assumes that you have a developmental problem (what Freud calls a "fixation") in one or more of those parts of your personality that accounts for your strong positive or negative attitudes toward these subjects.

For the Freudians, jokes represent a way for a person to express unconscious feelings of aggression or sexuality. They are an indirect, and therefore safer, method of expression. Directly engaging in such behaviors as an adult is usually illegal and highly socially inappropriate. So the process of humor making actually saves us from getting into big trouble with the authorities in society (the police or mental hospital admission doctors). However, the joke telling itself can lead to many negative consequences. As we have been discussing throughout *Just Kidding*, faulty humor use can be inappropriate, off-putting, cruel, ineffective, and destructive to personal relationships. We obviously want to encourage the good, not the bad, aspects of joke telling.

According to Freud, *wit* is the safe expression of evil. These forbidden impulses of sex and hostility are biologically driven and are present in everyone. They must be expressed—that is, the built-up tension must be released in one way or another. This principle is true for all humans, even preachers and politicians. We can satisfy these drives safely via the processes of dreaming when sleeping, or while awake via humor making, which allows those feelings to be released in a controlled manner. If the joke itself is too direct, it may not sufficiently disguise the impulses in question and therefore does not serve the needs of the teller's personality very well. Ultimately, the humor efforts may just be perceived as painful or profane and not very funny.

Another interesting indirect way to express these "bad" impulses is via a mechanism Freud called *sublimation.* Sublimation is one of the major defense mechanisms in his theory, which operate to help a mature personality function successfully. To illustrate, when you choose an occupation, the behaviors required of that particular occupation are clearly understood and approved by society at large. For example, physicians are held in high esteem in our society. Surgeons can be very helpful to their sick patients by carrying out the necessary process of cutting them open and thereby causing severe pain, while simultaneously relieving themselves of their own unconscious hostile impulses in a socially approved fashion.

Another rather obvious medical example occurs when you meet a physician for the first time, and within minutes you willingly disrobe for a visual and physical examination of your body. Usually this happens in a medical office rather than at a party. Regardless, it is a highly unusual social interaction for two strangers. It is permitted in society because it is regarded as professionally necessary for a proper evaluation of a patient and occurs with the tacit understanding that the physician receives no personal psychological satisfaction from the procedure. That assumption may not always be valid.

In these two examples, the physician's basic psychological needs are sublimated into performing socially valuable activities. Other approved activities and occupations that serve to sublimate a person's basic hostile impulses include contact sports like boxing, ultimate fighting, and football; military service; some aspects of law enforcement; or even critiquing books, movies, or plays with heavy doses of sarcasm.

Another example of sublimation through work choice is the women's shoes salesman who also happens to have a foot fetish. The job requirements include looking at and touching women's feet. He has found an ideal occupation in which to gratify his unconscious sexual impulses. Note that certainly not all shoe salesmen have foot fetishes—at least not when they first take the job.

Sexual impulses can be gratified in other workers via the process of sublimation in these occupations: life model artists and photographers; massage therapists; producers of porn magazines, movies, and websites; romantic novelists; and even obtaining the necessary sexual histories during interviews by clinical psychologists, probation officers, lawyers, pharmacists, nurses, and public health social workers. It might be fun to brainstorm a list of other completely "normal" jobs in our society that at the same time can satisfy certain personal psychic needs and interests of the individual worker.

Another humor-related concept from Freud's theory is called *parapraxis.* Parapraxes are verbalizations or overt behaviors that are unintended expressions of either of those two basic drives of sex and aggression. For example, a physician was describing an alcoholic patient and inadvertently used the phrase "a bottle-scarred veteran." Or a beautiful female patient indicated an unwanted sexual interest in her by her male therapist when she referred to him in writing as "the rapist." In these instances the errors in speech or motor behavior are examples of parapraxes, which in Freudian theory are assumed to reflect unconscious desires or attitudes. Funny errors can also occur when typing on computer keyboards. Whether occurring verbally or via typing, these "slips of the tongue" have become widely known as "Freudian slips." However, you will never find them for sale in Macy's or Mervyn's lingerie department.

Freud wrote, "The interpretation of dreams is the royal road to a knowledge of the unconscious activities of the mind."[6] Analyzing a person's dreams and noting their symbolic meanings can help the therapist understand all levels of the patient's personality. Analyzing the content and forms of a patient's humor preferences is also a direct road to the unconscious. Undoubtedly that path is also a shorter road because the psychic material (the patient's preferences, drives, and defenses) is less hidden in jokes than in our nightly dreams.

The kinds of jokes you tell or like to hear from others, according to Freud, are revelatory of your own personality structure. If you prefer hostile jokes or sexual jokes, there is a corresponding personality feature within you to account for that preference. Jokes that are patently racist or sexist are considered to be reflections of hostile impulses that have not been satisfied elsewhere. This process applies to both the joke teller and the audience. Interestingly, Freud's theory can ascribe specific meanings to your personality whether you really enjoy a particular kind of joke or you especially do not enjoy it. This flip-flop flexibility can sound like a matter of "the patient can't win." That's because it is true.

To Freud's credit, he is one of the few theorists to have given much consideration to the importance of humor in a comprehensive theory of personality. He discusses humor's functions, its manifestations, and its unique meaning for the person. Of course, it is very important to realize that his clinical interpretations, despite being intricately described, are not necessarily valid and await more scientific proof. However, Freud's views certainly have stimulated additional research by psychological scientists for many years and continue to do so. That itself is definitely a valuable contribution to our eventual understanding of humor preferences by different personality types.

TECHNIQUES TO DEVELOP THE ILLUSION OF SPONTANEITY

Become a humor spotter. Constantly be alert to discovering humor stimuli around you. The best examples are those that were not intended to be funny. Jay Leno's "Headlines" segment on *The Tonight Show* is a good illustration. Viewers send in the headlines from newspaper stories or published picture captions that have unintended humorous meanings. You can be a humor spotter as you read your daily paper or drive around town being exposed to innumerable commercial and traffic signs. An example of the latter was a sign on the Interstate 5 freeway in San Diego that suggested "CRUISE SHIPS USE THIS EXIT." Rarely do cruise ships travel that particular highway.

Sometimes billboards along the road have unwitting humorous messages. Along Interstate 95 in Florida was a notice in large letters with the advice "DON'T LIVE WITH NAGGING PAIN." Did this good advice come from a divorce lawyer or a chiropractor or a drug company or an Internet dating site?

Another billboard along the same highway asks, "LONELY? DEPRESSED? ANGRY? JESUS IS STILL THE ANSWER." We are left to ponder whether Jesus really caused all that grief. No wonder he wants to help. He must be feeling guilty about it. After all, he did have a Jewish mother.

Admittedly billboards along the highways are designed to capture our attention and to deliver their message quickly. There is no time for explanatory language. Thus, the short burst of information may be ripe for alternative (that is, humorous) meanings. The old standard sign of "Eat Here—Get Gas" does not sound as appealing as the merchant might have intended.

Thousands of people see those same signs every day and don't detect the humor in them. You can do it with just a little focused attention and practice. It should be a source of fun for you and can help you navigate otherwise boring routine duties. To others, you will appear witty and spontaneous.

As a humor spotter, you can also spot signs that are intended to be humorous and mentally make up your own new punch line to piggyback on the original one. For example, some churches (and dry cleaners) are now putting brief, mildly humorous messages on their marquees as a way to reach a wider audience. Let us give praise for that! The First Christian Church in Selma, California, posted "EXERCISE DAILY. WALK WITH JESUS."[7] As we pass by and read this suggestion, what if we respond to ourselves, "OK, but what if Jesus decides to take another walk on the water that day?" It can be a fun humor exercise for us to add a punch line to a punch line. The task can even be done without any blasphemy—most of the time.

Tex Petersen, who creates the funny marquee messages for his Harmony Free Will Baptist Church in Fresno, California, believes, "The Lord wants us to laugh and smile."[8] I, for one, am thankful to hear that God endorses what all of us amateur and professional humorists are trying to achieve with our effective humor techniques. The Lord would certainly not be "just kidding" us.

What to do if you feel "joke challenged" when in the company of your jokester friends? Everyone may be going around telling a stock joke they've heard. You may have trouble remembering jokes, as many people do, and so don't have much to contribute. There is no law saying your contribution has to be a formal joke. Most people tell jokes that go on far too long, include irrelevant details, and become boringly obvious because the setups lead to predictable punch lines. Or you and others have already heard the joke elsewhere. Instead, it is often easier for you to mention a funny quote or the hilarious punch line from a different story when it is your turn to contribute. A single sentence is easier to come up with than some long and well-traveled convoluted tale requiring lots of rehearsal to pull off well.

An extraordinarily useful technique for improving your humor making is simply to hang out with funny people and listen carefully. They will inadvertently be modeling their storytelling skills and joke repertoires for you to learn from. Humorists love an appreciative and attentive audience. You can enjoy their humor while picking up bits of delivery styles and funny content all at the same time. It's all part of your humor immersion process of education.

TYPES OF NEGATIVE HUMOR THAT "SPONTANEITY" MIGHT TEMPT YOU TO TRY

When you are joking without preparation, you are at risk for trying certain forms of humor that are more likely to be received as inappropriate and offensive by your audience. Even with preparation, some people will choose to indulge themselves in these negative types of humor. Why? Most likely, such individuals are personally and professionally insecure. These jokes surely will bring surprise and shock to the audience, thereby giving the jokester some desperately needed attention.

The phenomenon is like that of people who use curse words unnecessarily and overly frequently because they apparently do not have sufficient vocabulary skills to communicate emphases without those words. Cursing for no reason or too frequently dropping in filler words and phrases, such as "you know" or "you know what I'm sayin'," just detracts from the main message and annoys the listeners. That's not an effective way to get laughs.

Thus, the types of negative humor described below should be avoided if you are interested in maximizing your humor's effectiveness and keeping your audience.

- *Sick humor*: This category includes jokes and stories that are especially disgusting and distasteful to most audiences—for example, dead baby jokes; jokes about Chernobyl, the *Challenger* disaster, or the Holocaust; quips regarding the deaths at the World Trade Center, the Pentagon, or the planes on 9/11; and AIDS and cancer jokes.
- *Scatological humor*: Generally, this form includes what is known for children as "bathroom humor" and includes the biological functions performed in that room. For adults, the jokes can become more specific in descriptions of the processes and products of defecation, urination, and flatulence, as well as eating excrement or using it and urine as part of consensual sexual play. Now, do you see why it might be offensive to some prudes?
- *Paraphilia humor*: This type of humor involves funny stories and jokes about any of the variety of paraphilias. A paraphilia is an abnormal source of sexual gratification for human adults that is different from that of another living human adult. Examples include fetishistic objects, such as rubber clothing or raingear, underwear, high-heeled shoes, or beef liver, and a variety of socially inappropriate outlets for sexual release (animals, children, blow-up dolls, voyeurism, exhibitionism, rubbing against someone in crowded venues, deceased partners, masochistic or sadistic behaviors involving the receiving or inflicting of pain and cruelty, crossdressing for arousal purposes, and assorted other practices "not otherwise specified" in the language of the current *Diagnostic and Statistical Manual*).

  Although most of these topics are ripe for humor making, most people are likely to find them offensive regardless of how clever the joke is. Unusual sexual interests can be made funny, but it is not easy to do so successfully and far too risky for nonprofessionals.

- *Shaggy dog stories*: This type of humor is not ethically or morally offensive like the preceding types, but these jokes are only very slightly more appreciated by audiences. There are several different explanations of the origin of the term, but the general description of this type of humor is a long and convoluted boring story filled with irrelevant details and transitions often lasting several minutes, finally leading to a conclusion that may be mildly amusing because the meaningless, anticlimactic punch line is totally unexpected by the audience. Such stories are not recommended because they are the opposite of spontaneous humor and tend to alienate your listeners due to their growing boredom and ultimate ennui.

- *Joking at the airport*: Since the tragedies of 9/11, airports throughout the world prominently post anti-humor signs. The security authorities are super-sensitive about detecting any hint of funny comments even remotely related to possible criminal behavior. San Diego International Airport as you approach the screening area features a clearly unfriendly total ban sign: "NO JOKING." Airports in Australia, New Zealand, and Great Britain have joined those of the United States in their zealous efforts at detection and arrests of spontaneous jokers at their airports. One Australian airport features this sign: "WE TAKE JOKES SERIOUSLY." Wouldn't it be better and more accurate if their sign read "WE DO NOT TAKE JOKES SERIOUSLY"?

  A scene from the hit TV comedy *Friends*, which was never actually broadcast because of its proximity to the 9/11 events, featured the newly married Chandler and Monica being detained by security at the airport for joking in front of this sign: "FEDERAL LAW PROHIBITS ANY JOKING REGARDING AIRCRAFT HIJACKING OR BOMBING." This sign implied that some joking would be permitted as long as it did not involve the taboo topics of hijacking or bombing. Chandler argued to the security officers that the sign was misleading because it said you couldn't make jokes about bombs, when, in fact, the sign really should have said "NO BOMBS."[9] Even attempting a well-reasoned and thoughtful discussion with airport security personnel about the semantics of their warning signs is not a wise strategy. You are very likely to be chosen for a more thorough examination, even internally, and will probably miss your flight.

- *Anti-humor or unjokes*: This form of humor requires the listener to be familiar with conventional joke structures and setups. The joke is begun in accord with a common setup narrative, but the surprise is that it anticlimactically violates that expectation in the listener. The punch line may simply be a *non sequitur* or may not be a punch line at all. It becomes the ultimate twist, a bad joke parody. Comedians Norm McDonald, Jimmy Carr, and the late Andy Kaufman are noted devotees of anti-humor. One could argue, though, that anti-humor is generally unfunny humor. It's all paradoxical.

Our eleven-year-old son Sam proudly told us a new joke that he had written: "A young boy was having a birthday and so his father said 'Let's go shopping. What would you like?' The boy replied, 'A golf ball.' Father said, 'OK.' On the way to the store, the boy got hit by a truck! And it was a golf ball truck!" Sam thought his joke was hilarious and laughed heartily when he told it. At first, we couldn't even muster a courtesy laugh for Sam and carefully explained to him that with such a sad ending it wasn't a very good joke. However, upon reflection we realized that the story was actually a great example of an anti-joke and was indeed funny. We couldn't stop laughing every time we retold his joke to other people. Sam really has learned to be funny and is even writing his own material, although I'd rather have him move on to standard-format jokes.

My recommendation for adults is to plan your humor sufficiently to avoid *all* of these irregular forms and topics. Your probability of effectiveness will be increased markedly. For example, only an audience filled with psychologists and psychiatrists would likely laugh very much at jokes illustrative of any of the paraphilia humor topics. Even some of these serious mental health professionals would fail to see the humor in any of the bizarre behaviors. They even might be inclined to attribute the unusual behaviors to manifestations of mental illness instead of just amusing quirks. It is not socially appropriate or PC to laugh at sick people. You can trust me on this judgment call because I know many such overly sober and nearly humorless health professionals from a lifetime of work experiences with them.

NOTES

1. E. Shanaphy, ed., *The Encyclopedia of One Liners by Henny Youngman* (Katonah, NY: Ballymote Books, 1989).

2. www.brainyquote.com/quotes/authors/m/mark_twain_11.html.

3. R. Nordquist, "On the Difference between Wit and Humor, by Charles S. Brooks," About.com, http://grammar.about.com/od/classicessays/a/brookswithumor.htm.

4. S. Allen and J. Wollman, *How to Be Funny: Discovering the Comic You* (New York: McGraw-Hill, 1987), 3.

5. L. Wilde, *The Larry Wilde Treasury of Laughter* (Carmel, CA: Jester Press, 1992), 7.

6. H. Reich, *Don't You Believe It! Exploring the Myths behind 250 Commonly Believed Fallacies* (New York: MJF Books, 2010), 144.

7. R. Orozco, "'The Lord Wants Us to Laugh and Smile,'" *Florida Times-Union*, November 12, 2011.

8. Orozco, "'The Lord Wants Us to Laugh and Smile.'"

9. www.youtube.com/watch?v=4uw08PX9gi8.

EIGHT

How You Can Be Even Funnier

Laughter and play . . . are an entrée into being more human . . . [and] the only way to keep a sense of fun and play in your [work] life is to consciously choose to make it a priority.
—Matt Weinstein, management consultant and author[1]

In this chapter we will identify the specific skills and personal qualities you need to be funny and the best techniques to deliver humor. We will also examine how to determine what is funny and what is not. Finally, you will learn how to raise your Humor Quotient (your HQ, but not necessarily your IQ, since it may be far too late for that). There is no standardized test to assess your HQ, but business humor consultant Ann Fry suggests that you can find it out simply by asking a number of your friends, family, and social contacts this question, to be answered on a scale of 1–10: "How much fun am I to be around?"[2] Then calculate your average score from all their ratings. By the way, ten 1 ratings do not make you a "perfect 10"!

Let's assume that everyone is already funny to some degree (at least most people think they are). This book, and this chapter especially, is designed to *increase* your current level of funniness from wherever you already are on that scale. As it is with the money in your bank account, your tennis skills, and your reservoir of self-esteem, there is always room for some improvement in your sense of humor. Even the professional comic or the best office jokester doesn't hit the humor jackpot every time. We'll begin with a brief discussion of the sense of humor construct and then review how to determine what is funny. Finally, I'll describe the best personal qualities and the specific comedic skills necessary for delivering humor effectively.

The major focus of this book is to help adults use humor in beneficial ways. For anyone interested in fostering the development of the sense of humor in children, in all modesty I can strongly recommend my earlier book on that topic: *Kids Who Laugh: How to Develop Your Child's Sense of Humor.* That task can be accomplished with your young children or students by following a simple seven-word formula: "Model it. Reward it. Don't punish it."

DETERMINING WHAT'S FUNNY

When you plan to do or say something you think is funny, you are making a prediction that your audience will likewise perceive it as funny. This process is much more complex than you might think. Many variables enter into the equation (few of which can actually be controlled), and only some of them can be known to the speaker. We need to mention and discuss these variables to fully understand the process of being funny and how to make your prediction reasonably accurate. How all these variables interact is, in fact, highly subjective.

The only guarantee is that the analysis itself will not be very funny. American writer E. B. White long ago warned, "Analyzing humor is like dissecting a frog. Few people are interested and the frog dies of it."[3] Luckily, you and I are among those who are interested in understanding humor in order to use it more effectively, both for fun and sometimes even for profit.

We usually conclude that something is funny when we and others laugh in response to a remark, a cartoon, or some incident. But even that criterion for funny is not foolproof. We have seen, for example, that members of laughter clubs laugh regularly and heartily in the absence of any humor stimulus. They derive tremendous personal benefits simply from the physical act of laughing. In addition, we all know some people who will laugh excessively loudly at even mild humor. They seem to prefer drawing everyone's attention to themselves and away from the speaker or comedian, rather than laughing unobtrusively in mild amusement. For instance, the classic comedian Phyllis Diller has always used an exaggerated laugh as part of her comic persona, although she claims it is natural for her.

Conversely, sometimes we may judge a comment or joke to be quite funny without actually uttering a sound. We definitely appreciate the humor of it but respond only internally. This outcome is most likely when we are alone.

The widespread use of modern social media has created a new way to express amusement—the familiar acronyms LOL and LMAO. They are conventionally expressed in written or texted format. However, an episode of HBO's hit comedy *Curb Your Enthusiasm* extended its usage when a woman at a dinner party shouted "LOL" whenever she thought something was funny, rather than smiling and actually laughing out loud, as most people do. Her verbal habit was so annoying to her husband that the script called for him to forgive a $500 debt owed by the star Larry David, *if* Larry could get his wife to stop yelling "LOL."

Science has now quantified the simplistic view that someone is funny when other people laugh at what they have said or written. Steve Roye has invented the Comedy Evaluator Pro, which is applied to evaluate stand-up comedy performances. With computer software and a quick finger, he can measure the ratio of the audience's laugh time to the comic's overall performance time. A similar ratio can be calculated for audience applause time to the total performance time. Roye claims that a comedian needs to reach a goal of at least 30 percent on these measures to qualify as a comedy club headliner. Lower percentages indicate that the performer's skills are currently at the (middle) featured act level or the opening act–emcee level. [4]

Roye's program takes into account an interesting phenomenon that has emerged recently in comedy audiences' reactions. Formerly, when people found the comedians' routines to be funny, they simply laughed. The laughter could range from polite chuckling to uproarious fall-to-the-floor-with-tears-streaming-down-their-cheeks levels of laughter. Now audiences may smile and laugh a little while applauding loudly or whistling to show their appreciation of the joke or wisecrack. I'm sure that comedians appreciate the applause—that is, the "love" of the audience—when they finish their acts, but immediate responsive laughter is their preferred drug (at least while on stage), more so than polite clapping.

Interestingly, professional comedians rarely laugh heartily themselves when in an audience of fellow comedians. Perhaps it is due to rivalries, jealousy, or simply taking a strict cognitive-analytical approach to the comedy being presented. Professional comedians are notoriously stingy with their own laughter when not performing themselves. They may just comment dryly, in their intellectual analysis, "That's funny" or "Very funny" or even "Hilarious." If it's not funny to them, they may say just that and then simply scowl or silently cringe.

Tina Fey, winner of the 2010 Kennedy Center Mark Twain Prize for American Humor, commented in an interview, "Someone once said that to make a regular person laugh, you need to dress a guy up like an old lady and push him down the stairs. To make a comedy writer laugh, you have to push a real old lady down the stairs. I don't know who that's attributed to." [5] Answer: W. C. Fields, perhaps the greatest of all movie comedians, has been credited with the same comment in relation to comedians, when he pointed out, "To make the average person laugh, all you need to do is dress a man up like an old person and push him down the steps. To make a comedian laugh, you have to push an old person down the steps." Comedians and comedy writers definitely have different standards for laughter for themselves than for the general public. Most likely they are all more jaded or have heard nearly all of it by now.

Another example of this distinction is that professional humorists, unlike most nonprofessionals, are nearly all aware of the iconic joke that uses the most extreme vulgar language and disgusting visuals imaginable, called "The Aristocrats" (see chapter 4). This classic joke lowers the humor bar to several stories below ground, just under the septic tank. The documentary movie of the same name, consisting of a large number of comedians telling this improvisational story in their own distasteful ways, is a big hit among professionals and an equally big turn-off for most lay viewers.

VARIABLES AFFECTING FUNNINESS

A large number of specific variables determine whether something is perceived as funny or not and then just how funny it is. It is a very complex process and essentially impossible to calculate exactly how successful any joke or remark will be. One of the frustrating features of performing comedy is that the same joke that just killed the last time you told it to a similar group surprisingly bombs this time. And you have no idea why that happens. It's also rather funny that the language of comedy uses the verbs "kill" and "bomb" so freely when referring to the funniness of a performer or a routine. And these two violent terms have exactly the opposite meaning! The best way to proceed is to be aware of what factors are relevant to the overall comedic process and make your best prediction on whether the humor will "work" this time.

Among the relevant factors for funniness, in no special order, are the setting, speaker to audience gender or age congruency, and the audience.

The Setting

If you are in a comedy club or at a stand-up concert, the setting helps produce laughter more easily than in a classroom or business seminar presentation. People in the club are there wanting to laugh and expecting to laugh. In fact, they have paid money to have a fun experience. The availability of alcohol definitely helps as a social lubricant.

The opposite is true in a college class, church, or business meeting, where humor and laughter are traditionally seen as inappropriate to the main mission of the group to learn, worship, or help the company be more successful. Of course, most humor experts disagree with that traditional belief and are sometimes called upon to help make humor and fun more acceptable within the institutional culture. With some prominent exceptions, the task of incorporating more humor into the historically conservative medical, legal, educational, and business communities is a titanic task that might have stymied Hercules himself.

Interestingly, sometimes the very inappropriateness of the setting can set off laughing jags among vulnerable people who may be experiencing heightened emotionality. For example, the setting of a church or a mortuary during a solemn service, wedding, or funeral would ordinarily be seen as the least likely place for humor to appear. Yet it can happen there, and the phenomenon of contagious laughter soon emerges.

For example, one of the classic scenes in the history of TV situation comedy occurred on *The Mary Tyler Moore Show*, when the cast attended the funeral of Chuckles the Clown. Chuckles had died when he was dressed in a peanut suit and was accidentally killed by an elephant that mistook him for a large peanut. After his death and prior to the funeral, Mary had been admonishing her colleagues for inappropriately joking and laughing about the circumstances of Chuckles's death. However, at the funeral itself it was Mary who broke up laughing uncontrollably. The attending minister even invited her to stand up and laugh in front of all the mourners because the late Chuckles loved laughing and hated crying (at which point, of course, Mary began to cry). The clip is available on the Internet.[6] It will be very funny both to those who saw it originally and to anyone for whom it would be new.

Even professional actors and newscasters periodically have their bouts of breaking up on stage or TV. It seems that the harder you try not to laugh, the more likely it is that you will laugh. The data also indicate that the younger you are, the more likely you are to be affected. We can call this the "irreverence of the young," something we might all aspire to.

Speaker to Audience Gender or Age Congruency

If the speaker is of the same gender as all or most of the audience, there is more shared commonality and it is a bit easier to have your humor efforts perceived as funny. The same effect occurs with age similarity. You also have more freedom in presenting material that may be somewhat controversial or risqué. Sometimes any incongruencies are of little or no consequence, but in some situations the differences can have a dampening effect on perceived funniness. Betty White, for example, in her elderly years gets a lot more laughs than a woman decades younger would get with the same material.

Audience

An audience can be just one person or it can be an arena of thousands or a TV or Internet audience of billions of people. Such a range of differences permits a parallel range of intimacy. Speaking to a lover in bed (a great place for humor as long as no one is pointing at body parts and laughing sarcastically) is obviously a different level of closeness than reading scripted jokes or dialogues to a worldwide TV audience at the Academy Awards. The key to maximizing the funniness of your humor making is to gear it to the interests, values, expectations, and background knowledge of your audience.

"Inside" technical jokes from within the movie-making industry would not do well outside of a movie awards audience. Humor based on the content of popular movies or the personas of the stars is much more likely to be successful with general lay audiences. Similarly, the personal preferences and any quirky aspects of your mate's lovemaking can be great opportunities for shared genuine laughter—but revealing them to friends at a dinner party would likely have unpleasant emotional effects.

Knowing the nature of your audience is one of the most critical aspects of using humor effectively. This issue is discussed in detail in chapter 9.

TEN THINGS WE KNOW FOR SURE ABOUT FUNNINESS

What is funny and why it is funny are difficult to explain. There is a lot we don't know about funniness, but some things we can be fairly certain about now. These are guidelines that, when understood and accepted, will help you use your humor more effectively.

1. Nothing Is Funny All the Time

Repetition dulls the edge of humor. You can enjoy a painting or a piece of music repeatedly with little loss. But with humor there is little surprise the second or third time around. It can still be amusing with no shock or surprise left, but the remark will no longer be so totally outrageous or hilarious.

2. Nothing Is Funny to All People

Because of individual sensitivities and unique personal histories, nothing really is universally funny. Someone will always have an objection, feel slighted, or claim to be offended for some reason. Further, some people just may not get it, regardless of how witty and clever we are. It is best to try to amuse most of the people all of the time.

3. Pain Is Funny—If It Happens to Someone Else

If the pain happens to you, at least you can take comfort in that it is most likely funny to someone else. The German word *Schadenfreude* defines this genre of humor, in which a person feels joy or delight in the misfortunes that happen to others. The Greeks also have a word for this phenomenon—*epikhairekakia*—which may have come from Sophocles's description of Athena, who asked if laughing at one's enemy is not the sweetest form of laughter. This experience of joy at the expense of others is very common in the world of humor, even though it does not seem to reflect our highest ethical or moral values. Mel Brooks defines tragedy versus comedy quite clearly: "Tragedy is when I cut my finger. Comedy is when you fall into an open sewer and die."[7]

4. The Unexpected Is Funny

This is especially true if it involves some aspect of pain or the embarrassment of someone else. Classic joke structure involves sending the listener down one cognitive trail and then springing a surprise at the end, which prompts hearty laughter. This technique is also known as *misdirection*. A good example is this joke from South African white comedian Chris Forrest: "Recently I have actually met a new girlfriend. She's black. My parents are really shocked. . . . They thought I was gay."[8]

5. Lies, Such as Exaggerations, Are Funny

Hostile lies are not funny, at least to the recipient. Interestingly, the book written by comedian Chelsea Handler's friends and family, *Lies That Chelsea Handler Told Me*, immediately reached best-seller status. Each chapter recounts multiple hurtful lies that were perpetrated by Chelsea, essentially for her personal amusement (see chapter 2). Despite the pain caused by her elaborate pranks and lies, all of the chapter authors profess their love for Chelsea. No doubt it helps that Ms. Handler is a rich, international star with her own TV program, so obtaining forgiveness from her victims comes very quickly.

6. Puns Are Not Funny

Sometimes puns are clever and intelligent, but rarely funny to anyone but the punster. I'd suggest avoiding them unless you are a full professor of English literature or classics having lunch with colleagues at the university faculty club. Admittedly, not everyone shares my cynical, devalued view of punning. Musician and humorist Oscar Levant once said, "A pun is the lowest form of humor—when you don't think of it first."[9]

If you are interested in pursuing puns, I'd suggest checking out the title, and perhaps the book itself, of John Pollack's *The Pun Also Rises: How the Humble Pun Revolutionized Language, Changed History, and Made Wordplay More Than Some Antics*. The book also discusses several unique forms of wordplay such as *spoonerisms* (e.g., transposing "a blushing crow" for the intended phrase of "a crushing blow"), *wellerisms* (in which a common phrase is spoken and followed by a facetious one, such as "'It all comes back to me now,' he said as he peed into the wind"), and *Tom Swifties* (a form of wordplay in which the following adverb reveals a punning relationship to the speaker's statement, such as "'I know who turned out the lights,' Tom said darkly").[10] As always, there may be different strokes for different folks, your author agrees swimmingly.

7. Some Words Are Simply Funnier than Others

Examples of inherently funny words are *midget, corkscrew, scrod, titty, titter, peepee,* and *cock* (the fowl). Your word choice can be the key to creating a successful witty line . . . or a dud.

In Neil Simon's play *The Sunshine Boys,* the character Willy gives his nephew a lecture about comedy and how to tell which words are funny:

> Fifty-seven years in this business, you learn a few things. You know what words are funny and which words are not funny. Alka Seltzer is funny. You say "Alka Seltzer" you get a laugh. . . . Words with "k" in them are funny. Casey Stengel, that's a funny name. Robert Taylor is not funny. Cupcake is funny. Tomato is not funny. Cookie is funny. Cucumber is funny. Car keys. Cleveland . . . Cleveland is funny. Maryland is not funny. Then, there's chicken. Chicken is funny. Pickle is funny. Cab is funny. Cockroach is funny—not if you get 'em, only if you say 'em.[11]

8. Self-Deprecation Is the Safest Strategy for Getting Laughs

Making yourself the butt of the joke does not threaten anybody else. It capitalizes on the *Schadenfreude* phenomenon (the tendency to feel pleasure when others suffer misfortune). After all, it is not the listeners, for example, who are fat or hapless in their relationships and dating behaviors. Therefore, the story is likely to be perceived as all the funnier by the audience. A good example of self-deprecating humor is Gary Shandling's quip: "After making love, I said, 'Was it good for you, too?' She said, 'I don't think it was good for anybody.'"[12]

As with most things in life, it is possible to overdo the self-deprecation in humor. Some professional comedians dwell on their own obesity or other physical impairments so much that their audiences can become uncomfortable. A better example is Josh Blue, who has cerebral palsy but quickly acknowledges his physical differences by stating them at the outset of his act and making a few jokes at his own expense. He then goes on with standard comedic material that is totally unrelated to his CP.

The basic message is that self-deprecation within limits is a wise plan in funny storytelling. It communicates that you are aware of funny things and stupid behavior, even when they happen to you. People who can't laugh at themselves leave the job to someone else, as "Anonymous" once wisely proclaimed.

9. The Degree of Funniness of the Humor Messenger Is the Number One Key to Funniness

The messenger's funniness consists of two major components: personal qualities and humor delivery skills. Let's examine each of these components in detail. Is a sense of humor innate or learned? Clearly, our premise is that it is a learned skill, which may come as a surprise to many people. No one is born funny. You learn to be funny by trying to be funny, usually beginning in childhood, and getting feedback on your efforts. You can model yourself after well-known funny people or even funny family members. By informal trial and error and incorporating helpful feedback, you then modify your efforts at joke telling, riddles, impressions, and physical humor. You know quickly when it works well and when it doesn't. Your reward is the laughter and appreciation of other people.

Professional comics work at their comedy for the laughs they can get far more than for the money and fame (or so they claim). That laughter equals love from their audiences. It doesn't hurt for the humorist to enjoy the attention of the spotlight and have that rare ability to get everyone in the room to laugh. That is the greatest reward possible, although great sex and enormous paychecks are not too far behind.

10. You Must Practice, Practice, Practice

Practice is indeed essential for you to be effective in your humor making, even if you have no goal of getting to Carnegie Hall. Saying funny things is a skill like any other skill. The more you do it, make corrections after feedback, and then do it again, the funnier you will be. Naturally you must practice the right things: knowing your audience, knowing your material, delivering the humor succinctly with proper timing, and including a reasonable amount of self-deprecation and PC awareness for seasoning.

A BAKER'S DOZEN OF PERSONAL QUALITIES AND DELIVERY SKILLS NEEDED TO BE FUNNY

As in many axioms in life, many of my recommended personal qualities for an effective humorist are much easier to describe than to achieve. Certainly they are goals toward which we all can enthusiastically strive. These qualities will also be beneficial in many other areas of life in addition to humor making.

1. Personal Likability

If people like you, your efforts at humor will be much more readily accepted and appreciated. The easier you establish a strong rapport with your audience, which could be as small as one other person, the more effective your humor will be. Your goal is to come across as someone the other(s) would like to have as their friend . . . now. How do you do that? Smile a lot. Make eye contact immediately. Be open and candid in your language. Appear transparent. And, if necessary, fake the sincerity! You don't have to be of the same race, gender, religion, sexual orientation, or any of the other major demographics as most of those in your audience. It may help in the beginning, but very soon the audience will decide to like you or not. If it is the latter, your task of humor making will be all the more difficult. In sum, be nice and communicate that quality to your listeners.

2. Vocabulary Breadth and Word Knowledge

Another advantage of reading as much as possible is that this habit will expand your vocabulary and give you more word choices when creating your humor. What you read isn't that important. It could be novels or current events or works from any academic discipline. It is not necessary to learn extremely obscure words and their definitions. In fact, that could inhibit your humor effectiveness by causing your joking to stray too far from what is common knowledge. Taking this advice will help keep you from being the real-life butt of linguistic-based jokes, such as this one: The employment interviewer asked the job applicant if she was bilingual. She replied nervously, "Well, just once in college."

3. Verbal Fluency

As with any public presentation, when delivering humor, it is crucial to eliminate speech filler phrases and sounds, such as "you know" or "ummmmm," which will annoy and wear down the patience of listeners. Any humor that can break through all that noise will be much less effective. Most people are unaware of how often those filler sounds appear in their speech. Recording your practice sessions will allow you to learn just how often you use these disruptive fillers, which definitely impede your communication effectiveness.

One personal anecdotal story on the topic of verbal fluency: In a psychology of humor class, I was working with a student on his stand-up routine. He stuttered very badly but had a surprisingly positive attitude about his "disability" and his potential for performing in public. I told him (in retrospect perhaps a bit too spontaneously) that he was very fortunate because due to his stuttering, he only needed to prepare five minutes of material for his fifteen-minute routine. Both he and I, and all the class, laughed heartily.

4. Ability to See Things Differently

This skill is sometimes called thinking crookedly. It simply means that your perceptions go beyond the obvious and intended ones. When you communicate that difference in your humor, you create "aha" experiences in others, who quickly are able to see things in that new way too. The phenomenon is similar to seeing an illusion figure in only one way until someone points out how it can also be viewed in a different way. From then on it is easy to see both forms of the perceptual illusion. When you see the world in a slightly skewed way, rather than in a tremendously different way (as does a psychotic person), your reality contact remains intact. You have gained grist for your humor mill. This quality is essential for the humor-spotting technique discussed below.

5. Acquiring a Feel for the Basic Structure of Jokes

After hearing enough formal jokes and after practicing writing jokes, you will soon learn the sense of their basic structure. Another technique is to read joke books regularly, not to learn and tell those same jokes, but to learn the various joke structures. Examples would include the "rhythm of threes," where two similar setups precede the third, which produces the punch line. The setups prepare you for the laugh (expectations), and then the punch line (the surprise) delivers the laugh. One illustration of this form came in a speech given by Senator Bob Dole when he quipped that three ex-presidents attended the same Washington party—Carter, Ford, and Nixon: See No Evil, Hear No Evil . . . and Evil.

The rhythm-of-threes type of joke is probably the most common form among jokes told to friends or passed along via e-mail. These jokes, though, are usually too long to maintain the listeners' attention sufficiently and hence are not recommended for effective humor use in person. One typical example joke from this category, with a notable PC upgrade:

> A young Native American brave asked his father how all of his family got their names. His wise father explained, "Son, it is very simple. Your grandfather was born when the sun was just coming up, so he was called Rising Sun. I was born during a great thunderstorm, so I am named Black Cloud. But, tell me, why are you asking about this, Broken Rubber?"

Funny material can come in the form of one-liners, formal jokes, humorous writing, allegedly true stories, life observations with a comment, quips, limericks, puns, pranks, and physical humor. Not everyone will enjoy delivering (or even hearing) all of these forms. We all have our preferences as appreciators and initiators of humor.

Another aspect of a successful joke structure is placing the key punch line word at or very near the end of the joke with no unnecessary words following. It is critical not to hurry the punch line by increasing the tempo of your setup lines. From Steve Martin: "Sex is one of the most beautiful, wholesome, and natural things—that money can buy!" Using *incongruity and resolution* are also part of standard joke formatting, as illustrated in Martin's very funny line. Many jokes develop an incongruity that must be followed by a resolution of that difference, thereby creating the satisfactory and humorous end to the mini-story.

6. Knowing What to Eliminate and What Not to Add in Your Humor Making

Leave out all the unnecessary words and comments, such as "Did you hear the one about . . . ?" or "That reminds me of . . . ." or "Stop me if you've heard this one." Avoid long, repetitious, and predictable prologues to your humor. Attention deficit disorder is epidemic in America now. The audience's attention can quickly waver, and listeners may try to anticipate the punch line. Whether their guess is successful or not, the humor is definitely diminished. Be succinct to be funny.

What *not* to add to your story or joke? Leave out embellishments— any unnecessary details, irrelevancies, or verbal self-distractions. Telling a joke is not a stream-of-consciousness exercise. Too many people, sometimes abetted by a nitpicking "helpful" spouse, add information that only prolongs the story and does not serve the critical goal of parsimony. For example, the day of the week or the time of day, who else was there, and the reaction of the others as the event transpired (if the tale is true) are probably not relevant to the intended humor.

7. Timing

Timing is a technical skill in humor that is absolutely vital. Comedian Larry Wilde defines *timing* as "the art of delivering words, phrases, and sentences in a rhythmic or varying tempo with calculated emphasis in order to heighten their effectiveness."[13] Delivering the setup and punch line of the joke with the proper pacing and pauses and then hitting the emphasis at the end constitute this critical comedic skill. Timing is just as important as the content of the material to produce its funniness.

One of the most important aspects of comic timing is the pause. Pausing at key points in your message for just a second or two can enhance your humor more than steroids. Pause at points in your phrasing that are natural to the tempo of the setup. Jack Benny and Johnny Carson were masters of the pause. Imagine being a great comic success without uttering a word!

Professional comedians are masters of comedic timing, while amateurs frequently fail on this dimension even with good or great material. Timing takes practice and is integral to having the basic feel for effective humor delivery. A good example of timing comes from A. Whitney Brown: "I saw my grandmother the other day—probably for the last time. . . . She's not sick or anything—She just bores me to death."[14]

The importance of comedic timing in the performance of jokes is universally agreed upon by humor theorists, teachers, comedians, and audiences. The consensus view is that in comedy "timing is everything." Yet, surprisingly, very little scientific research on this key aspect of humor has been conducted to verify this proposition.

In the most recently published paper on joke delivery timing, linguists Salvatore Attardo and Lucy Pickering analyzed twenty prepared and spontaneous joke performances by ten nonprofessionals. The authors expected that the speakers would raise or lower their speech rate at the point of the punch lines and that pauses would precede the punch lines. To their great surprise, they found no evidence whatsoever of these clear predictions derived from the theory of timing.[15] Our surprise is that perhaps for the first time in the history of science, the researchers could not confirm what everybody already knows.

8. Spontaneity

Being funny without merely repeating a prepared joke is especially difficult, yet an extremely powerful comic tool. Humor created spontaneously is the essence of wit. Wit connects disparate ideas and perceptions in unusual and funny ways. When wit is expressed spontaneously in verbal interchanges, it is most impressive as a comic art. To demand spontaneity is an oxymoron. The description of my interchange with the stuttering comedy student above is an illustration of spontaneous wit. For more discussion on the topic of spontaneous humor, see chapter 7.

9. Sensitivity to Offensive Humor Domains

You should always be aware of what areas may well be offensive to members of your audience. The offensiveness may be partly due to the content of the material, but it can also arise from having established insufficient rapport or from the perceived intrusion upon an established social group. Obviously it is necessary to know the current guidelines of political correctness. PC standards change as well.

Earlier in my career I conducted a survey of topic interests that were relevant to a serious book I was planning on bizarre psychological syndromes. One of the choices under consideration was bestiality (sex with animals). Reportedly, this behavior is more common than most people think, especially among teenage boys reared on rural farms. But since the survey results indicated that there was very little interest in reading more about this topic, it was not included in the book. It is safe to say that bestiality is clearly an offensive humor domain for most people. However, comedian Dave Attell boldly claims, "I would have sex with a horse.

Because it's a beautiful animal, and when you have sex with a horse, you know you always have a ride home."[16] He might have added, "And the horse doesn't expect you to call in the morning or nag you about when you will be coming back out to the farm."

Given sufficient awareness of potentially offensive topics, you then must make the conscious choice to proceed with that material, to dilute it to reach more acceptability, or to delete it entirely in favor of safer, less personal targets of humor. Ultimately, it's your choice.

10. Personal Assertiveness

It can be daunting for someone to take on the comic role in any social setting. To use humor effectively in a job interview setting or as part of a professional role such as a health care provider can be a risky undertaking. You are being assertive when you are willing to speak up and try to make others laugh. One of the hardest tasks in show business is to enter a room filled with many strangers and within a minute or so get those people to like you and laugh when you tell them stories. The job is made more difficult because the audience members may hold a variety of agendas. Some are there to impress their dates; some are there under mild coercion; some are there primarily to eat and drink; some are there to get their money's worth from admission and cover charges; some are there to find love; and some may be there just to get in out of the rain. To win this disparate group over to have a good time with you as their comic entertainer in a very short period of time takes immense courage, comedic skills, good material, likability, and the personal assertiveness to step up and be funny.

Personal assertiveness is another way of saying "a willingness to take social risks." Usually to make significant gains, you have to take significant risks. Some people are not even willing to try to use humor in their daily lives. As a result, those people tend to be timid socially, less likely to be hired, less likely to make the sale, and less likable or fun to be with because they are too sober, serious, grim, negative, depression prone, and lonely. Who wants that? Who wants that in their friends? Answer: No one, other than perhaps a paid therapist. Take a chance. Life is short and just like a roll of toilet paper—the closer you get to the end, the faster it goes.[17]

11. Before You Speak—

Successful humor making is contingent upon knowing what you are going to say *in its entirety* before you start your story or joke. Repeating a joke that you have heard or read is especially risky because there is a set order for the setup and punch line. If you go blank in the middle and cannot recall the finish or omit a key preparatory piece of information, it will create a most uncomfortable deadness for both you and your listeners. Telling a humorous story about a true experience you actually had is less prone to this memory problem, although a smooth delivery nearly always requires a little prior practice before trying it in public.

12. *Before the Story Begins*—

Do not overpromise your listeners, claiming that the story you are about to tell will "knock your socks off" or send them to the floor laughing. You definitely will not get them *literally* to laugh their asses off, even if you succeed in accomplishing that physical goal figuratively. Enjoying excellent humor never leads to loss of bodily integrity or even noticeable weight reduction. It can, however, weaken the appreciator's knees, stimulate tears of joy, and create an asthmatic gasping for air.

During your presentation, there is no need to warn the listeners with distracting phrases such as the following: "Are you ready for this?" "Listen carefully now." "This will kill you." "Sit down for this." "Pay attention to what I say." All of these errors create unhelpful expectations and interrupt the fluid delivery of the humor. Usually the best strategy is to tell your story with no verbal preface at all other than a big smile, which signals everyone that something funny is coming.

13. *Knowledge of the Major Characteristics of Humor as a Phenomenon*

The following is a brief list of the most common and the most important qualities that contribute to funniness:

- *Exaggeration of a real or stereotyped quality*: This includes jokes or comments about the greed of lawyers, doctors, and business executives; the absent-mindedness of university professors; the craziness of psychologists; the misbehavior of the clergy's children; leaky faucets in the plumber's own home; or mechanics' cars being frequently out of service.
- *Understatement*: Twisting a cliché one might say, "There is less here than meets the eye." Another illustration is the true story of the rookie major league baseball player who naively asked his new manager, Frank Robinson, who was already in the Major League Baseball Hall of Fame, if he had ever played the game. Robinson drily replied without elaboration, "Yes, I played some."
- *Ambiguity or double entendre*: This type of humor is based on a word or comment that has more than one meaning, one of which is humorous. In the case of double entendres, one of those meanings is usually sexual. For example, certain words can be defined in a straight way or a sexual way: "Do you *come* here often?" or "I love to *eat* at the Y" or "The party last night was really *gay*."
- *Targeting superiors*: The butt of these jokes is someone in a superior position, such as the boss, the president, military officers, superin-

tendents, government officials, and so on. Those in inferior roles also can be joke targets, such as fast-food workers, poor people, or the homeless, but it creates a greater risk of social unacceptability. Louie Anderson does get away with this funny observation: "Don't you hate it when the homeless guys get all the best shopping carts?"

- *Wordplay*: Often bumper stickers or clever commercial ads reveal funny wordplay lines. A septic tank cleaning service ad: "We're #1 in #2." Painted on a tow truck: "Support your local repo man. Miss 2 payments." Bumper sticker insightful accuracy: "I'm hung like Einstein and I'm as smart as a horse." Double meaning: "I child-proofed my home, but they still get in."
- *Surprise*: An unexpected twist at the end of the sentence or story produces the funniness. With the surprise element going for you, the humor impact will be greater. When one of comedian Greg Proops's jokes bombed, he politely commented to the audience, "You guys are real nice. You honor everything I say with a moment of silence."[18] His unexpected retort brought huge laughs.
- *Irony*: In this type of humor, the literal meaning of a comment is the opposite of the intended message. For example, during a fierce thunderstorm someone observes, "Beautiful weather today." Or someone asks, "If I bought something at the Container Store, what would they put it in and would they charge me for it?" Irony is often part of related aspects of humor, such as *sarcasm, satire,* and *wit,* usually intended to mock or ridicule something or somebody. Here are some future news headlines: "U.S. Supreme Court Rules Punishment of Criminals Violates Their Civil Rights"; "Heterosexual Couple Petitions Court to Reinstate Legal Marriage."
- *Effects of your own mood*: You can be funny regardless of the personal emotions you may be feeling at the time. Psychologists call these *organismic variables,* a term that can be made funny by tapping into its similarity to the word *orgasmic.* Your own mood definitely affects the tone and type of your humor at the time. For example, if your mood is positive and upbeat, your jokes and observations will likely be heard as witty and clever. Good examples here are the monologues of late-night TV hosts Jay Leno, David Letterman, Jimmy Fallon, and Jimmy Kimmel. If your mood is negative—sad, angry, or frustrated—your humor will likely be more in the form of a rant, complaining and yelling in outrage. Prominent examples here are Lewis Black, Dennis Miller, and Bill Maher.

NONVERBAL HUMOR BEHAVIOR

A key part of effective humor is to make your nonverbal behavior congruent with your verbal humor. That is, to be sure your audience understands that your impending remarks are intended to be humorous, it is vital to *signal* the audience of your intent. The easiest and best way to do that is to *smile* just before and during your speaking. Sometimes, adding a few words to support your signal can be helpful, such as "That reminds me . . ." or "Conan [or Leno or Letterman] said last night . . ." Then deliver your joke or comment. Many times, though, the amateur humorist will make that preliminary signal far too lengthy and the audience's attention will quickly begin to drift away.

Here is a *bad* example of verbal signals that go on too long: "Before I came over here tonight, I was reading this funny article in the paper in the Letters to the Editor section. It had to do with the lack of formal education of so many of our political candidates. For example . . ."

Another typical error many people make is advising their listeners beforehand how hilarious the next joke will be and then providing a lot of irrelevant details before getting to the meat of the joke. "This is really funny. My priest told me this one after church last week. He's such a funny guy in real life. His joke, which is really hilarious, is about a minister, a rabbi, and a priest playing golf on a weekend late in December, and . . ."

Usually an extensive verbal humor signal is not really necessary and tends to lessen the humor effect, even when the material is very good. As indicated, it is also very easy to go on far too long with a wordy introduction prior to the actual humor making.

DEADPAN HUMOR

The major exception to the importance of humor signals is when you use deadpan humor (not to be confused with bedpan humor). This style refers to delivering the humor expressly *without* signaling that humor is coming. Use a monotonic voice and no smiling. It is more difficult to pull off successfully, but it can be especially funny because your audience is not expecting the humor. However, the risk of failure is also greater. One of the best professionals to use the deadpan style of delivery is Steven Wright, with a more intellectual, yet usually illogical, wordplay in his series of random comic observations. Two representative samples from Wright: "The New Testament is actually pretty old" and "What did Jesus ever do for Santa Claus on his birthday?"[19]

OTHER NONVERBAL HUMOR FORMS

The most effective forms of nonverbal behavior to aid humor are the eye roll, the eyebrow lift, lip pursing, and the "take." In this way you communicate the lack of seriousness of the speaker's message, whether you or someone else is the speaker. Steven Colbert is especially skilled in this aspect of humor delivery. The use of gestures is often the key to making a joke successful. An important caution is not to overdo gestures to the point of distracting the listener and thus weakening the humor's power.

In the history of comedy, two of the best comedians to perform the take were Jack Benny and Johnny Carson. A "take" or "double take" occurs when the performer gives an overly dramatic reaction to something being said or done in their presence. Their response is nonverbal and is communicated by their facial expression and posture.

A variation of the take is the "spit take," in which the comic's reaction involves spitting out a liquid that he or she has been drinking in an exaggerated spray. Someone else typically has said something outrageous or disgusting and the comedian lets go with the drink being consumed, perhaps hitting or just missing the speaker. Albert Brooks's film short *Famous School for Comedians* depicts a workshop for beginning comics on how to do the spit take effectively.[20]

The fun for those appreciative of slapstick physical comedy comes from pratfalls, such as those made famous by Chevy Chase on *Saturday Night Live,* and from buckets of slime that get dropped on kid contestants on the Nickelodeon cable channel's award shows. *America's Funniest Home Videos* is another great example of unintentional physical comedy. The hits to the groin, the slips and falls, and all variety of accidents are the super-dreams of America's liability lawyers. The rest of the viewing audience revels in an ocean of *Schadenfreude,* enjoying the misfortune of other people.

The first TV program featuring nonverbal slapstick humor was comic icon Milton Berle's variety show on his *Texaco Star Theater.* During a sketch he would casually mention the innocuous term "makeup," and then a comedy cohort would run on stage, yell "Makeup!," and hit him with a giant powder puff, engulfing Berle in a cloud of face powder.

Clowns and mimes often rely entirely on nonverbal humor to get their laughs. The classic clown scenarios include having many clowns emerge from a tiny VW Beetle, squirting seltzer water or whipped cream in someone's face, or gouging the eyes of offending others, as popularized in the Three Stooges movies. Hitting someone on the head with a frying pan may seem funny, as long as you are not the victim. In general, I do not recommend these forms of humor for amateurs and especially not for children.

Comedian Louis C.K. is especially negative in his view of clowns. He carps, "Clowns aren't funny. There's nothing worse than somebody who is not funny trying to be funny. That's what a clown is."[21] Jimmy Fallon agrees, but with less fervor: "When I see professional clowns, mimes, or people who make balloon animals, I think of their relatives and how disappointed they must be."[22] Cringe comic Paul Hooper scores a double anti-PC hit in his act, in which he calls a clown "nothing but a pedophile with war paint."[23]

I wonder if these comedians are aware of the psychological disorder of *coulrophobia*, the pathological fear of clowns, which affects a surprisingly large number of children and adults. There is even a website for them to share their concerns and stories: www.ihateclowns.com. Perhaps C.K. and Hooper are in denial about their own phobias, since there is only a very thin line between hate and fear.

Merely being aware of these categories of humor can definitely be useful, but that knowledge by itself will be insufficient to produce more effective humor making. It is most important, of course, to practice writing and delivering examples of these aspects of humor, so that their performance eventually comes easily and naturally. Be sure to review the other performance tips presented in chapter 9 and to practice the humor exercises in the back of this book.

NOTES

1. A. Fry, *Laughing Matters: The Value of Humor in the Workplace* (Austin, TX: Better Way Press, 2004), 74.
2. Fry, *Laughing Matters*, 91.
3. www.brainyquote.com/quotes/authors/e/e_b_white.html.
4. J. Brady, *I Am Comic*, documentary, Showtime Cable Network, December 18, 2011.
5. A. J. Jacobs, "The Real Tina Fey," *Esquire*, April 13, 2010, www.esquire.com/features/tina-fey-funny-quotes-040710.
6. www.youtube.com/watch?v=K8EUykajYWo&feature=related.
7. www.brainyquote.com/quotes/quotes/m/melbrooks161275.html.
8. www.youtube.com/watch?v=kgnOL0bEBRc.
9. http://thinkexist.com/quotation/a_pun_is_the_lowest_form_of_humor-when_you_don-t/186297.html.
10. J. Pollack, *The Pun Also Rises: How the Humble Pun Revolutionized Language, Changed History, and Made Wordplay More Than Some Antics* (New York: Gotham/Penguin, 2011).
11. N. Simon, *The Sunshine Boys* (New York: Broadhurst Theater, 1973).
12. D. MacHale, *Ready Wit: A Treasury of the Cleverest Things Ever Said on Any Subject* (New York: Barnes & Noble, 2004), 97.
13. L. Wilde, *The Larry Wilde Treasury of Laughter* (Carmel, CA: Jester Press, 1992), 5.
14. See http://www.scribd.com/doc/54540440/Greg-Deans-Step-by-Step-to-Stand-Up-Comedy.
15. S. Attardo and L. Pickering, "Timing in the Performance of Jokes," *Humor: International Journal of Humor Research* 24, no. 2 (2011): 233–50.

16. J. Wolk, "Gag Reflex," *Entertainment Weekly*, November 15, 2002, www.ew.com/ew/article/0,,388438,00.html.

17. Author unknown; www.quotegarden.com/age.html.

18. G. Proops, Sirius XM radio broadcast, 2011.

19. J. Delery, "What Did Jesus Ever Do for Santa Claus on His Birthday?," *Laughspin*, October 10, 2006, www.laughspin.com/2006/10/10/steven-wright-dont-call-it-a-comeback.

20. www.youtube.com/watch?v=HF7F57JY1OI.

21. L. C.K., "Talking Funny," HBO Cable Network, April 22, 2011.

22. http://thinkexist.com/quotation/when_i_see_professional_clowns-mimes-C.

23. See http://current.com/community/93030778_fox-news-boss-roger-ailes-to-be-indicted.htm.

NINE

Strategies to Avoid Humor That Fails

The old adage "It's not what you say but how you say it" is the very essence of communicating humor.

— Larry Wilde, comedian and humor author[1]

Among the pitfalls to avoid when humor making is offending listeners' sensitivities by using language and concepts that are not politically correct. No one wants to be publicly perceived as racist or sexist. Yet a real dilemma emerges for all entertainers and speakers because so much humor is based upon the characteristics of social group stereotypes.

To take just one example, religion (defined broadly as an active and organized group of believers in a deity) can be a very complicated topic to sort out socially. There are the large categories to consider, such as Christianity, Judaism, Islam, Hinduism, Buddhism, primal-indigenous, Chinese traditional, and many others. Within each of those are many different subtypes. And then there are also the atheists (a secular religion?), agnostics, humanists, New Agers, Scientologists, and Wiccans. There are literally hundreds of separate sects, cults, and religious societies (e.g., the Quakers) that are distinct in their beliefs. Each of them has followers who range from the very devout to those whose membership in the group is merely "cultural" or a result of an accident of birth to certain parents.

For example, even within a social setting of Christians only, a Christian speaker might safely make this comic observation: "An Episcopalian is just a Catholic who's going to hell." Some Christians, some Catholics, and some Episcopalians might laugh heartily and enjoy the comment immensely. However, realistically, some of them might become highly offended by the comment and then very unhappy.

Atheists and agnostics are in the unfortunate position of having no one to call out to during an intense orgasm. If they happen to be sufficiently narcissistic, though, they can call out their own names.

In 2005 the website Ship of Fools feared that the British government was planning to outlaw offensive religious jokes. In response the site conducted a poll of its readers to determine "the funniest religious joke of all time." The winner was this joke from the American comedian Emo Phillips:

> Once I saw this guy on a bridge about to jump. I said, "Don't do it!" He said, "Nobody loves me."
>
> I said, "God loves you. Do you believe in God?" He said, "Yes."
>
> I said, "Me too! Are you a Christian or a Jew?" He said, "A Christian."
>
> I said, "Me too! Protestant or Catholic?" He said, "Protestant."
>
> I said, "Me too! What franchise?" He said, "Baptist."
>
> I said, "Me too! Northern Baptist or Southern Baptist?" He said, "Northern Baptist."
>
> I said, "Me too! Northern Conservative Baptist or Northern Liberal Baptist?" He said, "Northern Conservative Baptist."
>
> I said, "Me too! Northern Conservative Baptist Great Lakes Region, or Northern Conservative Baptist Eastern Region?" He said, "Northern Conservative Baptist Great Lakes Region."
>
> I said, "Me too! Northern Conservative Baptist Great Lakes Region Council of 1879 or Northern Conservative Baptist Great Lakes Region Council of 1912?" He said, "Northern Conservative Baptist Great Lakes Region Council of 1912."
>
> I said, "Die, heretic!" And I pushed him over.[2]

Phillips's joke is indeed very funny and might have the positive social side effect of highlighting just how silly such subtle religious differences can sometimes become.

Stephen Colbert's appearance in character as host of the White House Correspondents' Association dinner in 2006 included a satirical joke about religion: "Though I'm a committed Christian, I believe in all religions—Hindus, Jewish, Muslim. I believe there are infinite paths to accepting Jesus Christ as your personal savior."[3] The joke is funny because the setup appears to be the standard-issue PC language of noncontroversial inclusiveness, up through the words "paths to." Most listeners expect the generic word "God" to follow. His surprise punch line instead reverts to a chauvinistic devotion to Christianity, which at a public event in Washington, D.C., is both non-PC and fitting with Colbert's comic character.

The main point here is that a joke that references religious faith in general or any particular religious group may easily run afoul of the PC police. The joke or comment may simply fall flat and be unappreciated, or, in the worst case, the speaker may be loudly condemned and shunned for making such blasphemous remarks.

Comedian Lewis Black concurs: "When you write about people's beliefs, you are asking for it. Every page here [in his 2008 book *Me of Little Faith*] has the potential to offend someone, somewhere, in perpetuity, throughout the universe." He believes that religion is taken too seriously, "and anything that takes itself too seriously is open to ridicule."[4]

Does this mean that we should ban all jokes relating to religion? Obviously not. Such a hypothetical ban would create a potential loss of millions of jokes and trillions of laughs. Some professional comedians whose acts and writings include much religious humor, such as Black, Jackie Mason, Bill Maher, or the late George Carlin, would essentially be put out of business. And certainly many amateurs and high-volume humor e-mailers would be seriously stifled.

Comedian Mark Normand in his act describes a loophole in the PC ban on humorous attacks on religion. He notes that most religions have advocacy groups who are alert to any hints of defamation. Normand suggests joking about Scientology works because their weird beliefs make it acceptable to make fun of them and everyone in your audience will jump on board. We might add that the Jehovah's Witnesses seem to have achieved the same easy-target status. Comic Bob Zany (what a perfect surname) jokes, "This week I made a killing in real estate. I shot a Jehovah's Witness on my front porch."[5]

If the topic of religion is acceptable for humor, what about rape? Is rape a sexist topic? Some zealous humor-content monitors consider it sexist, but in fact, the perpetrators and victims of rape can be either male or female. All combinations of gender and sexual orientation and victim and perpetrator have been reported in the news. Sarah Silverman is known for her very funny line: "I was raped by a doctor, which is so bittersweet for a Jewish girl."[6]

Louis C.K. also does a bit about rape that he claims has never generated a complaint from his audiences: "You should never rape anybody—unless you have a good reason—like you want to fuck somebody and they won't let you. What are you going to do? Not fuck them? That's no solution. You're going to have to rape 'em."[7] This is really strong material, and we hope that Louis is "just kidding."

Most professional comedians will maintain that *nothing* is off limits for joking. That degree of freedom is, to be realistic, just not there for amateur humorists. You *must* play by different rules than the pros. Your rules are unquestionably much more restrictive. If you do not abide by them, not only will your humor be ineffective, but you may also be severely ostracized in the process. Consider the issues of good taste and social appropriateness as well as your own relationship goals with the people who are listening to you. No laugh will be loud or long enough to be worth the personal costs of making most jokes about rape, child abuse, or animal abuse.

A popular humor resource website (www.jumbojoke.com) has posted what they describe as "the worst ethnic joke ever told." Note: I don't want this book to be a collection of bad jokes—there are far too many competitors in that book category. In this case, though, this very mildly funny joke is a bit of a spoof on the PC restrictions regarding identifying specific ethnicities in humor. I don't recommend trying to memorize it to repeat at cocktail parties. Besides, I've definitely heard lots of much more offensive ethnic jokes than this example:

> An Englishman, a Scotsman, an Irishman, a Welshman, a Latvian, a Turk, a German, an Indian, several Americans (including a Southerner [but certainly not a redneck!], a New Englander, and a Californian), an Argentine, a Dane, an Australian, a Slovakian, an Egyptian, a Japanese, a Moroccan, a Frenchman, a New Zealander, a Spaniard, a Russian, a Guatemalan, a Colombian, a Pakistani, a Malaysian, a Croatian, a Uzbek, a Cypriot, a Pole, a Lithuanian, a Chinese, a Sri Lankan, a Lebanese, a Cayman Islander, a Ugandan, a Vietnamese, a Korean, a Uruguayan, a Czech, an Icelander, a Mexican, a Finn, a Honduran, a Panamanian, an Andorran, an Israeli, a Venezuelan, a Fijian, a Peruvian, an Estonian, a Brazilian, a Portuguese, a Liechtensteiner, a Mongolian, a Hungarian, a Canadian, a Moldovan, a Haitian, a Norfolk Islander, a Macedonian, a Bolivian, a Cook Islander, a Tajikistani, a Samoan, an Armenian, an Aruban, an Albanian, a Greenlander, a Micronesian, a Virgin Islander, a Georgian, a Bahamian, a Belarusian, a Cuban, a Tongan, a Cambodian, a Qatari, an Azerbaijani, a Romanian, a Chilean, a Kyrgyzstani, a Jamaican, a Filipino, a Ukrainian, a Dutchman, a Taiwanese, an Ecuadorian, a Costa Rican, a Swede, a Bulgarian, a Serb, a Swiss, a Greek, a Belgian, a Singaporean, an Italian, a Norwegian, and forty-seven to fifty-three Africans walked into a fine restaurant.
>
> "I'm sorry," said the snooty maître d', "but you can't come in here without a Thai."[8]

It is truly a complex terrain of humor here, and the treacherous footing is constantly changing. What suggestions can we offer to help you achieve PC respectability in your humor?

Lewis Black capitalizes on his persona of the raging, sputtering, nearly out-of-control observer and victim of society's outrageous injustices and irrationalities. Thus, he gains both personal benefits and professional esteem from loudly venting his complaints on stage for big money. Talk show icon Larry King praises Black: "Nobody makes anger funnier. He may be the angriest man in America."[9]

SAFE HUMOR MAKING

A keen sensitivity to your audience's religious and other deeply held moral values, along with what is currently PC in our society, will help ensure that your humor making is successful.

The following two principles are especially vital to being funny with full social acceptance.

The Mother Rule

The Mother Rule can be a useful major arbiter in those PC dilemmas of "should I use this joke or not?" The Mother Rule is this: Would you say it if your mother were there to hear it? This rule will be more influential to amateurs than to the pros, who by definition are more likely to say or do *anything* for money and to produce all potential laughs out there.

The Whisper Rule

Whenever a storyteller or jokester changes his or her voice to a whisper, the speaker is likely at some level to be aware that the coming comment could be offensive or over the line. The whispering is likely to be accompanied by furtively looking around to check whether someone else might be within earshot. Of course, these behaviors are more likely to occur in non-stage appearances. Such hallmark signs of an intention to use socially inappropriate humor content are surprisingly unknown to most speakers. You should be aware of this rule when listening to others or when tempted yourself to whisper certain words, even relatively innocuous words correctly used, such as "the blacks," "minorities," "Mexicans," "the Jews," "Catholics," "Tea Partiers," and so on. The desire to change your voice to a whisper means that the ideas or concepts to follow are probably offensive.

THE FUNDAMENTAL PRINCIPLE OF KYA

"Know your audience" (KYA) is *the* most important concept to apply in deciding whether to make a comedic observation or joke. You can usually quickly assess whether it is probable that your audience will even understand and then be socially accepting of your humor or not. It's helpful, of course, if your remark is funny, but funniness is definitely a subjective perception of your listener(s). Your audience, as always, may range from just one other person to a large group at a meeting. The setting can be very informal, such as speaking with a waitperson or store clerk, or quite formal, such as a wedding toast or an after-dinner speech.

Some variables to consider when evaluating your audience:

- *Intellectual level*: Are the topic content and your word choices within the audience's comfort level? Using foreign or abstruse language (such as the word "abstruse") with people of limited education is not recommended. Your comments will not be understood and perhaps will not be well received simply because they had the effect of belittling listeners whose vocabularies are more limited. At best you might receive a courtesy laugh.
- *PC concerns*: Are your humorous comments within reasonable PC guidelines? Are they attacking certain groups of people unfairly? Might they be perpetuating negative stereotypes? Is the target of the humor characteristics that are not readily changeable, such as a person's race, gender, sexual orientation, or body integrity, as opposed to specific behaviors that are habits or quirks?
- *Setting*: Is the humor delivered in a relatively private one-to-one setting, such as with a waitperson (one of the newest PC job titles) or in conversation with a friend? Or is it part of a public statement, such as a speech or interview with the broadcast media? The more public the setting, the more attention your comments will receive. Remarks that are intended to be humorous, but fail to be, will produce greater negative effects when spoken on the air, tweeted to acquaintances, or reproduced in interview transcripts.

The general concern in this area of PC is to avoid humor that sounds degrading to any group or that implies that people who are different in some noticeable way from the majority of people are somehow inferior as a result. Your choice of words is critical. Slang and pejorative words must be avoided both directly and indirectly.

The following guidelines represent the best ways to avoid humor that is most likely to fail. Professionals sometimes can skirt these pitfalls successfully, but even then they can alienate large portions of their audience, if their edgy humor falls off the ledge. Here is our best advice:

- *Do not use stereotypical offensive language.* The best example here is the "N-word." This word is so non-PC that it is now known only by its initial letter. The word has long been judged acceptable only when used by African American comedians in their acts, but obviously not when used by non–African Americans. Eddie Griffin, for example, offers to hand out a "nigga card" to anyone in his audience after the show. He claims the card will entitle anyone to "five free trips to the hood without an ass whoopin'. For a white man, he can only pick up one sister. For a white woman, she can have up to five young bucks."[10] Griffin's language is not unusual in comedy club performances of black comedians today. I'm sure these cards are entirely mythical.

Mike Birbiglia does a satirical bit in his stand-up act about using the word "cracker." He claims that if only blacks can use the N-word, by analogy, only whites can use "cracker." He goes on to parallel the other clichés about who can use each racial slur with whom.[11]

In contrast, Lisa Lampanelli claims another special entrée for using the entire word: "I've banged a black guy for two years now, which is nine and a half years in black. I figure I've done my time, so I can do all the nigger jokes I want. Also, black people usually love me."[12] It is no accident that her 2009 memoir is titled *Chocolate, Please*, which does not refer to her asking for a piece of candy or a milkshake. Interestingly, Lampanelli recently committed marriage to another Italian American, whom she affectionately refers to as "Jimmy Big Balls."

Comic Jabari Asim has published a history and discussion of the usage of the N-word in America. Interested readers may want to check out his book *The N Word: Who Can Say It, Who Shouldn't, and Why* or Harvard law professor Randall Kennedy's *Nigger: The Strange Career of a Troublesome Word*. Kennedy also traces the history of this word throughout American society, referring to it as the "paradigmatic racial slur in the English language." His book's description of the word on the amazon.com website is enlightening: "It's 'the nuclear bomb of racial epithets,' a word that whites have employed to wound and degrade African Americans for three centuries. Paradoxically, among many black people it has become a term of affection and even empowerment."[13]

In 2011 two new editions of Mark Twain's *Adventures of Huckleberry Finn* were published. Twain is widely regarded as America's greatest humorist author. In the original 1885 U.S. publication of the book, Twain deliberately used the N-word 219 times to spotlight nineteenth-century racism. In one of the new editions, a zealous PC-conscious editor replaced every instance of "nigger" with the word "slave." The second new edition is a hipster version of the Twain classic with the replacement words being "H-words" (hip words) throughout. Mark Twain scholar Robert Hirst, the official curator of the Mark Twain Project at the University of California, Berkeley, argues that the changes are stupid because it weakens the message of how bigoted the character Pat Finn really is, as revealed in his drunken tirade about meeting an educated "nigger" who votes.[14] Does no one worry about perpetuating the stereotype of drunken Irishmen?

Comedy clubs will occasionally promote certain special events that they call "cultural nights." For example, the show on Latino Night might feature all Hispanic comedians with heavy doses of Spanish-language humor. Comedian Leslie Jones reveals the open secret in the business that when clubs feature a night of all African American comedians, the event is known by insiders as "Nigger Night," but they advertise it euphemistically as "Urban Night."[15]

The comic genius Richard Pryor was a very successful stand-up comedian and actor, frequently using the N-word long before it was just a euphemistic initial. Comedy Central cable network in 2011 rightly awarded Richard Pryor the number one position on its list of the all-time greatest stand-up comedians.[16] Interestingly, toward the end of his life and after an educational trip to Africa, Pryor gave up using the word "nigger" in public because he believed it was too derogatory and hurtful. Some other prominent African American comedians, such as Bill Cosby and Paul Mooney, are now trying to discourage its use by all their fellow black comedians. Mooney admits to having been what he calls an "ambassador" for the word previously. He now argues that its continued use in professional comedy has the undesirable effect of desensitizing listeners to the full N-word and results ultimately in perpetuating a negative image of this ethnic group. I agree.

Even the competition for the Republican presidential nomination for the 2012 election has created an "N-word" controversy. One-time candidate Rick Perry of Texas belonged to a private club there with the name "Niggerhead." His father eventually purchased that club and painted over the name, which had been prominently displayed on a large slab rock sign at the entrance. Even after the painting, the offensive original words were still visible and so they turned the rock over. Some of the other candidates strongly chastised Perry for joining a club with such a name. (The parcel is now known as the "North Camp Pasture," if you find yourself looking for it in West Texas's Throckmorton County.)

The historical details of the incident during the debate and its analysis are of minimal relevance to our present purposes. What is of most interest to us is how those candidates and the media commentators in their post-debate analyses all refused to state the actual name of the club because of their PC concerns. Their verbal tiptoeing became quite funny to the audience at large, who heard just how convoluted the commentators' speech could become to avoid saying the actual original name of the Perry family's hunting camp. The sole African American candidate at the time, Herman Cain, courageously and boldly announced the full name of the club soon after on a national news interview program.

Referring to the "N-word" term achieves nothing except creating the illusion of a person's PC sensitivity. In fact, saying the euphemistic "the N-word" actually serves to instill the word "nigger" in everyone's mind. Presidential candidates surely should be aware of their language and tone as well as the overall content of their public speeches. However, this word is creating so much controversy and anxiety, let's suggest a simple guideline: When discussing the issue of using that word or reporting a news incident, it should be OK to use the word in its entirety, IF it is somehow important to use it at all. Make it a positive usage. However, if you are using the word to indicate your hatred, distrust, or antipathy to black people, it is not OK to use the word, even in humor making. That is a negative usage.

The "N-word," of course, is not the only stereotypical offensive label that should always be avoided to ensure some social acceptance of your humor. A *partial* list of disparaging slang for particular groups also includes chink, spic, wop, dago, Polack, Hebe, wetback, beaner, kike, jigaboo, faggot, homo, Lesbo, jungle bunny, slant eyes, slope head, *schwarze* (for Yiddish speakers), and all related adjectival forms of these words. There are more, but I don't want to give anyone any more bad ideas. Offensive words such as these are certainly shocking and attention-getting, but it is not necessary to use them in order to be funny. Larry Wilde adamantly advises, "Keep it clean. Never tell a story that might offend."[17]

English comedian and actor Ricky Gervais created comedy controversy with his bawdy and personalized jokes as host of the 2011 Golden Globes Awards on American TV. Despite the uproar, Gervais was hired to host the 2012 program, presumably by a close vote. Later in the summer of 2011, on *The Marriage Ref*, a comedy-advice program for couples' semi-serious problems, he commented, "It's funny to be racist."[18] Although it was an isolated odd remark worthy of some further explanation, which did not happen, Gervais most likely was "just kidding."

Formal and public comedy roasts are a special genre of humor making. There are no language limits and no concerns for displaying any hint of good taste. Roastmaster Ross calls himself an "equal opportunity offender" and truly means it. His teacher, Lee Frank, in a New York City stand-up comedy class, taught Ross and the others, "If it doesn't offend somebody somewhere, then it's not a joke."[19] That philosophy was the perfect motivation for the future roaster.

- Generally, with the exception of the first item discussed above, *it is permissible to make fun of a group of which you are a member or with which you are closely identified.* For example, telling a bald joke, even to a bald person, will usually work if you yourself are bald. Telling a joke about Jewish American Princesses will work if you are Jewish or a Gentile married to a Jewish woman. It is critical, though, that the audience be made aware of those factors, or they may not be forgiving.

Comedian Russell Peters is a Canadian of Indian heritage. He argues that even when he makes a joke about some stereotypical characteristic of his own ethnic group as an insider, he really wants to make a *cultural* point applicable to everybody. All human groups are more alike than different. That is why both insiders and outsiders can enjoy the humor.[20]

Jeff Foxworthy from Georgia can make fun of unsophisticated "rednecks." Larry the Cable Guy can make fun of poor white trash. Actor-comedian Denis Leary routinely capitalizes on the foibles and stereotypes of his own Irish heritage. Ralphie May can make fun of fat white Southerners. Even Don Rickles will sometimes be self-deprecating in his act and make fun of old Jewish men. The late Richard Pryor made fun of life as a black man in America. We accept these comedians' targeting these specific social groups because they are presumably talking about themselves and their own subculture. Of course, while Ralphie May remains morbidly obese, Larry the Cable Guy is nowadays a very long way from being poor.

Comedian, author, and film producer Paul Provenza is an Italian American white guy. Comedians from other ethnic backgrounds at times use Caucasians as the outsider group in their humor. As an audience member, Provenza himself has experienced being a part of the group that was the butt of the joke. He admits empathically that it didn't feel so good.[21]

- Generally *it is not PC to target any characteristics of a person or group that are not changeable,* such as a specific person's intellectual capacity, height, physical deformity, race, or facial ugliness. Using pejorative terms to describe that person, such as "retard" or "crip" or "vegetable" or "Jew-boy," should obviously be avoided. The word "midget" is simply a funny-sounding word, but the PC proper language now is "little person" or "dwarf," according to the association Little People of America. Unfortunately, the more acceptable terms, from the perspective of humorists, are just not very funny-sounding. Rather than target physical characteristics, it is much preferred to target people's behaviors. Almost any behavior *can* be changed, and so it is fair to critique it humorously, especially when people act stupidly or speak foolishly.

What about someone's weight as a topic for humor? That is a changeable characteristic, but certainly not easy to change, as many of us are so well aware. Fat can be funny. Even the word "fat" is funny. Some comedians, such as Ralphie May, John Pinette, and Lavell Crawford, play up their own obesity as part of their comic persona and wear oversize clothes, both to emphasize their bulk and to provide needed coverage. However, the acceptable PC term for the obese is a "person of size" (presumably without adding adjectives such as "incredibly large" to the noun "size"). Using a PC phrase often dilutes the humor, unless it is itself the target of your humor. "Person of size" is a good illustration of that effect.

The Big Four topics that are sure to bring the speaker to the ever-changing borders of the non-PC arena are *race, sex, religion,* and *politics.* Everyone soon realizes that these topics are volatile, sensitive, and likely to raise strong emotions instantly. For the same reasons, these topics are extraordinarily fertile ground for humor. We should all be aware of the advice of Bill Maher and others: "Denying racism is the new racism."[22] If, in the context of telling a joke or relaying a true personal incident, you preface your comments with the phrase "I'm not racist *but* . . . ," you are about to throw your holy self-appraisal into serious question.

Professionals nurture those four fields and happily harvest jokes and full routines from them. However, the metaphor that best fits the amateur is that these are also dangerous minefields capable of detonation without warning, thus leading to the destruction of old friendships and other important relationships. That which might indeed be the funniest territory available is also likely to be the riskiest. Proceed with caution.

- Specific *psychological "buttons"* are the unusually sensitive areas specific to a given person. They may even seem irrational to most people, but some people have certain trigger points whereby humor making on that topic will create exceptional upset and hurt in those persons. When you know a person well, you will know what their hot buttons are. It could be weight, food preferences, hobbies, interests, religion, mannerisms, historical humiliating incidents, experiences of abuse, or countless other possibilities. When you make someone's button the target of your humor, you are taking advantage of your special knowledge about that person, which really is simply being unfair, hostile, and cruel. No one wants that.

- Avoid jokes reflecting *international disdain.* Joke genres are faddish. Periodically, these classes of jokes have featured morons, elephants, light bulbs, feminists, dorks, blondes, psychiatrists, and citizens of certain countries. The latter genre is more of a curiosity in the historical development of humor than a genuine source of funny or witty material. What is interesting is that when it comes to jokes reflecting international disdain, usually the citizens of one country make the joke and the citizens of another country serve as the preferred target because of their alleged stupidity or buffoonery.

  For example, Americans typically told "Polack" jokes. The French told jokes about the Belgians. The Eastern Canadians told jokes about the "Newfies" of Newfoundland, while the Western Canadians targeted the Ukrainians and the Icelanders. The English told jokes about the Irish. This genre came to be labeled "international disdain," and the jokes were rarely very funny.

Welshman Christie Davies, an international humor scholar, conducted a comparative analysis of ethnic jokes told in most countries of the world and the countries that were targeted because their citizens were allegedly either stupid or canny. There is a long tradition of such derisive humor, with the stupid and canny jokes being overwhelmingly dominant in their frequency and persistence.

The Jews have been disproportionately represented as the butts of jokes that depict people who are "canny, calculating, and craftily stingy." Davies considers "canny" to be the opposite of "stupid." He explains, "Canniness implies cleverness and rationality, but it is a shrewd cleverness, and a calculating rationality applied in the pursuit of personal advantage . . . [with] their alleged disposition to use these qualities in ways and in contexts that others find ludicrously inappropriate and excessive."[23] Other nationalities and groups are targets of canny jokes as well, but the high frequency of Jews as the targets suggests possible anti-Semitism in the origin of these jokes and riddles.

Davies recognizes that some observers might claim canny jokes reflect or encourage anti-Semitic attitudes. He argues that any such contribution by humor to the long and vicious history and hatred of the Jews would be "utterly trivial." The propagandists have other, more potent weapons and disguises to promote their animosity, such as anti-Zionism, Nazi Holocaust denials, punishment of economic crimes, and political denigration. Such people, he believes, are "disdainful of jokes" anyway. Davies is a very intelligent man and a respected scholar, but few humor experts believe that repeatedly targeting Jews with negative stereotypes and as butts of jokes has no deleterious effects in the attitudes of worldwide audiences. Most of us recognize the psychological principle that telling big lies often enough and long enough leads to more believers.

Jon Stewart, host of the Comedy Channel's *The Daily Show*, picked up on *New York Post* columnist Steve Dunleavy's negative generalization about French citizens: "The French are against everything, including that curious American habit of showering every day." Stewart noted the irony of Dunleavy's curious "habit of employing crude stereotypes to sum up an entire nation."[24] Such sweeping observations reflecting international disdain are both unfair and unfunny. They are not easily swept under the table or eliminated by regular bathing.

Thankfully, this form of derisive joking is dying out, despite the occasional uncovering of a gem of real humor. No one really believed that all Poles are stupid, for example, but native Poles and Polish Americans suffered from some harsh kidding that bordered on humiliation during the heyday of such jokes and riddles.

- It is safer to attack general *concepts* rather than specific individuals or groups by name, unless your humorous point is related to some widely known incident, such as a philandering politician in the news. After all, why target one political party or one ethnic group or one religion, and thereby risk alienating and reducing the size of your audience by the size of that group? Professional comics, such as late-night TV hosts, carefully try to balance their humor to give roughly equal ill treatment to all.

In summary, you flirt with non-PC danger zones when your humor making involves the following:

- Offensive language as defined by social consensus
- Attacks on people or groups unlike yourself

- Targeting unchangeable negative qualities in people
- The Big Four topics for humor (sex, race, religion, and politics)
- Psychological hot buttons
- International disdain
- Attacks on specific people rather than concepts

Old-fashioned cursing is common in current comedy. Swearing is particularly funny when it comes from someone unexpected, such as the cussing children seen on many online videos or the elderly (see comic actress legend Betty White or the profane comedian Grandma Lee Strong, the seventy-five-year-old semifinalist on the 2009 *America's Got Talent* competition). This classic joke also illustrates the point: "How do you get a seventy-eight-year-old woman to say 'Fuck'?" "Yell, 'Bingo!'"

In general, when you abide by the above warnings of the standard PC pitfalls, you are likely to avoid humor that fails. It is also extremely useful to monitor yourself to keep from expressing anger-driven humor and any associated tendencies toward scapegoating. If there is a group of people with whom you have had some recent difficulty for any reason, it is easy to use hostile humor with them and with others in referring to them. Not a good idea.

We all face frustrating or anger-arousing situations from time to time in our daily lives. It can be useful to look for the humorous absurdity or the irrationality or the bizarreness in those situations, as a psychological coping mechanism. That technique is highly recommended as a stress reducer. It can help you navigate the negative encounter at the moment with much less felt tension and anger. It can also yield many funny stories (usually a while later) that you can use in a formal routine, or at least to amuse your friends at a party more easily than ever.

Ineffective humor results from failure to follow these guidelines or perhaps from poor comedic delivery skills. Larry Wilde defines "delivery" as "the articulating of words in manner or style that is convincing, authoritative, dramatic and entertaining." He cites four major benefits of delivering humorous material properly:

1. *The deliverer commands attention.* The audience is "with" the speaker and takes in each word and its tone. Their attention and empathy are maximized and the message is fully accepted.
2. *Intimacy is established.* A smooth and polished delivery establishes your rapport with the audience. They then listen with pleasure and interest.
3. *The audience laughs easily.* Close listening to well-delivered humor paves the way for genuine laughter.
4. *Competency is conveyed.* Skillful delivery shows the audience that you are competent and authoritative. They become comfortable with you and are convinced of the validity of your message.[25] This

effect, of course, occurs with all captivating messages, humorous or not.

Wilde presents four basic speechmaking techniques that are essential to achieving a great delivery style. He warns us that the most success will occur only after years of concentrated effort and rehearsal. Since it must be concentrated, it might help to add a pint of purified water to facilitate the process. To improve your delivery of humor, be sure to practice these elements:

1. *Gestures*: Augmenting your message with the calculated use of your hands and arms is extraordinarily valuable. That is, don't use gestures randomly, which could create distractions. Plan ahead and use your finger pointing, fist clenching, and arm waving to illustrate and emphasize your points.

2. *Body movement*: Beyond mere gestures, use whole body actions to bolster your message. Any of these actions can help: posturing, posing, strutting, staggering, shrugging, bending, kneeling, or bowing as appropriate.

3. *Facial expressions*: An animated, expressive face can help your humor. Sometimes the expression can replace your words temporarily. Good examples include raising an eyebrow, squinting, sneering, smiling, grinning, and more. Watch the expert Stephen Colbert's facial expressions, especially during his comedic monologues on *The Colbert Report*. Colbert's nonverbal comedic skills rival those of the late Johnny Carson.

4. *Vocal variety*: Intentionally lowering or raising the pitch and sound of your voice; changing the tone from sweet to angry or vice versa, then whispering or yelling; or judicious pausing for effect are all valuable to keeping your audience's attention. Voice training coaches and active participation in any of the Toastmaster International Clubs can be extremely useful in building your speaking and humor delivery skills.

Larry Wilde's expertise in humor making is built upon his experiences from many years in show business and as the author of more books on humor than anybody else in history. He strongly recommends diligent daily practice of your burgeoning humor skills, first in front of the mirror and then in front of anyone who will listen to you.[26]

The delivery is at least as important as the joke itself. Anyone can learn to write or read a joke and then recite it. But you must *deliver* it effectively to produce the laughter. It's all about getting the laugh. You really don't have to take a cream pie in the face or drop your pants to do that. Of course, that often works too.

DREAMING AN IMPOSSIBLE DREAM?

This is my personal dream for the broader acceptance of humor: In an ideal world, we all could appreciate and initiate humor that is funny, positive, and constructive with no occurrences of their opposites. Successful humor making can definitely forge permanent close relationships, improve our physical functioning toward greater health and longevity, or simply result in exponentially more enjoyment of life (yes, hedonistically). Maybe we could even enjoy ethnic humor, for example, without guilt or fear of being accused of some undesirable personal traits. If something is funny, even if it's about our own group, let's all laugh heartily.

A good illustrative example comes from a bit in one of African American Eddie Murphy's stand-up routines: "Black folks have big lips. That's not racist. It's just a fact. And white folks can't dance! It's just a fact."[27]

Let's vote for funny over PC! Yes, a joke or story may have some racist, sexist, ageist, or similarly undesirable overtones, but it does not have to be overwhelmingly offensive and disgusting. Agreed, we should not tolerate any blatant, excessive, unfair, or discourteous attacks on anyone. However, funny is funny. We should all be able to enjoy practically all humor without fear of being chastised for laughing and without implying any hint of truly believing or holding any of the stupid biases and prejudices being exploited for their humor value. We definitely should vigorously fight discrimination of any kind and ensure that strict laws are passed protecting all individuals in our society from anything less than fair and equal treatment. At the same time, we can enjoy humor, even if a particular joke or remark is directed toward our own personal group, whether it is our race, religion, sexual orientation, national origin, or political affiliation. Let's not let the PC Police armed with their super-sensitivities stifle our appreciation and creation of witty remarks or funny stories.

We already know that laughter feels good, even without any specific humor stimuli. It works even without any preceding jokes, riddles, or pratfalls. Steve Wilson, leader of the World Laughter Tour, suggests that the more people laugh together, with or without a reason, the closer we will be to a world of peace. Who can deny the value of that? It definitely sounds a whole lot better than "bombing for peace."

We also already know that merely watching other people laugh is great fun for the observers, who most likely will soon begin to laugh themselves. This effect occurs in person or even watching professional comics or the typically serious newscasters on TV who sometimes just can't seem to stop laughing. Laughter is contagious, and no one wants science to discover any immunization or cure for it.

Comedian and comic author Chelsea Handler advocates the following:

It's so relaxing to laugh really hard. I mean, there's no better feeling, even if you are not in on the joke, to see someone else hysterically laughing when they can't contain themselves. We've all had that, where you really think you're going to pee . . . you're laughing so hard and you can't get it together and you know it's totally inappropriate. That's what I want people to be doing.[28]

Me, too, Chelsea.

NOTES

1. L. Wilde, *The Larry Wilde Treasury of Laughter* (Carmel, CA: Jester Press, 1992), 2.

2. P. Barkham, "Bigot on a Bridge Wins Poll for Funniest Religious Joke," *The Guardian*, September 25, 2005, www.guardian.co.uk/uk/2005/sep/26/religion.world?INTCMP=ILCNETTXT3487; E. Phillips, "The Best God Joke Ever—and It's Mine!," *The Guardian*, September 28, 2005, www.guardian.co.uk/stage/2005/sep/29/comedy.religion.

3. http://video.google.com/videoplay?docid=-869183917758574879#.

4. www.lewisblack.com/Me-of-Little-Faith.aspx.

5. J. Brady, *I Am Comic*, documentary, Showtime Cable Network, December 18, 2011.

6. Quoted in J. Zinoman, "Female Comedians, Breaking the Taste-Taboo Ceiling," *New York Times*, November 15, 2011, www.nytimes.com/2011/11/16/arts/television/female-comedians-are-confidently-breaking-taste-taboos.html?pagewanted=all.

7. L. C.K., *Talking Funny*, HBO Cable Network, October 10, 2011.

8. www.jumbojoke.com.

9. Interview with Lewis Black, *Larry King Live*, CNN, December 1, 2006.

10. E. Griffin, "Nigga Card," *The Message*, MP3 (Warner Bros., March 9, 1999).

11. www.youtube.com/watch?v=aRK5rU1ZPJc.

12. R. Shydner and M. Schiff, *I Killed: True Stories of the Road from America's Top Comics* (New York: Crown Publishers, 2006), 123.

13. www.amazon.com/Nigger-Strange-Career-Troublesome-Word/dp/0375713719/ref=sr_1_3?s=books&ie=UTF8&qid=1325356783&sr=1-3.

14. J. Del Signore, "Mark Twain Scholar Explains Why N-Word Is So Important," January 10, 2011, www.gothamist.com.

15. Brady, *I Am Comic*.

16. www.listology.com/list/comedy-central-100-greatest-standups-all-time.

17. Wilde, *The Larry Wilde Treasury of Laughter*.

18. R. Gervais, *The Marriage Ref*, NBC network broadcast, June 25, 2011.

19. J. Ross, *I Only Roast the Ones I Love: How to Bust Balls without Burning Bridges* (New York: Gallery Books, 2009), 84.

20. R. Peters, *The Green Room with Paul Provenza*, Showtime Cable Network, August 25, 2011.

21. P. Provenza, *The Green Room with Paul Provenza*, Showtime Cable Network, August 25, 2011.

22. B. Maher, *Real Time*, HBO Cable Network, 2011.

23. C. Davies, *Ethnic Humor around the World: A Comparative Analysis* (Bloomington: Indiana University Press, 1996), 15.

24. J. Raftery, "France Did Not Forget—Did You? A Response to 'How Dare the French Forget' by Steve Dunleavy," *New York Post*, February 10, 2003, http://roma-

na.now.ie/writing/francedidnotforget.html;   www.wsws.org/articles/2003/feb2003/
fran-f15.shtml.

25. Wilde, *The Larry Wilde Treasury of Laughter.*

26. Wilde, *The Larry Wilde Treasury of Laughter.*

27. Sirius XM radio broadcast, 2011.

28. L. Neary, "Chelsea Handler: Keys to a Multimedia Empire," NPR Books, May 16, 2011, www.npr.org/2011/05/16/136363758/chelsea-handler-keys-to-a-multimedia-empire.

TEN

Getting the Last Laugh

He who laughs, lasts.

—Mary Pettibone Poole, author[1]

Mary Pettibone Poole's astute observation on laughter reflects our society's widespread views on positive humor as well as illustrating a comedic twist on a cliché. English poet and novelist John Masefield's original quote of "In this life he laughs longest who laughs last"[2] has become commonly shortened to the cliché "He who laughs longest laughs last." Poole's modification above, though, diminishes the observation even further to emphasize the salubrious effects of laughter. Another version, which increases the overall humor value, might be this: "He who laughs last . . . [pause] . . . is the slowest to get the joke."

In honor of this the last chapter in the book, let's look at some humorous famous last words. One of my personal favorites is "Hey, guys, watch this!" (preceding some stupid stunt ending in death). Of course, treasure troves of last words are found on tombstone epitaphs, which may be fictional or not, and in reports from bystanders at deathbeds.

It is extremely hard to determine the "truthiness" (Stephen Colbert's neologism) of inscriptions on cemetery monuments many decades postmortem. Truthiness refers to something that *seems* to be true in terms of a person's perception or opinion but has no regard to logic or factual evidence in the matter. Kathleen E. Miller noticed the humor potential in this area and put together an amusing collection in her book *Last Laughs: Funny Tombstone Quotes and Famous Last Words.*

Some of us have the foresight to write our own epitaphs as part of our final instructions, while others leave any tombstone writing to the whims of their survivors. After all, monument companies charge by the letter and digit when they add these inscriptions. It is always wise to maintain good relationships during life with your likely epitaph writers, as this

169

represents our last chance to display our sense of humor to the world — sort of a communications gift from the beyond without having to hire some pricey psychic medium.

Beyond the basic name and dates of birth and death, inscriptions on graveside monuments may be comments on the decedent's life and manner of death or his or her effects on the surrounding friends and family. The late humorist Irvin S. Cobb described an epitaph as "a belated advertisement for a line of goods that has been permanently discontinued."[3] Funny, but not exactly uplifting. Regardless of the extent of our worldly status, fame, or portfolio, death is definitely the great equalizer. No one escapes it, and no one returns afterward (if we may exclude certain biblical examples and several other best-selling contemporary books).

How many of us share Woody Allen's views on death? He explained, "I don't mind death. I just don't want to be there when it happens. On the plus side, death is one of the few things that can be done lying down."[4] Steven Wright muses, "How young can you die of old age?"[5] The same concern happens to show up in Drake "Light Up" lyrics featuring the rapper Jay-Z.[6] Another unknown wag claimed that he would prefer to die when he's around age one hundred — after being shot by a jealous husband.

Rarely do we know exactly when our time for living will expire. (Note: The term *expired* is technical medical language for "we made a big mistake and the patient died.") Even a judge's court order setting an execution date for a guilty prisoner is hardly ever carried out at that particular time or even that same decade. Steven Wright claims to be an exception: "I know when I'm going to die. My birth certificate has an expiration date on it."[7] If you, though, are unsure of that exact end date, you may want to prepare your epitaph in advance. W. C. Fields did just that (see below), as did Benjamin Franklin, who foresaw himself eventually becoming "food for worms." Not such a pleasant image, but a humorously accurate one. George Carlin proposed this epitaph for his tombstone, if he had had one: "Gee, he was here a moment ago. . . ."[8]

The headstone of "real cowboy" Russell J. Larsen, currently a resident of the Logan City Cemetery in Logan, Utah, reveals his sense of humor in the "pre-need" epitaph that he wrote: "Two things I love most, good horses and beautiful women, and when I die I hope they tan this old hide of mine and make it into a ladies riding saddle, so I can rest in peace between the two things I love most."[9] It is unclear whether Larsen's survivors carried out his wishes for a good tanning, but his writing was sufficiently impressive to win an award for the "Coolest Headstone" in a contest held twenty-five years after his departure from this earth.[10] Great writing is not always recognized by society immediately. I've noticed that myself with previous books.

Many, but not all, epitaphs are humorous. Many of those so-called humorous ones are clearly not hilarious. A number of the funnier examples, many from Miller's book,[11] follow:

- Here lies Johnny Yeast. Pardon me for not rising. (Johnny Yeast)
- I don't want to talk about it now. (Bonnie Anderson)
- She did it the hard way. (Bette Davis)
- One less fool on earth, one more in Heaven—or somewhere. (Unknown)
- Stiff at last! (Unknown—for good reason)
- Here lies an honest lawyer. That is Strange. (Counselor John Strange)
- Hurry! The party's started. (Elsa G. Schaper)
- To the short memory of Marvin Trueham. Regretted by all who never knew him. (Marvin Trueham)
- Tears cannot restore her. Therefore I weep. (Anonymous)
- Here lies the body of Emily White. She signaled left, and turned right. (Emily White)
- A victim of fast women and slow horses. (Milt MacPhail)
- Looked up an elevator shaft to see if the car was on the way down. It was. (Harry Edsel Smith)
- What are you looking at? (Comedian Margaret Smith's Uncle Sammy, allegedly)
- I told them to bury me face down so the whole world can kiss my ass. (Unknown)
- Gone underground for good. (Unknown)
- Here lies the Marlboro Man. Ashes to ashes. (TV commercial)
- Go back. It's dark in here. (Unknown)
- Published and still perished. (Not mine, I hope)

The brief, humorous inscription on his marker in Union Cemetery, Ft. Edward, New York, indicates an unfortunate premature end to Mr. Lawrence L. Cook Jr.'s complicated love life:[12]

> MA LOVES PA — PA LOVES WOMEN
> MA CAUGHT PA, WITH 2 IN SWIMMIN'
> HERE LIES PA . . .
> 10-29-1934 8-1-2004

Miller's book also includes a number of allegedly true humorous last words spoken on the speaker's deathbed. Surely some of their words came during their last days rather than their last moments. Many times, when death is imminent, due to incapacity and low energy, most "stars of the show" are not sufficiently coherent or even able to speak, let alone be funny. Regardless, it would be the preferable way to go in my view, as long as the laughs generated were long and hearty.

Some examples of last words from *Last Laughs*:

- W. C. Fields's well-known epitaph was actually suggested by him forty-one years before it was needed: "On the whole, I'd rather be living in Philadelphia." As it turns out, his real tombstone at Forest Lawn in Glendale, California, simply shows his name and dates of birth and death.[13] Fields's actual last words were as follows: "God damn the whole world and everyone in it. . . . Except you, Carlotta."[14] (Carlotta Monti was Fields's mistress, who was both an afterthought and his final thought.)
- Henry John Temple, a former British prime minister, said to his physician, "Die, my dear doctor? That's the last thing I shall do."[15] Definitely true.
- Orson Welles, star-producer-director-screenwriter of the black-and-white movie *Citizen Kane*, fearing the future colorization of his classic film: "Don't let Ted Turner deface my movie with his crayons."[16]
- Winston Churchill, British prime minister during World War II, spoke his very memorable last lines not exactly at the end, but near his end: "I am ready to meet my Maker. Whether my Maker is prepared for the great ordeal of meeting me is another matter."[17]

On their deathbeds apparently some people can still be witty and mildly funny, but usually not hilarious. Let's try to raise the standard for humor, when we try the epitaph-writing exercises to improve your Humor Quotient that are included in the appendix. After all, W. C. Fields's suggestion for his epitaph was very funny, especially if you've ever been to Philadelphia, and to this day it is readily associated with him. He prepared sufficiently well in advance, since his line wasn't actually needed until over four decades later, and then it wasn't even used. Fields's proposed epitaph has even spawned imitators who modified the message to other destination preferences (e.g., Isabelle Keneston's "I'd rather be at the mall"[18]).

GALLOWS HUMOR

Gallows humor literally is humor that appears surrounding formal executions. The prototypic gallows humor joke involves the prisoner who was offered a cigarette immediately prior to his execution and refused it by saying, "No thanks, I'm trying to quit." Of course, the mode of execution for this form of dark humor is not restricted to death by hanging, but it can occur prior to death by electrocution, guillotine, firing squad, the gas chamber, or the currently popular method of lethal injection. ("Popular" is ironically the correct descriptive term here because most U.S. states allow the prisoner to have a choice in the method.) To no one's surprise, "none of the above" is not an option on this questionnaire. There are no known reports of humor making, though, from condemned individuals due to die in countries that still practice stoning.

Actually, the term *gallows humor* is not even restricted to situations of execution. It is sometimes associated with the humor used to cope with situations that are serious and negative but not necessarily fatal, such as impending surgery, unusually long or short jury deliberations in noncapital cases, or even opening the mailed results of college or graduate school admission tests and bar exams.

Here are some examples of real-life gallows humor reportedly occurring just prior to the acts of their actual execution:

- James Rogers, facing a firing squad, on being asked if he had any last requests, replied, "Why, yes, a bulletproof vest." [19]
- George Appel, about to be electrocuted, said, "Well, gentlemen, you are about to see a baked Appel." [20]
- James French, also prior to his electrocution, supposedly said, "How's this for a headline for tomorrow's newspaper? 'French Fries.'" [21]
- Robert Childers gave lethal advice to his Irish firing squad: "Take a step forward, lads. It will be easier that way." [22]
- William Palmer walked to the gallows and inquired of the hangman, "Are you sure this is safe?" [23]

Comedian Dick Gregory tells a death penalty joke: "Just as the prisoner was being strapped into the electric chair, the priest said, 'Son, is there anything I can do for you?' The prisoner said, 'Yeah, when they pull the switch, hold my hand.'" [24]

We can never be totally sure that these prisoners' execution quips are, in fact, true as recorded and passed down. Regardless, they are fun to read and do illustrate gallows humor. If we are ever faced with life-threatening situations or even imminent death, we might well want to try some humor to ease our own physical suffering and the emotional suffering of those in attendance.

Gallows humor is a genre in which the humor serves a coping function for powerless individuals mired in extremely serious situations such as facing impending death. For example, there is a joke in which two Jews were lined up against the wall by the Nazis, who were planning to execute them by a firing squad. Before he gave the order, the commandant approached the men and asked if they had any final words. One man turned and spat into the face of the executioner. His condemned colleague instantly admonished him: "Moishe, don't make trouble!"

This kind of humor also might appear in military troops just before engaging in a battle. It can help them cope with the anxieties of their immediate perilous situation as well as serve as a check on the feelings of their comrades at the same time. Gallows humor can also be a type of social probe to assess whether the others are also upset and scared. It is a genuine "misery loves company" matter, and any joking might help defuse the tension and share that misery. This is certainly a constructive use of humor. Would it not be great if the need for this form of joking would diminish in a more peaceful world? Unfortunately, that prospect remains unlikely for the foreseeable future.

Any laughter from gallows or black humor presumably arises from the joker's cynical and sarcastic perspective on ordinarily taboo topics, such as death and mocking victims and their suffering. The emotional sympathy may even be more with the victimizer than the exploited ones. The effect of black humor is to generate laughter and discomfort simultaneously in the audience. By definition, black humor makes audiences uncomfortable, which is the opposite of your usual goal in using humor to become more personally effective. This is a good form of humor to leave to the professionals. Don't try it at home or with friends, unless you are facing combat together.

Humor is a much better strategy at the time when death is imminent than cursing God, scaring away solicitous clergypersons, condemning your personal enemies, continuing any ongoing feuds with estranged family members, or other acts of vengeance. It is also a really great time to make huge purchases and large donations to worthy charities on your credit cards.

WHAT HAVE WE LEARNED IN *JUST KIDDING*?

My overall goal for this book is to add you to the growing group of happy people who enjoy humor and practice it well as a vehicle to enrich your life, especially your relationships with those people with whom you most often interact. Humor can bring you happiness on a daily basis, and most likely a myriad of health benefits too.

On the negative side, humor probably cannot add a single cubit to your stature or a second to your life. I think that is mentioned in the Bible. If you can't find it in your copy, go ahead and write it in on the margins.

In addition to the provision of an incalculable amount of general wisdom and good cheer, the following learning points were presented in *Just Kidding: Using Humor Effectively* and hopefully will be retained in your memory bank with high interest for the rest of your natural life:

- Humor is a powerful force in individual personality development and in promoting physical health.
- *Effective humor* is doing or saying stuff that is funny, is considerate of others who may be different from you in some ways, and is the kind of humor that results in greater social cohesion without engendering feelings of embarrassment or humiliation in other people.

- Laughing together can bring us all closer together as individuals in a diverse society and the world at large.
- Self-deprecating humor (within limits) is the safest form of humor. No one will get upset when you make fun of yourself. It also saves them the trouble.
- Humor making is a skill that can be increased and strengthened to maximize its effectiveness.
- The principles of humor making apply equally to amateur and professional humorists, although performance freedoms and social acceptance are definitely greater for the professionals.
- More effective humor skills result from good information, instruction, modeling, feedback, and diligent practice followed by more practice.
- A sense of humor consists primarily of both initiation and appreciation skills. This book happens to emphasize the former.
- Many situational variables contribute to whether a given humorous observation or a formal joke will be successful or not.
- Success is measured by the degree of amusement generated within the audience and is shown by either (or both) overt laughter or internal pleasure. Professional comedians often garner actual applause in response to their funny comments, but don't expect clapping from humor use in your routine daily interactions.
- Humor can be positive, energizing, and constructive, or it can be negative, demeaning, and hurtful to its targets.
- Humor can be applied in a large variety of settings, including health care professionals' offices, business organizations, sales, e-mail and phone communications, and most daily social interactions with friends and new acquaintances.
- The many forms of humor include formal jokes and riddles, storytelling, irony, malapropos, satire, sarcasm, slapstick, intellectual, philosophical, physical, wordplay, nonsensical, sexual, obscene, scatological, hostile, ethnic, demeaning to men or women, gallows, sick, rough, and practical jokes.
- Freud's theory of personality, albeit somewhat dated now, has elaborated the role and meaning of our use of humor more than most other theories. It also accounts for the predominance of jokes involving aspects of hostility and sexuality.
- Political correctness values periodically change in society, but they always play an important role in the success and acceptance of humor making.
- Attempts at humor sometimes fail and can have unintended negative consequences, including both figurative and literal explosive bombs.
- Politicians, athletes, and professional comedians have set off some memorable humor bombs and surely will continue to do so. Such

unintended gaffes are a daily occurrence. The supply seems unlimited, as will be our enjoyment.

- Determining what is funny is a very complicated question, but in the end the matter is necessarily situational and subjective.
- Do our humor preferences reveal our true feelings about a subject or is something just funny regardless of the content?
- Should we laugh at off-color or inappropriate joke topics that are otherwise funny?
- Taboo topics historically play a major role in humor making, but other, more neutral topics can be made funny as well.
- Wit is the admirable, spontaneous, and clever creation of verbal humor, but it can be sarcastic and barbed as well as positive and inspiring.
- The construction and delivery of humor are teachable skills that can produce effective humor making for anyone willing to learn. See the appendix to get started now.
- Successful humor production is a result of specific strategies designed to create humor and avoid specific pitfalls that result in humor failures.
- The end of life does not mean the end of inducing laughter as long as epitaphs can be inscribed on tombstones, which should last for at least two centuries. Your final thoughts can also be kept and expressed forever via recordings and books.

Surely there are many more valuable points of information (if not, light) contained in the preceding chapters. However, in keeping with what my clinical supervisor in a mental hospital taught me long ago about how to end my formal psychological reports, I will follow his valuable lesson. He advised, "Never write a summary because that's all they'll read. If they want to know what your opinion is, make them read the whole thing."

My final suggestion is for everyone to heed the advice from Oscar Wilde and Mark Twain, respectively: "Laughter is not at all a bad beginning of a friendship, and it is by far the best ending for one,"[25] and "Let us endeavor so to live that when we come to die even the undertaker will be sorry."[26] Certainly a reasonable goal for anyone who hasn't joined Steven Wright's appealing longevity plan: "I plan to live forever. So far, so good."[27]

NOTES

1. www.quotationspage.com/quotes/Mary_Pettibone_Poole.
2. www.brainyquote.com/quotes/authors/j/john_masefield.html.
3. www.brainyquote.com/quotes/authors/i/irvin_s_cobb.html.
4. www.brainyquote.com/quotes/authors/w/woody_allen.html.
5. J. Brown, *The Comedy Thesaurus* (Philadelphia: Quirk Books, 2005), 101.

6. www.directlyrics.com/drake-light-up-lyrics.html.

7. www.wright-house.com/steven-wright/steven-wright-Mi.html.

8. http://thrillingdaysofyesteryear.blogspot.com/2008/06/gee-he-was-just-here-moment-ago.html.

9. www.estatevaults.com/lm/archives/2003/05; K. E. Miller, *Last Laughs: Funny Tombstone Quotes and Famous Last Words* (New York: Sterling, 2006), 44.

10. http://pecozbill.blogspot.com/2008/05/he-won-coolest-headstone-contest.html.

11. Miller, *Last Laughs*.

12. http://ginva.com/2011/01/creative-gravestone-architect-and-design.

13. H. Reich, *Don't You Believe It! Exploring the Myths behind 250 Commonly Believed Fallacies* (New York: MJF Books, 2011), 138.

14. Miller, *Last Laughs*, 142.

15. Miller, *Last Laughs*, 144.

16. Miller, *Last Laughs*, 145.

17. http://thinkexist.com/quotation/i_am_ready_to_meet_my_maker-whether_my_maker_is/9539.html.

18. www.freesurnamesearch.com/epitaphs/surnames-k.html.

19. Miller, *Last Laughs*, 152.

20. Miller, *Last Laughs*, 151.

21. Miller, *Last Laughs*, 152.

22. Miller, *Last Laughs*, 145.

23. Miller, *Last Laughs*, 149.

24. Brown, *The Comedy Thesaurus*, 101.

25. E. Esar, ed., *The Dictionary of Humorous Quotations* (New York: Dorset Press, 1989), 219.

26. http://quotationsbook.com/quote/10097.

27. See http://quotes.prolix.nu/Humor/Steven_Wright/quotationsbook.com/quote/10097.

Appendix

Humor Development Exercises to Raise Your HQ

Your HQ is your Humor Quotient—your ability to create and appreciate humor that is positive, constructive, and facilitative of your personal relationships. Humor making requires a variety of specific skills to attain the overall result of effectiveness: verbal fluency, timing and pacing, speech-making, felicity, and, above all, cognitive skills. It is vital to learn to think funny—that is, to think in ways that are different from most people's styles. The goal is to discern what might be funny in your environment, especially things that other people don't necessarily regard as funny. You develop a unique perspective, even though you have access to the same information and perceptions as everyone else. Some refer to this ability as cognitive flexibility, or, more colloquially, thinking crookedly.

The exercises in this section are designed to promote that kind of flexible thinking. These are not tests. They are exercises for you to try out, play with, modify, seek feedback on, and repeat. Of course, you don't *have* to practice, but if you *want* to practice (which is the real key), you will get better. Doing the exercises along with one or two buddies can make them all the more fun, just as it is more fun to go to the gym with friends for demanding physical exercise than to leave your home and go out alone on dark and stormy nights.

The goal here is to make your responses as funny as possible. It often will be relatively easy to give a response, but to create one that is really funny can be a much tougher assignment. In this case it is the journey *and* the destination that count.

Even if a particular exercise at first glance doesn't appeal to you, please give it a try anyway. You may never have a need for those responses in real life (other than the "Famous Last Words" exercise), but the humor creation process practice will be invaluable.

One of the lessons that you will gain from these activities is that writing comedy is not very easy. However, the more you practice, the easier it will be, and then the more fun it will be. The serious effort you put in to these humor exercises should raise your Humor Quotient by a significant number of points.

THE EXERCISES

Twisting the Cliché

Task: Here are a dozen familiar phrases that have become part of cliché expressions. You are given the stem of the phrase or saying and are asked to complete each one in a novel and funny way.

Samples:
You are what you eat, so . . . I'm staying away from fruits and nuts.
She was an earthy woman and so . . . I treated her like dirt. (George Carlin)

Carlin's completion of the sentence is funny and even a bit hostile. Hostility is not a requirement for this exercise, but, as always, it could help.

1. My body is a temple, so _____.
2. After that incident, I am sadder but _____.
3. Some day your chickens will come home to _____.
4. Don't put all your eggs in one _____.
5. A penny saved is _____.
6. Don't make a mountain out of _____.
7. Blessed are the _____.
8. The meek shall inherit _____.
9. If you can't say something nice about someone, _____.
10. For every drop of rain that falls, _____.
11. Strike while the iron is _____.
12. It's not over until _____.
13. Winning isn't everything, it's _____.
14. You can't buy love, but _____.
15. Let a smile be _____.

Famous Last Words

Task: What would you like your last sentence on earth to be and whom do you want to hear it? Write it out and don't forget the funny.

Epitaph Writing

It's OK to name names on these. The results can be totally fictional. Thoreau has assured us that "the rarest quality in an epitaph is truth." No need to change anything about that.

Task 1: Write a funny epitaph for your best friend or loved one.

Task 2: Write a funny epitaph for your worst enemy.

Task 3: Write a funny epitaph for yourself. (No need to use it immediately. It can be stored.)

Bumper Stickers

Task 1: Start keeping a list of especially funny bumper stickers that you have actually seen.

Samples:
"My kid is an underachiever at the _____ School and we're proud of it."

Seen on the *same* bumper:
"Vote Democrat—It's easier than working."
"Vote Republican—It's easier than thinking."

Task 2: Create some bumper stickers that reflect your philosophy on the value of humor. Limit the funny message to eight words or less.

Headline Improvements

Task: Look at your daily newspaper's lead headline on page 1. Obviously, it will be about a serious matter. Change the headline in ways to make it funny. Don't worry about space limitations, but keep your modification to a single sentence.

Movie Plots

Task: In two sentences or less, describe a comedy movie plot you would like to see. Be fanciful and funny. Do this for three separate films.

TV Game Shows

Task: Invent three separate TV game shows with rules and tasks that would be funny to play and to watch. Requiring nudity would be permissible, but no physical pain allowed.

Double-Speak: Creating Euphemisms

Task 1: Take some everyday objects and create an alternative description (which is usually more cumbersome and indirect). If you get really good at this, you will be qualified for a job in the military or government, where wordy euphemisms flourish. Add humor to your creative descriptions whenever possible.

Samples:
Briefcase: a data transport device
Security guard: loss prevention officer

Task 2: Create a PC consistent double-speak euphemism for the following everyday items:

- Bed
- Camera
- Desk
- Phone
- Book
- Donkey
- Computer
- Calendar
- Church
- Golf ball

Oxymorons

Task: Create a list of ten *new and funny* oxymorons (terms or concepts that are mutually incompatible).

Samples:
- "jumbo shrimp"
- "bad sex"
- "mandatory options"
- "plastic glass"

Double Entendres

Task: Create a list of ten double entendres—that is, words or phrases that have a second meaning, often risqué (in keeping with the French theme here). In many cases, this form of wordplay is too easy to create and thus too frequently heard. Watch for them in ordinary conversation and seize upon them, if the audience is appropriate, for the resulting humor. Sometimes it is better to let it pass (I'm not referring to gas).

Regardless, here are some standard English words that readily lend themselves to dual interpretations. Feel free to add more examples to this short list.

Samples:

- To come
- To do
- Balls
- The Y
- Wood
- Hot

You Might Be . . .

Task: Starting with Jeff Foxworthy's classic setup line, this exercise uses additional setups to be completed for developing your humor thinking and writing skills. Remember, the goal is for your punch lines to be *original and funny.*

1. You might be a redneck, if _____.
2. You might be from California, if _____.
3. You might be from New York City, if _____.
4. You might be getting old, if _____.
5. You might be getting too heavy, if _____.
6. You might be losing your sense of humor, if _____.
7. You might be going broke, if _____.
8. You might be addicted, if _____.
9. You might be spending too much time online, if _____.
10. You might be dreaming, if _____.

Create an Acronym

Task: Make up a phrase or sentence based on the five letters in the word HUMOR that communicates a funny message. Create at least two different messages for this acronym. Take your time.

Your Funniest Teacher

Task: Who is the funniest teacher you ever had in your life? List three different concrete ways that he or she displayed that funniness to you and your class.

Book Titles Become Punch Lines

Task: Below are a dozen real book titles. Your assignment is to create a funny question, setup line, or riddle for which the book title is the answer. If you happen to be familiar with the actual book, ignore that information, since it is not relevant to this humor creation task. None of the titles below are related or even friends with each other.

Sample:

Book title *Last Call*: "In addition to 'No, thank you, I'm going home alone,' what are your least favorite words to hear in your local bar?"

Invent an even more hilarious setup, if you can, for which the following real book titles are the answers:

- *Starting Over*
- *The Finkler Question*
- *One Day It'll All Make Sense*
- *Eat Naked*
- *Here Comes Trouble*
- *Half in Love*
- *The Great Hangover*
- *On Second Thought*
- *The Sixth Man*
- *Unfamiliar Fishes*
- *Happy Accidents*
- *Driven to Distraction*

Humorous Icebreakers

Task 1: Generate five original *humor-based* opening lines that you would be willing to use in a bar to begin a conversation with a stranger whom you might have a personal interest in.

Task 2: Generate five original *humor-based* openers to use with someone you meet at a mutual friend's house party. You have no particular personal interest agenda at stake here.

Thought Questions about Humor

No need for any writing here, just some thinking.

1. Who is your favorite comedian? Why specifically do you like his or her humor?
2. By laughing at inappropriate, but funny, jokes, do you believe you are indicating agreement with their content or the values portrayed?

3. Who is your funniest personal friend or family member? Why is this person's humor successful?
4. What role do you think humor should play in the school system? How is it used or regarded now in your local schools?
5. How can you incorporate more humor in your intimate personal relationships as a way to strengthen them?
6. What can you do to encourage more humor use in your children, grandchildren, or young students (if you are a parent, teacher, coach, youth group leader, or mentor)?
7. Do you think that a keen sense of humor is an important personal quality for a president of the United States? How might it add to or detract from a president's job performance?
8. Do you believe more humor in your workplace could have positive effects? What might those effects be? What could be the reasons for those positive effects, or what could be the reasons if the effects of more humor were not positive?

Suggested Readings

For readers interested in more technical sources and elaborations of the material in *Just Kidding*, I would suggest consulting the following eighteen books or any issues of the research-based journal *Humor: International Journal of Humor Research*, which claims it "reflects the standard of knowledge at the time of publication."

Berger, P. *The Last Laugh: The World of Stand-Up Comics*. New York: Cooper Square Press/Rowman & Littlefield, 2000.

Carter, J. *The Comedy Bible*. New York: Fireside/Simon & Schuster, 2001.

Davies, C. *Ethnic Humor around the World: A Comparative Analysis*. Bloomington: Indiana University Press, 1990.

———. *The Mirth of Nations* (reprint ed.). Piscataway, NJ: Transaction Publishers, 2010.

Helitzer, M. *Comedy Writing Secrets*. Cincinnati, OH: Writers Digest Books, 1992.

Knoedelseder, W. *I'm Dying Up Here: Heartbreak and High Times in Stand-Up Comedy's Golden Era*. New York: Public Affairs, 2009.

Lewis, P. *Cracking Up: American Humor in a Time of Conflict*. Chicago: University of Chicago Press, 2006.

Martin, R. A. *The Psychology of Humor: An Integrative Approach*. Burlington, MA: Elsevier Academic Press, 2007.

McGhee, P. E. *How to Develop Your Sense of Humor: An Eight-Step Humor Development Training Program*. Dubuque, IA: Kendall/Hunt Publishing Company, 1994.

———. *PUNchline: How to Think like a Humorist if You're Impaired*. Dubuque, IA: Kendall/Hunt Publishing Company, 1993.

McInnis, J. *Finding the Funny Fast: How to Create Quick Humor to Connect with Clients, Coworkers and Crowds*. N.p.: Cubicle Comedy, 2009.

Mendrinos, J. *The Complete Idiot's Guide to Comedy Writing*. Indianapolis, IN: Alpha Books, 2004.

Minkoff, D. *OY! The Ultimate Book of Jewish Jokes*. New York: Thomas Dunne Books/St. Martin's Griffin, 2005.

Perret, G. *The New Comedy Writing: Step by Step*. Sanger, CA: Quill Driver Books, 2007.

Provenza, P., and D. Dion. *¡Satiristas! Comedians, Contrarians, Raconteurs, & Vulgarians*. New York: HarperCollins, 2010.

Provine, R. R. *Laughter: A Scientific Investigation*. New York: Penguin, 2001.

Shore, S. C. *Sandi C. Shore's Secrets to Standup Success*. Cincinnati, OH: Emmis Books, 2004.

Shydner, R., and M. Schiff. *I Killed: True Stories of the Road from America's Top Comics*. New York: Crown, 2006.

Index

About the Author

Louis R. Franzini is emeritus professor of psychology at San Diego State University, and a licensed psychologist in California and Florida. He has published over seventy-five articles, chapters, and books in the scientific and professional literature of psychology. He received his doctorate in clinical psychology at the University of Pittsburgh and completed a post-doctoral fellowship in behavior modification at Stony Brook University. He has also lived and taught abroad at universities in Belgium and Singapore.

He is the senior coauthor of two books: *Eccentric and Bizarre Behaviors* (translated into Italian, Turkish, and Bulgarian) and *Convention Survival Techniques: Practical Strategies for Getting the Most Out of Your Professional Association's Meetings*. His third trade book, *Kids Who Laugh: How to Develop Your Child's Sense of Humor*, won a Bronze Medal in *Foreword* magazine's competition for parenting books, and has now been translated into Korean and Spanish. Dr. Franzini has also published in the popular press: *American Way, American Health, Today's Manager*, and the *San Diego Union-Tribune*. Finally, he has won several humorous caption-writing contests, both locally and nationally.

Dr. Franzini is a member of the interdisciplinary International Society for Humor Studies and has presented to this association at its conferences in Sheffield, England; Paris, France; Ithaca, New York; Youngstown, Ohio; and Oakland, California. He has published humor research in the scientific journal *Humor: International Journal of Humor Research* and serves as an ad hoc reviewer for that and other journals and book publishers. He has also presented on humor issues internationally in Windsor, Ontario, and most recently in July 2012 at the Paris International Congress of Humanities and Social Sciences Research, in addition to presenting at the Association for Applied and Therapeutic Humor's annual conference in San Diego, San Francisco, Austin, Las Vegas, and Chicago.

Dr. Franzini is past president of Laughmasters, at the time the only Toastmasters International Club specializing in humor. He has performed stand-up comedy at conventions in Los Angeles, San Francisco, Reno, and San Diego and at other comedy showcase venues. He currently resides in St. Augustine, Florida, and claims to have found the Fountain of Youth there.